A PHILOSOPHY FOR THE HUMAN WORLD

About the Author

Denis White, a strategy planning pioneer and speechwriter for Prime Minister Malcolm Fraser, was Director of Fraser's Private Office, Exec Director of Foundation Studies at Trinity College at Melbourne Univ, Warden of Deakin Hall and Politics Senior Lecturer at Monash Univ, Philosophy Tutor at Queens College and Melbourne Univ. White holds BA(Hons), MA and PhD degrees from Melbourne Univ., and Grad Cert in App Sci from CSU. Married and with three children, White and his family established an olive grove in Victoria's Strathbogies for producing extra virgin olive oil.

Also by Denis White

The Philosophy of the Australian Liberal Party, Hutchinson, 1978

Malcolm Fraser on Australia (co-written with David Kemp), Hill of Content, 1986

The University Dream: Creating Trinity Foundation Studies, Trinity College, 2021

Fraser in Office, Jeparit Press, 2022

A PHILOSOPHY FOR THE HUMAN WORLD

Denis White

Connor Court Publishing

Copyright © 2023, Denis White

ALL RIGHTS RESERVED. This book contains material protected under International and Federal Copyright Laws and Treaties. Any unauthorised reprint or use of this material is prohibited. No part of this book may be reproduced or transmitted in any form or by any means, electronic or mechanical, including photocopying, recording, or by any information storage and retrieval system without express written permission from the publisher.

CONNOR COURT PUBLISHING PTY LTD
PO Box 7257
Redland Bay QLD 4165
sales@connorcourt.com
www.connorcourt.com

Front cover image is licensed under the Creative Commons Attribution-Share Alike 4.0 International license.

An abstract orange man with a rope arrow tangled in a knot with a posterior arrow indicating an infinite loop. Bespoke futuristic children's illustration style.

Date 10 January 2023, Author: Wesxdz

Background colour changed from orange to blue by the front cover designer.

ISBN: 9781922815729

Printed in Australia

I dedicate this work to my dear wife Carnie, and to my family

Contents

Letter To The Reader	9
Thanks and Acknowledgements	17
Chapter One: Beginnings	19
1. Making Ways Of Life	20
2. Being On Our Own	21
3. So What?	24
Chapter Two: The Measure Of All Things	31
1. Humans As The Measure	31
2. Humans As Measurers	49
3. Humans And Their Measures	63
Chapter Three: Machinery	81
1. Machinery In General	81
2. Types Of Machinery	96
3. The Impact Of Machinery On Humans	112
Chapter Four: Mystery And The Facts	127
1. Facts And Mysteries	129
2. The Need For Knowledge	142
3. People's Dependence On The World	156

Chapter Five: The People   169

   1. Individuals And Groups   173

   2. The Dynamics Of Groups   191

   3. The Effectiveness Of Groups   206

Chapter Six: The Politicians   225

   1. The Nature Of Politics   229

   2. The Impact Of Politics   261

Chapter Seven: The Determinators   277

   1. Calling The Tune   280

   2. The Role Of Government   304

   3. The Impact Of Tune-Calling   327

Chapter Eight: Humans   331

   1 Threats To Humans,

   And Conditions Of Achievement   349

   2 Humans On Their Own,

   And Making Ways Of Life   357

End Notes   375

Bibliography   381

Index   387

A Letter To The Reader

Dear Reader,

I hope you will find interest and value in these ideas about human life and its organization. I think of them as 'human philosophy' – philosophy that fits people's aspirations and circumstances. They range beyond traditional political philosophy, which is about politics and government.[1]

This philosophy is intended to make sense of today's and tomorrow's human world. This world is profoundly different from anything experienced in the past. Three examples – all followed up in the text – illustrate the need to break new ground. First, productivity increases over the last 150-200 years mean that 'quality of opportunity' should replace mere 'equality of opportunity' as a benchmark aspiration for future generations. Secondly, globalisation cries out for organizational understanding that is more accommodating than has previously been contemplated. Thirdly, interdependence means there is nothing simple that can govern the nature and limits of interference with others.[2]

The objective of the following chapters is to build a logical structure with propositions about humans and their nature, human relationships, human organization, the dynamics of change, and the kind of life which befits human beings. The resultant philosophy is about what people are, and what they do. While encompassing politics and government, this philosophy goes further and deeper, by exploring foundations for understanding, managing and organizing our world. Like traditional political philosophies, it includes one or two supposedly incontrovertible assertions about human beings and human affairs; it frames a particular understanding of its era; it draws attention to issues that matter and call for action; and I hope it identifies some priorities and directions.

The philosophy elaborated below does not tell us what to do – that is not philosophy's role – but how and with what to **think out** what to do. This role includes helping us take proper account of human nature - including people's needs and wants, their hopes and fears, their ideas, their capacities, and their weaknesses. Its role includes helping people to take enlightened account of the environment in which we live, including the earth, space and time, history and the past, the present and the future. Its role includes relating and assessing conflicting ideas and approaches. To be worth its salt, this philosophy will need to be able to inform consideration of issues ranging from world order to primary education, from peace to true prosperity, from political obligation to social harmony, from population objectives to economic management, from force to freedom, from structures of government to limits on power, to name just some of the issues that humanity needs to address and deal with.

It helps in reading these chapters to have in mind a sense of the truly extraordinary world for which they have been written. This world's population is some eight billion people, with burgeoning worldwide communications and communication systems. It comprises around two hundred nations, each with its own system of government, its own practices and approaches, its own language or languages. It has divergent and evolving economic structures, practices and beliefs; multiplying international authorities and organizations;

many belief systems and religions; proliferating education arrangements and accomplishments including sport; expanding R&D systems and general expertise. It is a world in which prodigious new centres of power and influence have recently taken shape – a world in which surveillance and internet innovations are transforming the ways in which people relate to each other, both individually and collectively. It is – almost if not quite - a world in which agriculture has the capacity to feed everyone, and medicine to control disease worldwide. It is a world in which a small number of power holders have the capacity to wipe humanity out altogether. It is a world in which co-operation, conflict, and 'live and let live' wax and wane. It is not a world in which politics or government are on top of the games they play, nor improvement always on the top of agendas. It is a dynamic, relentless and constantly changing world.

This world's potential is prodigious, and its dangers are dire. It beggars belief that humanity puts so little effort or resources into raising the standards of politics and government.

A truth which stares humanity in the face is that some sort of sound, benign and encompassing 'human' philosophy is a precondition of a happy future for our world. If ever there was a time to pay attention to such philosophy, now is surely that time. If ever our world needed fresh thinking that is true to contemporary life and that might lead to good and beneficial outcomes, now is that time. For the fundamental issue before humanity is how to organise ourselves and our affairs so that we can advance or at least hold our ground – so that we do not blow ourselves up or fragment into new dark ages – so that the whole world and all its people can benefit, in some measure at least, from the advances that are taking place in so many fields of human endeavour.

Prominent in the philosophy below are ideas about human nature, including peoples' thinking, activities, values and relationships; ideas about human organization including its dynamics, structures and impacts; and ideas about the character and drivers of the kind of life which befits human beings.

This attempt at a fresh philosophy began in 1979.[3] For the previous twenty years, I had been teaching and reviewing previous philosophies. Through all these years, I had been following the lead of others in deciding where to start my thinking. I realised that if I was to develop a fresh philosophy as we approached the Twenty First Century, I would need to determine its starting point myself. Taking advantage of the freedom offered by a sabbatical year as part of my employment in the Monash University Politics Department, I took up that challenge!

For two months I sought my starting point. I did my best to follow the example of Descartes, the founder of modern philosophy, who sought an indubitable starting point for his thinking, and devised the famous *cogito*: "I think, therefore I am". I had in mind a memorable comment of my grandfather Charles Atkinson that lighting on the *cogito* was for Descartes like stepping on a solid rock while trying to cross a turbulent river.[4]

What was the rock from which I could start? To begin with, my thinking was fathomless. Finally the notion 'ways of life' came to mind. It was fundamental, and it seemed right. So I made it my starting point: 'people make ways of life'. Expressed thus, it is a mind-blowing idea. For people have long been willing to die for their ways of life.[5]

Next, the idea that 'people are on their own' came to mind.

This is existentially more challenging than the first idea, for it throws us back on ourselves. Without denying or supporting religion, it asserts human responsibility. Chapter Four's emphasis on mystery confirms that religion and conviction are as much at home in this philosophy as uncertainty and denial. For 'responsibility' means there is no escaping ourselves or reality.

Thus the upshot of my two months reflection was a dual starting point - two Cartesian rocks instead of one. Two was better than one, because more congruent with the diversity of the real world.

"Humans make ways of life, and humans are on their own." These ideas are truly true to life as starting points for a fresh "human philosophy". They emanate from human nature and from the human situation. They are solid ground. Nothing is or can be more solid – or more comprehensive.

I adopted them, happy that they rang true, and not unhappy they were commonsensical. I was more interested in where they would take me than defining them.

They actually took me all the way. They determined the scope of the book, which is spelled out in the title. Then they led me to the successive chapters.

Chapter One is called 'Beginnings' because it explains the two foundational ideas just introduced. Chapter Two is called 'The Measure of All Things' because in order to make a way of life – or anything else – in a world where they are on their own, people need ways to measure things. Chapter Three is called 'Machinery' because nobody can make anything – much less a way of life – without tools. Chapter Four is called 'Mystery and the Facts' because while people are on their own, they inhabit a world of which they know something but not everything. Chapter Five is called 'The People' because it considers how individuals and human groups are structured, how they interact, and how they achieve. Chapter Six is called 'The Politicians' because moderating between people is a fundamental and inescapable aspect of human life. Chapter Seven is called 'The Determinators' because in all the diversity of modern life, there are many creators and arbiters (including government) of the rules and other determinants by which we live. Chapter Eight is called 'Humans' in order to focus all these elements back on the real subject of the book.

The book thus presents a human philosophy that is original – my thinking, coming from my experience plus other influences. On a personal note, this philosophy has served me well for forty odd years – and I have no regrets about its emphasis on freedom. All up, the book took about fourteen months to write from start to finish, during which time I read virtually nothing and discussed what I was doing with no one. In its first edition, the book was titled *The World of Man*, and – in line with convention at the time - 'man' (and cognates) rather than 'person' (and cognates) was used in the text. I have enjoyed what has happily been the straightforward activity of de-gendering the text for this edition.

Like any original philosophy, this work tries to develop its own basic ideas, its own categories, its own conceptual framework. It frames its own questions, develops its own criteria, and reasons in its own way to its own understandings and conclusions. I am speaking of philosophy in the classical sense, as a coherent edifice of thought - a systematic attempt to comprehend and address with abstract reasoning the fundamental issues that humans face.

Because it is new, this philosophy will likely feel unfamiliar. And because it is framed by abstract reasoning, the book is not an easy read, even though it is written in everyday language. My suggestion to a reader is that it often helps understanding to put aside presumptions, suspend judgment, and read such works on their own terms. I hope readers will find this philosophy 'fit for purpose' in the Twenty First Century. For as noted earlier, our troubled world is desperate for fresh thinking that is benign and compelling.

Thank you for your interest, and I hope that *A Philosophy For The Human World* will be of interest to you. I would be pleased of course to discuss any questions you may have.

Denis White

December 2022

Thanks and Acknowledgements

It is uniquely gratifying to thank all who have influenced the development of this philosophy. I pay tribute to the groundbreaking thinkers who created philosophy as a way of coming to grips with human life, and who have taken it to new heights over many centuries. I think of fine lecturers and teachers. I thank the scholars and researchers who bring knowledge to the world. I am greatly beholden to students who have asked perceptive questions.

I wish to recognize my good fortune. I think of family, especially my wife Carnie, our children and grandchildren — also my parents, and theirs. I think of the kindergarten, schools, universities, colleges, churches and clubs I have attended and belonged to, including places of employment. I think of access to fine libraries and galleries and performances and sports. I think of my good fortune to be an Australian — and of the scholarship schemes of Sir Robert Menzies and his Government, which gave me the privilege of attending university.

We are privileged with a rich inheritance, including the arts and sciences, sport, religion, technology, practical skills, common sense, and many disciplines. A particular debt with regard to *A Philosophy For The Human World* is to scholarly writers who have sought broad but reasoned answers to serious questions about the meaning and fundamentals of human life, about human relationships and human achievement, about politics and government, about human nature and freedom.

I thank the many friends and colleagues who have supported and contributed to this work, especially David Runia, Tony Staley, Philip Ayres, Harry Redner, Neville Crago, Simon Johnson. Without the inspiration of the late Professor Rufus Davis of Monash University, who saw to the heart of politics and human life, I would never have contemplated this work. I would never have carried this work through without the unswerving encouragement of Dr David Kemp, who has been an indefatigable and authoritative apostle of freedom in Australia for half a century.

While acknowledging how much I owe to others, and the shortcomings of what is here, I take this opportunity to make it clear that responsibility for this work rests with me.

Denis White

1

BEGINNINGS

This book pursues the consequences of two simple but far-reaching truths. The first is that humans make ways of life. The second is that humans are on their own.

There is little novelty about either proposition. But together, they provide the foundation for a philosophy which is both comprehensive and relevant for our time.

This philosophy offers a dynamic viewpoint on human activity. It underpins a commitment to freedom. It gives substance to the importance of opportunity. It harmonises the status and relationships between individuals and groups, organizations and institutions. It puts the aspirations and dreams as well as the problems and shortcomings of human beings into perspective. It contains a wealth of insight into the most effective ways of arranging human affairs.

The sphere of interest of this philosophy is the world which is continuously being made by human beings. Its point of departure is that human beings themselves must have pre-eminence for human affairs and objectives to be successfully evaluated.

The human world is made by the way people think and act and live. It includes everything that people make in order to live as they want. It encompasses each person's lot in life, both when they take it as it comes, and as they make it for themselves.

It incorporates physical reality as experienced, comprehended and adapted by humans. It includes social reality as created and developed, experienced and internalised by humans. It includes everything that moulds individuals and groups, as well as what they themselves mould. It is a world which is collective and collegial as well as individual and personal; public as well as private; theoretical as well as practical.

1. Making Ways of Life

The primary simple truth on which this work is based is that humans make ways of life.

As a minimum, the elements of a way of life must add up to something more than simply "one damn thing after another". There must be relationships of mutuality in people's activities and attitudes for their lives to be ways of life.

Ways of life embody a degree of pattern and coherence, harmony and rhythm, integration and flow, development and continuity. Ways of life have their own style, their own perspective, their own pace. They are typically in large measure made up as they develop, and they are built up upon themselves.

In short, a way of life is intelligible, and as such is totally distinct from a fragmented smorgasbord of pieces of living. And while a way of life may not necessarily be conspicuously consistent from an external point of view, it will substantially hang together in its own terms at least.

Ways of life need not be self-conscious, although they must be active as well as reactive. They need not be consciously reasoned, although they must be deliberative as well as habitual. They need not be planned, although they must be regular as well as spontaneous.

Ways of life do not simply happen. Nor are they chosen, or settled upon, once and for all, at a single point of time. Human beings make them, and do so on a continuing basis as they go along. We make them as individuals, we make them as groups, we make them as nations.

In making ways of life, we humans are neither wholly programmed nor wholly random in what we do. Ways of life are made, adopted and entered upon continuously – sometimes gradually and steadily, sometimes by fits and starts. A way of life gives form to the content of life. The shape and character of a way of life typically firms up over time, although the direction it will take in the future is never totally predictable.

2. Being On Our Own

The central thrust of saying that humans are on their own is that they have to be their own masters and mentors. In the end, humans have nothing to fall back on except themselves. The question 'what is human life all about' can only be answered in terms of what we do and think, of people's activities, ideas, interests and objectives. There is nothing like guidelines or standards to be discovered independently of ourselves.

The inevitability that certain consequences will flow from certain actions is something that people will normally want to take into account, assuming that they know about them. But we must remember that the conclusions drawn about these consequences are drawn by people. There is no inevitability about what conclusions people will draw. Any response which people make to inevitable or likely consequences is a human decision, and cannot be anything else.

There are four time honoured ways of trying to find independent standards or reference points which have inherent intrinsic authority. These four are reason, nature, religion and history. Each is considered individually below. But the essential point about all of them is that they are all used and brought into play by human agency and as a result of human decision. It is human beings, and human beings alone, who decide whether to use them, and if so how to use them. In use, they are what human beings make of them, and they cannot be anything else. They are not to be discarded on this account, and are none the worse for it, but it is important to recognise them for what they are.

Reason tells us what we think and how we think. And logic tells us something about how to make our thinking processes effective on the basis of given premises and assumptions. But reason does not and cannot of itself tell us what to think or what to do or what to be. While Socrates talked of following arguments where they lead, he was usually involved in dialogues — and it is people, not reason itself, that take arguments in particular directions[6].

A line of thought can yield a conclusion which is inescapable in terms of the argument presented. But when the conclusion is reached, a reader or listener can just as easily turn around and reject either the starting point or the basis of the argument. While it is true that people can be persuaded by reason in important matters, the fact is that few people are. It is inescapable that reason persuades us only if we let it. Thus reason leaves the mastery of humans intact, and leaves humans on their own.

Nature is like a shop which sells everything. Because it is totally undiscriminating, it gives the buyer no advice and no direction.[7] It sometimes says no, and possibly even "don't try", but it never says yes.

The more we learn of nature, the greater our sense of its directionless variety. Nature often facilitates the activities of humans. And it becomes a most potent instrument for human purposes the more we master it. But nothing is pre-eminent in nature, nor is nature ever unidirectional. Humans must take nature as we find it, and through scientific or any other kind of interpretation which we are able to construct, make what we will or can of it.

Religion is neither a solution to life nor, as some would say, an escape from life. It is itself a way of life. And while various gods may die, religion itself will never die.[8] For so long as there are mysteries to be embraced, believers will be found to weave ways of life around them.

Even if there is a God, even one who reveals God's purpose for humans, it would be up to them to interpret and live that purpose. And insofar as humans said no, this independent purpose of God would stand apart from them among the facts or the mysteries. Whether humans have control over any ultimate destiny they may have is left as an open question. But the point on which there is no question is that, in biblical terms, humans must work out their own salvation.[9]

History is no mystery – except perhaps the history we ourselves make. Humans always stand at the end of what history there is, and are always poised on the brink of future history. The direction in which history is heading is no guide to humans, for that direction is decided and determined by where they take history.[10]

There are other related points of reference by which people often try to guide their star. There are standards and morality, principles and traditions, feelings and emotions, education and knowledge, art and culture. Such factors enter into the very being of a great many people. For it is one of the great truths about humans that they have a history. This history is predominantly made up of the morality, traditions, knowledge and culture of earlier generations as expressed in their lives and behaviour.

But these elements have no life of their own, at least none to which people can appeal independently of their own decisions. Each generation must keep alive, for itself and in itself, the history of earlier generations. Human history is otherwise a contemporary irrelevance, even though it may remain retrievable at some point in the future.

This is not to say that the activities of earlier generations have no impact on the present. For the consequences of earlier human actions are facts to be taken into account in the present.

Unless history is continuously revitalised by present generations, unless we draw our own conclusions from it, then it will simply impinge upon us as other facts do. And granted that history is made up of morality, traditions, knowledge and culture, it is far more fruitful to consider what can be found in it and done with it, rather than simply to let these factors have their inevitable effects.

3. So What?

The substance of the foregoing remarks is perfectly commonplace and familiar in human experience. One initial point to emphasise is that humans are on their own and make ways of life both as individuals and as group beings.

Individuals and groups are interdependent, and it is misguided to construct theories which make them appear antagonistic.

On the one hand, the human individual is a group being. On the other hand, groups are made up of individuals. Any questions about which has priority are futile in the abstract. It is relationships that matter, as considered further below.

The eight chapters of this book fall into two groups. The first four chapters set out a number of basic considerations about humans themselves, the mechanical side of their life making activities, and their relationships with the world they inhabit. The later chapters deal with humans and their ways of life in their political and social dimensions.

The inescapable starting point in making sense of humans and their lives is that we measure things, in the widest and most comprehensive sense of this term. Chapter Two, 'The Measure Of All Things', tackles this fundamental subject.

As a race, humans have an ineradicable disposition to size things up and get their measure by classifying, comparing, numbering and evaluating them. Not only do human beings measure things, they also make the measures required to do what they want done.

More than this, humans are themselves the ultimate measure. The ultimate reference point of human beings has to be themselves — their own perceptions and attitudes, their own capacities and concerns. There can be no other point of reference if only because human beings would have to weigh up any proposed alternative by reference to themselves anyway.

With themselves as the ultimate albeit developing standard, humans decide not only what to measure, but also the kinds of measurements to make, as well as the units and scales to be used.

Machinery, including everything designed or used to achieve some purpose beyond itself, is equally indispensable in making ways of life. The nature and role of machines, along with the ways in which people relate to them, are the subject of the third chapter.

Machinery in this broad sense has an impact on almost every sphere of human life. It is both an element and a product of the human world, and also a major influence upon it. Machinery is a spur to inventiveness, and often a force for liberation. It enables difficulties to be surmounted, and gives humans unparalleled mastery over their own circumstances.

There is, of course, another side to this equation. Machines which outlive their usefulness can become a drag on human development. In addition, there is a potentially uncontrollable quality about certain devices – and organisations – created by human beings. This makes an overall perspective on the role of machinery in human affairs doubly important.

While humans can achieve tremendous mastery over their circumstances, they are equally subject to restrictions and limitations in what they can do. These limitations are sometimes quantifiable, and sometimes immeasurable.

Chapter Four, entitled 'Mystery and the Facts', is concerned with the boundaries of the human world and the limits on human activity. We inhabit a world of unshakeable fact on the one hand, and impenetrable uncertainty on the other. In a very large number of our activities, we come up against elusive qualities just as much as identifiable quantities.

Human knowledge has considerable reach, but we are often

uncertain about whether our knowledge is sufficient for the practical purposes in which we are engaged. Human achievement can extend in endless directions, but there is a great deal that we always have to allow for and take into account in whatever we may be doing.

If there was nothing that humans needed to take into account, they would be in an impossible and nonsensical position. We would have to create a world from nothing in every generation. There could be neither history nor improvement. And people's uncertainty about what might come next would be boundless. On the other hand, however, inconvenient facts are unquestionably an irritant to us, for they limit us even though they may also enable us to act with confidence within various limits. Disruptive uncertainties are also an irritant, for they foil human plans even though they may also enable humans to hope and dream.

The function of these first four chapters, then, is to map the most fundamental features of the human world. They set out and amplify a series of considerations about human beings themselves, about the mechanics which underlie making ways of life, and about our relationships with the world we inhabit.

The following three chapters deal respectively with groups, politics and decision-making. These chapters are concerned with the nature of various human relationships, and with the issues of authority, influence and power.

In looking at each of these subjects in turn, the central objective is to explain what each of them does *to* people, and what they do *for* people. These matters are considered in the light of their implications for the two central truths that humans are on their own and that they make ways of life.

There are, for example, certain threats looming against

humans as the head and centre of their world. For there is, as noted already, an appearance of something uncontrollable about certain forces and devices constructed by human agency, and about certain organisational structures which human beings have created. Organisations, for example, can demand so much that people have little or no time to make or live their own ways of life. And some organisations have become endowed with a degree of functional autonomy which makes it well nigh impossible to rein them in.

In earlier periods, humans have always been able to reassert their mastery if they have been displaced from the centre. But there is no reason to assume that this capacity to rise again is necessarily indestructible in human beings. It is a daunting prospect that human capacity to make ways of life may entail a corresponding capacity not only to destroy ways of life, but possibly also to destroy the capacity to make them.

These are grim prospects. But there are also positive and encouraging implications to be drawn from the overall analysis. Humans undoubtedly do have the capacity to prevent the living of some ways of life. But it is equally open to humans, especially if they know what they are doing, to facilitate certain ways of life. We are able to act in ways which create the opportunities and secure the freedom which are needed if the two basic truths of this work are to have their fullest play.

While the philosophy which is developed in the course of this book is realistic, and while it inevitably sounds a number of warning bells, it is inherently a philosophy of optimism. For it implies that the mainsprings of civilization and development are always being renewed, always there to be revitalised. In the end, all these concerns come back to what human beings are, what they can do and be, and above all, how they need to act in order to remain themselves and retain their powers. And it is this primacy and pre-eminence of people that is reasserted and more fully explained in the eighth and final chapter.

2

THE MEASURE OF ALL THINGS[11]

1. Humans Themselves The Measure

People's most immediate consciousness is of themselves. We feel ourselves to be distinct, and we know that we are something in our own right. We can decide for ourselves, think for ourselves, understand for ourselves, act for ourselves.

We live in a world that is external to ourselves. It is a world that impinges upon us, a world of which we are a part. Yet we are distinct from it. Each one of us could imagine the whole world disappearing altogether – being completely obliterated – while we remained – at least for a time.

We do not feel distinct because we think and act whereas other parts of the world do not. Of course, the things that are unique to humans play a part in determining what they are. But the real point is that our thinking and acting turn us in on ourselves and back on ourselves. The very act of thinking contains within it a consciousness of one's own distinctness. It brings a sense of one's own identity, and perhaps also a sense of one's own integrity.

Humans are conscious of themselves, of being something. This consciousness is not merely of existence. Nor do humans conclude that they exist, for they take their existence for granted. Their more immediate and pressing question concerns what they are. And they cannot but wonder what they are both in relation to things around them, and also in themselves. What they are in relation to the rest of reality is one thing, and a very important thing. But what they are in themselves, as distinct and apart from everything else, is a different matter.

That we think, and act, and understand, and love and hate, and feel and have consciousness – what does that make us? 'Who or what am I, purely in myself and distinct from everything else that may or may not be' is a question that humans can be driven onto. And as humans, we must both find and give the answer to it from out of ourselves.

That we, as humans, relate to others and have experiences; that we need things outside of ourselves; that we are part of the world as well as distinct from it; that each of us is simply one person out of all the other members of the human race: we must ask ourselves what these 'things' make us.

Comparisons with non-human things may help us answer these questions. But such comparisons help us more to say what we are not than what we are. Real answers must come from within ourselves.

The question 'Who am I' is more basic than 'What are humans?' To be sure, we may derive some aid and comfort from a relapse into the latter question. But people cannot begin to answer this latter question except in terms of themselves, except from out of their own perceptions and conceptions. Each of us must answer the question about humans by using the resources of ourselves. The distinctness of each one of us – in every sense of the term – makes this inescapable. We simply have nothing else to go on, nothing else to start with, nothing else to use.

The pure being of a human person is wholly abstract.

Conceiving of ourselves in the absence of absolutely everything else is sheerly contemplative. For humans not merely are, but they live. And living is part and condition of their being in any substantive sense of the term.

People's living is their own affair. They are not caught in the toils of all absorbing instincts, nor do they follow some set pattern over which they have no say or control. On the contrary, humans make their own lives. They decide what they shall do and to some extent what they think. They adopt courses of life as their own. People make their own ways of life, and in the course of doing this they also make their own natures – of which more later. Humans do not live and act without any outside influences – and of that also, more later.

Humans live in a world, and they cannot live by the unknown, nor can they live adequately in a world of which they can make nothing. For granted that they must live in some sort of relationship, not to say sympathy with that world, they must be able in some sense to come to grips with it.

A being whose life followed some pre-determined pattern, a being that had no control over its own life, would have no need to grasp the way the world is. But any sort of mastery – and making one's own life even in the smallest measure must involve some degree of mastery no matter how slight – involves a need for some knowledge of the way things are.

Humans can do nothing until they have in some sense sized things up. We know this if we will but look at infants, who topple off chairs and merely cry instead of knowing that they must get down if they are to be able to walk away.

Humans must come to terms with their surroundings. In order to do this, they need to have some grasp of what they are. And in order to have such a grasp, they need to have some measure of their surroundings. The distinctness of humans from their surroundings makes it impossible for them to be in immediate harmony with these surroundings, to know them through and through in a way that might be called instinctive.

In infancy, of course, we can take much for granted, provided there is someone to look after us. In infancy, indeed, we die without someone to look after us. For humans cannot live without some sort of measure, and in infancy we cannot do our own measuring, so unless someone does it for us – and this is the real essence of being looked after – then we die.

Infants grow towards ways of life, they are led and initiated into them. And some people never succeed in casting off these swaddling clothes – they never live a life that is at all their own, they simply continue on, never acquiring any resources of their own, in some path to which they have been accustomed. These are the people who never grow up. They are in a way parasitic upon those who do grow to maturity and then find that they are in a real sense on their own.

In maturity, we humans have to fall back upon ourselves. It is not a question of solitude or isolation, for we are in the midst of a great deal, particularly if we are going all out in the general business of living. It is rather a question of independence, of superiority, of being the one whose business it is to be on top and to take charge.

It is not a shortcoming in the world that humans are on their own. People who feel that way are really not up to the role of being human. It is a mark of our eminence and our dominance, that we are on our own.

Humans would belittle themselves if they merely took things as they come. To do that is simply to be carried along on the road and at the pace of earlier generations. There is no sanctity in that, for those generations were not of giants any taller or stronger than ours.

By the same token to take anything for granted is to give up the fullness of one's own independence. That is a case, once again, of depending on others who cannot be presumed to be any better or wiser than oneself. This is not of course to say that one may not presume to put one's trust in someone else on some particular matter or type of matter – a case of delegation.

Humans are on their own and must fall back upon themselves in the world. They are not appendages, and they are independent in the sense that they decide what is what and what shall be – within limits of course. But they are dependent in the sense that they must make their way and live their lives in the world. They must come to terms with it no less than with themselves.

Humans cannot live by the unknown, and they cannot begin to make a way of life in the midst of the completely unknown. If people have no grasp of things, no sense of what might come next – none at all – then they can do no more than react. They can only live on a completely *ad hoc* basis. Their mastery and superiority become emasculated, and they become less than human. We know that this is so because we know that human beings have been deliberately subjected to this kind of regimen with precisely this consequence.

Coming to grips with the world and sizing it up is fundamentally a matter of measurement. We can understand nothing of the human situation if we fail to understand that humans compare things. They put things alongside each other, and determine this that or the other thing about one by comparison with the other. And they do this by reference to some unit or scale or standard of measurement.

Measurement is not just a matter of feet and inches, nor even of properties such as good or evil. To get the measure of something is to get at its inner nature, at its essential being, at its place in both the general and the overall scheme of things. The notion of the essential being of something that is external to humans will be seen to be a tricky one, for it must be realised that the being of things apart from humans has to do with humans and what humans make of them. So measuring even at this level is not simply a matter of discovering something that exists apart from people.

The heart of this opening section concerns units, scales and standards of measurement. When we put things alongside each other in order to measure and size them up, there is a virtual infinity of aspects we might choose to take into account.

To be even more fundamental about it, until humans develop some standards or measures, they could put things against each other to be compared, and not know where or how to begin to make a comparison. A thinking person might realise immediately that there are endless possibilities for comparison when two things are put beside each other. But points of comparison and bases of comparison do not appear to exist in the nature of things.

What is a reference point, or a unit or a standard? While they are all different from each other, they all have to do with the reality that measurement for its own sake is an incoherent notion.

Measurement must be for some purpose, must be related to something. For while there is an illimitable number of ways in which it would be possible to take note of the objects which the world presents to the attention of humans, there is nothing to show which of them would be illuminating, interesting, or worthwhile. Nature presents itself to us in an utterly raw form.

It needs some dressing – but does not tell us which dressings would be tasty or agreeable.

When its eyes begin to focus, a baby sees everything – and yet it also sees nothing at that stage, when it has no reference point, and nothing to tie its visual experiences up with. At that stage, the baby appears to have no sense even of itself, but only of its hunger. A reference point, at the most fundamental level, enables us to make something of what we experience, of what we feel, of what we think. Raw experience, raw feeling and even raw thought (to the extent that it differs from feeling) give every impression of being almost totally undifferentiated.

But humans hardly remain in that situation. They no sooner begin to experience than they begin to develop reference points and standards for things. We see this happening very quickly with children. Babies quickly develop some kind of orientation. Humans are unable to do other than relate the world to themselves.

A reference point enables us to identify things and say what they are. Initially at least, so far as humans are concerned, things are nothing in themselves. And what they are is intimately bound up with what they are for. Only when we have got this far can we begin to compare things. The notion of sizing the world up involves comparing the objects we find around us. But we can only begin to compare when we have become able to identify; and identification already presumes that we have – or are developing — reference points. We must be able to refer things to something that we know, something which is such that we have both an immediate and a definite sense of what it is.

It is not easy to discuss the notions of reference points, or basic orientations, in general terms. The phenomenon itself is extremely primitive, and something that humans obtain for themselves before they reach any level of sophisticated consciousness. We certainly do not cast about for a fundamental reference point, and choose the one that seems the best of the available options. On the contrary, we could not possibly do any choosing for ourselves without a point of reference of some kind.

This is the other part of why it is difficult to talk abstractly about reference points — namely that we can talk about them only from the vantage point of already having one. People can make nothing of their experience, their situation, or indeed, even of themselves, without some sort of reference point, something to which to relate what goes on with them, what happens to them and what they do.

People do not need to be particularly conscious of their own basic reference points. Indeed, such consciousness is hardly possible, granted that these points are so much the basis of all that they actually articulate. It is only when one becomes reflective, and stands somewhat apart from oneself – and then only if one is capable of a degree of detachment – that one is able to begin to articulate that which is really at the foundation of all one's articulations.

In a primitive sense, as noted, what things are, and what they are for, are closely bound up with each other. In the same way, how good they are is also integral to their being. Thus the notion of a standard is closely linked with that of a reference point. Whether either has the primacy is not really the point here, although I would incline to give it to the reference point. The real issue is that what things are, what they are for, and how good they are (perhaps I should say 'how satisfactory they are'), are all bound up with each other. In a primitive sense they may be said to be undifferentiated. The answer 'it is no good' in reply to the question 'what is that' could seem odd only to a philosopher. In all other respects, it may be a perfectly proper answer, one that saves both time and talk.

A standard is perhaps a trickier thing to identify than a point of reference. Certainly, a standard in the sense in question here need not be formulated, or even consciously identified or adopted. Again, whether it is utilitarian or absolute is of no real concern. The distinctions between various theories of morals and quality come rather late on the scene, and are themselves the product of considerable sophistication. The quality of a thing is, in a fundamental sense, a part or aspect of what it is. And a standard is that by which humans determine and discover what the quality of a thing is.

A standard in this sense does not allow for any simple definition or indeed application. (And it should not be forgotten that a standard, in the most general sense, is something that has to do with accuracy as well as quality.) The quality and goodness of things must be judged by reference to something. Or if 'judged' suggests too self-conscious an act, then we might substitute some notion such as 'viewed' or 'conceived'. In a sense, this kind of assessment is comparative, and the comparison between the items and objects that we find to hand doubtless comes quite early on the scene. But the very idea of making such comparisons depends on something more basic and fundamental. Humans have, or early acquire, a sense of there being quality and adequacy and goodness – without such a sense, they cannot proceed at all in sizing up the world and coming to terms with it.

A unit is a more sophisticated and 'civilized' phenomenon than either a standard or a point of reference – but it is by the same token their immediate if somewhat confused offspring. By the time that units come on the scene in any codified form, persons have advanced far along the road towards self-consciousness and mastery of their world – and indeed of determination of their world.

But there are also more primitive units — and more importantly, a sense of units before any codification of them. 'Bigger or truer or better' are the immediate offspring of 'big or true or good', and similarly, 'bigger or truer or better by how much' come immediately on the heels of the former. In the beginning, there is doubtless no capacity to define the units with which one works in going from gross to more refined comparisons.

But what cannot be escaped is that we no sooner start to make comparisons than we also start to make comparative comparisons. And the notion of comparative comparisons brings with it – or rather presupposes the idea of – units, and some sort of formulated or at least dimly conceived units must be at work or in operation concurrently with this.

Fundamentally, humans are themselves their own points of reference. Humans are themselves their own standards. Humans are themselves the bases of the units with which they measure. Humans relate things to themselves first and foremost and finally. For in the end – and probably in the beginning as well – there is nothing else to which to relate them.

It is as a consequence of the whole fullness of our nature that we are incapable of relating things except to ourselves. It is because we can think, because we can feel, because we are self-conscious, because we are aware of ourselves as distinct from anything else, because we can initiate, because we can decide and act – it is because of all these that we humans are ultimately our own reference points and our own standards.

Even if there were some focal point within nature, even if there is some God at the head of the universe (or of reality), humans could still not escape the fate of being their own points of reference. For we would still have to decide to go by this focal point or God. If we failed to do so, then our world would be a false one, and our lives would be something of a fantasy. Doubtless, too, we would pay the price of living a kind of lie inasmuch that our affairs would go awry and our perceptions be askew. Nevertheless, our lives would be our own. And in the same regard, persons who did accept the real focal point for what it is, and who in a sense gave way to it, would also be in the position of ultimate deciders of what <u>their</u> world is all about. They could always turn around and abandon the truth for the illusion if that was their wish or their conviction about where the truth of the matter lay.

I have spoken about a focal point as if, presuming one existed, it would be comparatively obvious to see. But the most conspicuous of facts about our situation is that even if there is a God or focal point – which of course is greatly disputed, and I do not mean to enter into this dispute – then it is not readily discernible. Even the greatest devotees of revelation all agree that some particular kinds of eyes are necessary in order to perceive the Truth – whether they be eyes that are opened by faith or by works or by grace or by contemplation or whatever. Standing off, and looking dispassionately at what all these eyes purport to discover, the conclusion seems inescapable that no focal point can be taken for granted, that is, if present at all, shrouded in very considerable mystery which is impenetrable so far as most people at least are concerned.

Whether God created "man" in "his" own image is certainly in great dispute. But there can be no dispute that humans have created many gods in their own image. These gods are not of course God. But they are not on that account to be rejected as sheerly delusive. For they become a shorthand for their creators. When humans use such gods as their ultimate point of reference, they are really doing nothing more than taking themselves as their points of reference. And in making gods, humans are setting up their own conception of what they themselves really are.

It is an amazing thing about humans that they have conceptions of themselves, that they are capable of asking 'who am I', that they form ideas about their own nature. And it is perhaps the more amazing that different people treat the question of human nature from almost entirely different and indeed conflicting viewpoints. Some people write themselves up to the stars, others write themselves down to the depths. But that humans can write in these terms at all – whether the terms used be elevated or degrading – is itself remarkable.

In relating themselves to the world, humans relate the world to themselves. Those who write themselves down write down the whole world. And those who write themselves up write up the whole world. People may beat their own breasts, and say that they are unworthy. But in saying that, they will usually be comparing themselves with other humans. There is a world of difference between saying that oneself is unworthy, and that humankind is unworthy. Unworthiness is a comparative idea, and presumes that there is something worthy.

There are many people who will say that humankind is nothing, but they are really saying in part at least that the world is of no account. They are gloomy all round. And there is something fundamentally incoherent about the view that beauty is all you need to know.[12] The incoherence rests in the fact that we have here a view to end all views – yet insofar as it is a view, and insofar as views are disputable and need to establish their credentials, such a view cannot really put an end to views; and so it cannot be the beginning and the end.

Humans conceive of themselves in endless ways, and see themselves in endless guises. The reality of human-ness, the essence of being human, what it is to be a human, what it is that makes people persons even — these various formulations are all different ways of coming at the question, the issue, of what people really are. They are different approaches to people's conceptions of what they themselves are.

Of course, in line with this, different people conceive of themselves (and thus of others too) in radically different terms. Some regard mind and reason as all important, others regard feeling and sense as all important. Some think thought important, others action. Some think that people's bodies, and their bodily functions, are the crux, others think that the body is almost an impediment (or at best a kind of necessary but unpleasant or irritating necessary condition) to the reign of the spirit and soul of human beings. Thus, insofar as people make explicit their conceptions of themselves, they disagree quite fundamentally.

But there is perhaps an even more fundamental divergence, which theorists can easily overlook. For it is of the essence of some conceptions of being human, (of some people's conceptions of themselves), that they are not explicit. Those who never theorise, or who never subscribe overtly to any expressed conception of what a human person is, do not on that account necessarily have no conception at all. Perhaps the term 'conception' is a misnomer here, but there is often present some sense or grasp of what being human is.

To conceptualize such grasps is not perhaps wholly impossible, if the greatest anthropological skill is employed. And the important point is that such conceptions cannot be expected to conform with the usual run of focuses – such as reason or action. On the contrary, one might very well expect something rather less finely formed, something that does not draw quite the distinctions which theorists draw. Furthermore, these inarticulate formulations are quite likely to relate being human more immediately to the world around them. For those who do not theorise are less apt to be introspective, and more apt to relate themselves directly to the world as they experience it.

That human beings have a conception of themselves is an integral part of their being human. Further, the particular conception that persons have of themselves is a vital ingredient of human-ness as the measure. It is not merely what we are that is the measure, but what we think we are. Indeed, the latter is the more important. There are clear correlations between the way in which different people think of themselves, and the way in which they size up the world. Those who stress the contemplative side of being human, for instance, tend to write down the material world, those who stress the active side of being human tend to stress the world's potential, those who see humans as beings of flesh and blood tend to view the material world as something of an extension of themselves.

These are extremely broad comparisons. People's conceptions of themselves ramify in far greater detail into their conceptions of what the world is. People relate the world to themselves because they can do no other. People see the world through their own eyes because they can attain no other view of it. For the world affords no perspective on itself.

The distinction between the objective and the subjective has no substance in the end. This is not to say that all views are of equal worth and weight, that no measures are more fruitful than others – though there is more to be said about that. What we need to seek is not some transcendent, totally objective view of the world, but rather something fruitful and illuminating. There is of course a degree of objectivity about certain kinds of measurements – such as length related to the standard metre – but this hardly takes us anywhere in terms of really getting a sense of the world. To know whether something is big is usually far more worth knowing than exactly how long it is. And knowing how long it is does not really help with knowing whether it is big. Furthermore, bigness cannot be wholly analysed away in terms of being a comparative notion.

Notions such as bigness – I choose this particular notion because it is at the basis of measurement as we generally conceive it – have a great deal to do with how the objects in question affect people. We deem a thing big if it dwarfs us, if we cannot control it, if it gets the better of us. And we deem ourselves to be affected, not just when something makes some kind of insignificant difference to us (although that is the strict meaning of the term), but when we are, in a manner of speaking, outdone; we are affected by forces that make their impact upon us regardless of what we may ourselves think or feel. And the things that we deem to be big are the things that are capable of doing this to us – the things that either do it, or that we believe capable of doing it.

Humans have an enormous tendency to view things insofar as they affect themselves. Indeed, they have no reason to view them in any other light. And people do not, nor should they, view such influences on themselves in a purely clinical way. They cannot be expected to engage in a purely cold kind of scientific appraisal of them. What things can do is what they do do to human beings. Things are strong if they have twice our strength, they are potent if they have an impact upon us even though they may have no impact whatever on anything else whatever. Correspondingly humans would think of lightning as merely a distant fact or even possibly a mystery if it were not that lightning sometimes strikes humans. People are wholly unconcerned with 'forces' which have no impact upon themselves, which have their being in a world which does not affect humans.

This is in no way surprising. The measure of something is its impact upon humans. And its impact upon humans is determined by humans themselves. Insofar as persons relate things to themselves, they themselves become their measure. The strength of things is weighed against people's own strength, their size against people's size, and their general significance against people's conception of themselves. In all of this, people's conceptions of themselves are of the utmost importance. In many ways, it matters not what the human person is (whatever that might mean), but rather what people think they are. Whether something matters depends upon what people think matters. And what people think matters depends in turn very immediately upon what people think they themselves are. The most mighty physical force is nothing much to persons who think their physical components have little importance. The most poignant poem is nothing to the people who pay no heed to any sensibilities that might have been developed within themselves. And the most horrendous brutality is nothing to people who take no thought of themselves as moral or feeling beings.

One of the most conspicuous indications of the human disposition to make ourselves the measure is our tendency to anthropomorphise the world around us. It is perhaps our greatest compliment to the world that we do so. In a sense, it may be said that we obscure the truth of other things by seeing them in our own image, for we thereby confound their essential nature. But that could be important only if things had an intrinsic nature of their own. By anthropomorphising, we bring the world closer to ourselves, we place it in a perspective which makes it immediately intelligible to ourselves. To impute feelings and understandings to beings which have none is of course to engage in a kind of unrealism. But on the other hand it has a considerable bearing on the way humans relate themselves to the things in question, and how humans treat them.

In any event, the question is hardly whether humans should anthropomorphize. The question is rather about the significance of the fact that we do anthropomorphize. We might ask why we do this. And the answer is surely that we do it in order to be able to bring ourselves into some more immediate kind of relationship with them. If that is the human way of coming to terms with them – or a way – then who is to gainsay it? Of course, it is not the only way which humans employ.

In a sense, the variety of measures is as great as the number of humans. There is no person but can be his or her own measure. Just as humans can see the world only through human eyes, so individuals can see the world only through their own eyes. Each person is his or her own measure. Each of us is the measure for ourself, so far at least as each of us is concerned. This does not mean that it is impossible to misread the length of a stick in metres. It rather means, in this context, that it is open to someone to decide whether or not to go by measurements in metres. One may not set much store by the length of things. We can see this illustrated in the case of houses. A thirty metre hall is thirty metres long whatever anyone may say. And to some, the fact that the hall of a house measures thirty metres may be of the last significance. But to a person who is concerned only about where a house is located, that measurement will have no bearing. Or again, in the case of a painting, the dimensions may be of major importance to some people, and of none to others.

That each person is his or her own measure does not signify bedlam. The human race could never have survived if there were no linkages, no connections, no interrelationships, between the individuality of the measures of every individual. Human beings do not constitute themselves *de novo*, nor do they develop a conception of themselves without the influence of historical factors and of their background generally. Individuals live their lives in groups, and come to maturity in the womb of groups. This detracts in no way from the fact that each person is individual. But there is no initial situation in which humans do or conceivably could begin to decide upon what they would be or how they would wish to relate to their fellows.

The influences to which we are subject in our relationships with other people have a prominent impact on how we come to conceive of ourselves, and on the factors around us which we decide to take into account. The measure that each person is has its own breeding line. It is itself despite this, but it is greatly influenced by this. Some such breeding lines produce progeny which are widely recognised to be of high quality in themselves, and these are then disseminated widely. By the same token, there are bad breeding lines which produce progeny which are, to be sure, themselves, and which may not die out, even though they may not do well in any sense at all. Again, there can be in-breeding, which creates peculiar distortions of many kinds, and which may be extremely difficult to do anything about when once it has happened.

So while there are as many measures as individuals, and

while each has its own peculiar authority, there are also connections and degrees of influence to be taken into account. All people relate things back to themselves, to what they think of themselves, to what they think they are. In the absence of any reference points, standards or units in nature, individual people have no option but to refer back to themselves.

The next section of this chapter looks at the kinds of measuring that humans do, and the third section then turns to the kinds of measures that humans make.

2. Humans As Measurers

That humans measure, and that they are themselves the basic measure, are matters of critical significance for understanding the status of each human being. It has already been noted that the fact that humans are the measure means that nobody can be gainsaid. This requires amplification, to tease out its implications.

Many attempts have been made to find a word or concept that encapsulates this high status of humans. It is different from the concept of human dignity. For fundamental as dignity is for humanity, it is not about what humans are or do, but rather about how they should be regarded and treated. It is not active and it is not dynamic.

The word that serves the present purpose most adequately is 'originality'. Every human, insofar as they are measurers and have themselves as the basic measure, is original. Each person is an originator, all people start with themselves, and no person can have any other starting point.

Turning this around the other way, what is being said is that there is no higher starting point than oneself. Nor can one tell others that there is any higher starting point than themselves. There is nothing above the human person, and no person is above other persons. All persons possess within themselves – indeed are by virtue of themselves – a kind of universality. Every person is the centre of the universe so far as they are themselves concerned. All persons are in a kind of supreme position by virtue of being the standard and point of reference for themselves.

The originality of each person is something different from notions such as integrity or autonomy or independence or uniqueness. Nor does it imply that each person is eccentric, or that there is no commonality to be found in human affairs. Again, originality is a different concept from dignity – as considered above — or inherent worthwhileness. But plainly, there is need to make connections with all of these (and similar) notions. They all go very much together, and the notion of originality forms a lynch pin and indeed a basis for all of them. The human person as measurer and as the measure has massive and profound ramifications in connection with the status of humans.

The originality of humans has much to do with individualism. If each person is their own standard and supreme, if no person can have any other starting point than themselves, if each person is the measure and measurer of all things, then the individuality of each person would seem to be a distinct possibility in fact, and certainly an unarguable legitimacy if it were to come to pass. If each person were to maximise the distinctiveness of their own lifestyle and take no account of the persuasions of others to conform to a certain pattern, of whatever kind, then there could be no basis for gainsaying them in this – except perhaps insofar as their own survival and that of others was brought into question. Further, although most may not seek to maximise the distinctiveness of their own lifestyles – indeed, though virtually all may choose to conform to a certain pattern or set of patterns – there is nothing to gainsay individuals who wish to do something in their own way. This is a point of vast significance, and is pursued further in the final chapter.

Most people in fact are disposed to conform in very considerable measure – they lack the interest, the will-power, and perhaps also the inventiveness to go it alone in any substantial sense of the term. But this does not detract from their originality. Nor indeed does the fact of their originality impose upon them any particular procedure. In the most extreme case, if persons simply allow themselves to fall into certain patterns of life – without thought or decision or any deliberation whatever – then there is nothing to gainsay their doing that. One might deplore such lethargy, and be saddened at such an outcome from originality – but their originality means that if that is what they do with it, if that is the way in which they measure things – then that is it for them.

But it must also be said that there are contexts in which conformism comes to be. Originality is not active or functional in humans at birth, and its fruiting can be held back, altered, or even altogether prevented. If people come to conform, not even because they allow themselves to fall into conformism, but because they are manipulated to the point of not being allowed (i.e. of being prevented from) attaining any sense of themselves as measure and measurer, then their originality has been subverted. It is often impossible in fact to determine whether a person has been manipulated to such an extent. And it is probably impossible to say whether all people are, from the outset of life, susceptible to such manipulation. It is probably even impossible to assert with any confidence that the originality which is latent in each person is actually capable of being brought to fruition. It is the highest calling of political science to reach sound judgments on these questions, and I return to them in chapters four, five and six.

Further to the earlier comments about it, human originality can also be shown to have much to do with the idea of human dignity. If one comes at the concept of dignity via the idea of originality, then one can begin to give some content to the former by reference to what I have already referred to as the individual not being gainsaid. The human person as measure and measurer counts for something. Each person is a source of universality – universality in the sense of being the potential constructor of what I might call here a general philosophy, i.e. a complete conception of what is, an account of the sense of human and other life. And it is the potentiality that is of real account in this connection. A potential source of universality counts for something whether or not the potential is realised.

In this view, the dignity of human beings consists in what they are no less than in what they do – indeed, the two go very much together, construing 'doing' in the widest possible sense. Human dignity, on this view, is a kind of compound. It stems from the originating potentials of human individuals. And it *is* one's being worth waiting upon, it is one's being a measure, it is one's being original. It is because humans are the measure of all things that they have dignity. This dignity consists essentially in a particular way of apprehending that they are the measure of all things. And this mode of apprehension consists in realization and appreciation of the truth that nothing could be greater, as a quality of conceivable beings, than their being the measure of all things – whether we regard such beings collectively or individually.

The integrity of the human person is consequential upon their originality, and depends upon the way in which they use it – on what they do with it. Integrity is a concept of limited range – persons of integrity may have little else going for them, and their integrity may not itself amount to anything much. There is both conscious and unconscious integrity. The former is particularly to be sought in those who think a good deal and who are self-conscious about their way of life. This kind of integrity is principally a matter, in the first place of honesty, and in the second of deliberate or attempted consistency. Persons who are aware of themselves as being a measure and measurer must be honest in what they say and do about measuring – honest both to themselves and to others, honest in relating their measurings to themselves and in relating both themselves and their measurings to others. But they must also relate their measurings to each other and thereby attain to consistency.

The unconscious kind of integrity is to be found in those who are not self-conscious as well as in those who are. Unconscious integrity has to do principally with coherence in the way in which one relates things to oneself. One can be one's own point of reference without thinking too much about what this amounts to or how one will go about relating things to oneself and oneself to the world. If there is coherence in the way that one relates to things, then one's life and oneself possess integrity. Coherence as used here has to do with harmony and congruence between the various measurings which one devises and employs. It is a kind of intangible and unwritten consistency.

Integrity is doubtless a good thing so far as it goes. But its limitation is that is does not in itself take account of the fittingness of one's consistency, coherence or even honesty. Integrity can be perfectly compatible with ineptness, with misguidedness, indeed with a life that is perfectly disgraceful at its very foundation.

Independence and uniqueness are closely linked with the notion of individualism. Originality does not mean either that one cannot link one's lot with that of others, or that one has to be different from others. Individuals can remain their own measures while binding their lot extremely closely with the lots of others. The division of labour – even the division of what may be called life – is perfectly consistent with the originality of each person. In addition, originality is no precluder of identical twins. Twins remain their individual selves, and the lack of uniqueness as between them in no way detracts from the fact that each is individual. Even the fact that at the physiological level each is virtually identical, even the fact that this physiological factor may have immense impact on the kind of measurings which they make and rely upon, does not impugn the originality of either in any way. For this originality has its being on an altogether different plane from that of physiology.

Every person, by virtue of their originality, may lay claim – and there exists no standpoint from which this claim may be contested – to have their own life and being. In a fundamental sense, the originality of none is greater than that of any other. And we certainly cannot foretell where a person's originality may or may not lead. There is only one perspective, as it were, from which a person may be banished, and that is the perspective of another person – who may equally be banished by the one. That humans are the measure of all things places humans in the highest possible or conceivable position. But it does not place humanity higher than individual humans, nor any human higher than any other human. Humans have a kind of greatly superior status by reference to everything but their fellow humans. In a sense we may say that the very elevating doctrine being talked about here has rather levelling consequences. The notion that humans are the measure of all things gives them the largest of advantages, but not over those over whom many humans would alone seek superiority, namely their fellow humans.

How far such claims may be allowed to go – granted the possibility of conflicts arising – is a theoretical problem for political science and a practical problem for governments. How extensively such claims will be asserted would appear to be a kind of reflection of the educational process which each person undergoes and which holds sway in any particular society. I talk of education to include virtually all experience in the formative years — for however long they may extend — and also to include all the inculcation in interpretation that befalls a person. How pressingly such claims may be pushed would appear to depend upon qualities such as determination, strength of will, and self-confidence. There are many kinds of pressing, some relentless, some intransigent, some quietly persistent, some lacking persistence. The sources of such qualities are obscure, and so it is difficult to say how they may best be generated – which means that the question of how far they should be generated is not one that needs to be confronted from a practical point of view.

In the foregoing discussion I have perhaps seemed unduly cavalier about moving between the language of description and that of assessment. I have certainly not preserved the sharp distinction, the logical gulf, that is so prevalent in much contemporary thought. But the point is – the gulf distinction seems not to work. The ramifications of humans being both measurer and measure do not confine themselves to either level of discourse. Indeed – to use a term which itself tends rather to go around the fact/value distinction – it is by no means clear whether we are dealing in the realm of fact or of value (as these realms are defined and divided by those who want to make much of them and keep them separate) with the statement that humans are the measure of all things. On the contrary, this statement seems not to fit into either category with any ease. It is neither fact nor value, but rather the fundamental nature, fundamental quality, a basic statement about what humans really are.

And so we come to the second part of this section. Humans measure and are the measure. But they are not themselves unaffected by their measuring. We must consider what measuring does to humans and for them. What enters into the soul of a measuring being? How do the distinctive measurings which individuals make enter into their souls and affect their being? What do humans lose when they begin to measure, and what do they gain?

The most fundamental feature of measuring beings is that they cannot simply take life as it comes. Upon measuring beings, as a result of their measurings, comes a sense of the reality of things, of the balance of things, of the differences and conflicts between things. To say that humans lose their innocence when they begin to measure is to put the point in too dramatic and obscure a way. But there is something important in this way of putting it. For it brings out the point that the measuring being is a calculating kind of being – and beings who calculate do not merely measure lengths and the like, they are on the road to weighing up everything that they may come across. And if the most calculating people are in a way the least attractive, they may also be said to be the most intense practitioners of humanness in its most distinctive aspect.

The thing is, here, that once people begin to measure, there is no saying how far they might end up taking their measuring. In a sense they themselves have no control over how far it might take them. Being the measure of all things does not tell you which matters are appropriate to be measured. Nor does it give much guidance on the question of the desirable transferral of measures from one kind of matter to another.

There is a sense in which the beginning of measuring marks a decline in the flexibility of a person. As soon as one adopts some particular kind of measure, then one suffers a loss of potential. For once having adopted a particular kind of measure for a particular kind of matter, one is hard put to see that matter in other terms. It is perhaps not impossible to ask whether the kind of measuring that one has adopted for a particular kind of matter is the most fruitful one: but it is extremely difficult, and calls for a rare degree of detachment, dispassionateness, and flair for comparative thinking.

As humans measure, as they relate the world to themselves and themselves to the world, humans themselves solidify. They assume a progressively and increasingly fixed shape. In terms of both form and content they become more set. They become more at home in the world, more at ease with it; but by the same token the world progressively loses some of its interest and excitement in the course of this happening. One becomes more confident in one's dealing with the world, and more able to manipulate it as one desires to do. But at the same time, one increasingly blinkers oneself to certain aspects of the world and to certain ways of seeing it; and there are fewer things that one would contemplate doing.

Measuring, then, results in humans pinning themselves down in the very act of defining themselves. But it need not lead to ossification. We cannot keep all our options open, except by failing to realize ourselves at all. But it is not impossible for humans to think of rethinking their whole position. If they have to do so in terms of the position which they have already evolved for themselves, that is perhaps not so much more limiting than having to measure *de novo*, i.e., with wholly unarticulated resources – which is after all the position in which humans necessarily have to start. In starting from the *de novo* position, we are not working with the bland sheet of <u>infinite</u> possibility. What we will be able to make of ourselves depends very considerably upon the capacities we have, the ways in which we can and do see things, not to mention the influences to which we are undoubtedly subject.

But measuring not merely pins humans down and defines them. It also enables and ennobles them. It gives them scope, and gives their activities range of a virtually incalculable kind. Measuring is the basis of persons becoming able to make, and to attain mastery. If humans were not measurers, their parts and attainments would be singularly inconsequential and ill-adapted to effectiveness. They might be able to follow bodily drives, and engage in certain physical exploits, except that it is doubtful whether they could survive at all.

For without measuring, humans would hardly be capable of <u>adapting</u>. And adaptation is surely that which keeps us going, which enables us to compete effectively with other factors and beings which compete for dominance and survival with ourselves. If humans were not measurers, they would simply be weaklings, singularly ill-adapted for life in the world in which they find themselves.

The impact of a person's measuring upon humans themselves is nowhere more conspicuous than in the differences between people and their lives that go along with the different measurings that they make. Clearly, there are interactions and interrelations between people's conceptions of themselves, their measurings, and their lifestyles. Those who concern themselves with the physical world in their measurings become quite different kinds of people, with quite different kinds of capacities, from those who concern themselves with the moral world in their measurings, or with the cultural world, or with any other aspect of life.

Of course, there are interlinkings between all these kinds of measurings as well. Plainly, nobody can ignore the physical realm completely, for it is in a way the most basic, the ground of everything else with which humans concern themselves.

As a consequence of their measurings – and in harmony with them and themselves with their measurings – humans head off in many directions; potentially, indeed, in as many directions as there are people. For each way of life is, in this connection, a different direction. And each way of life is in large measure based upon the measurings and kind of measurings with which it is associated. Humans as measurers not only have originality, but their originality is bound up in its concreteness with the measurings that people make and the ways of life that evolve along with them. In short, we may say that the fact that humans measure is no less amazing than the fact that they have conceptions of themselves.

It may also be illuminating to draw a correspondence between what I have been saying about the impact of measuring on people, and the notion of the 'shadow line', as discussed by both Conrad and Oakeshott.[13] When a person begins to measure, measuring brings with it the notion of balance, or realism. People who measure are not merely aware of the possibility of weighing things up – perhaps of needing to do so – but actual weighing up of things enters very immediately into their being. The rapture of the measuring person cannot be careless[14]. Calculation is liable to error, and the calculating person cannot but wish to avoid error. People who are aware of their limits and the constraints to which they are subject are very different kinds of being from those who are not. The measuring person, in a way, loses naivety in the nicest and most engaging sense of that term — and swaps it for maturity in the soberest sense of that term.

The whole being of humans becomes enmeshed in their measuring. It is not that the measures need to take over – although they can do that – but rather that the activities of measuring and the attitudes and activities, the approaches and preconceptions engendered by these measurings are all bound up with each other. As they measure, so do humans think and act and live; indeed, so do they have their being. And people's measures are an index no less than a determinant of their measure as humans. One's conception of what life is all about is virtually a direct product of the kinds of measurings in which one engages, of the way in which one comes to see the measures of life playing themselves out, or the kind of measures which one adopts and believes to be appropriate.

Again, nowhere is 'humans being on their own' more evident or conspicuous than in their measuring activities, predilections, and impulses. Humans are measurers and themselves the measure because they are on their own. If there was something else to which they could turn, then they could merely apply the measures which were brought to them, which they found ready made and awaiting their attention. If there were standards apart from themselves, then they could come to terms with the world in terms of these standards, and without having to be original, or having to turn themselves inside out in order to see what really is and the way things are.

As measurers, humans seem pre-eminently on their own – simply because measuring as considered here is a fundamental activity – fundamental in the sense that there is nothing to go on when one engages in it. The measures which others have devised might sometimes point the way towards what one is really after. But more often than not, the measures of others can throw one off the scent of what one is after. People commonly remain very much at sea, and fail to find themselves because they fail to cast off the spell of measures that are not their own, and that cannot do for them what they need measures to do.

One pre-eminent task of humans as measurers is to discover for themselves what they are competent to measure. Matters that are beyond their ken or their genuine appreciation, matters they cannot come to grips with, they should leave aside. Others may be able to make something of them, but everyone does not need to follow suit. The world in which a person lives cannot be the whole world. Some people live in larger worlds than others, and some can measure more comprehensively than others. Some people will construct for themselves more comfortable and accommodating worlds and ways of life than will others. People who are ill at ease with comfort may find a world in which things do not easily match, a world of disharmony and clashes and conflicts. They consign themselves to such a world: they cannot do otherwise, and that is how they will set up their own measures.

A major question that arises, granted that people are social beings, is the extent to which they can involve themselves in measuring the measurings of others. Is one bound, by one's own being, to mind one's own business? Can one ever really comprehend, much less be true to oneself in setting about interfering with, the world that others make for themselves? Can it ever be one's business to suggest to others that their measures are misguided?

The key notion here is integrity. Nobody is in any sense aided if an integrity that their own life possesses is taken away from them. But if their life lacks integrity, then it is perhaps possible that another may be of assistance to them, that the detachment and dispassionateness that another can call upon may help point them towards something that is more in line with what they really are.

The integrity of the interferer is also on the line in such eventualities. One can lose oneself, at the most extreme end of the spectrum — one can become bound up with another's life at the expense of one's own, and probably to the advantage of nobody. In a lesser degree, one can lose oneself by turning into a kind of chameleon – and this is the loss of one's own integrity, particularly in respect of coherence. The dangers of becoming involved in the business of others can hardly be overestimated. Nowhere, perhaps, is this more evident than in the life of politics. For politicians are interferers by trade – they are brokers of interference in the life of others. And the fate of their own lives is all too evident, in more than a few cases.

As measurers, human beings essentially stand alone, apart, and supreme. As they measure, humans become both more and less limited, more creators and more creatures (of their own measurings), more themselves and more determined. By measuring, humans become more able to cope with being on their own. Measuring is what enables humans to make something of their being on their own. In particular, it enables them to start on the road towards making a way of life. But the roads they will take, the directions in which they will move, and the destinations they will reach, depend very largely on the measures they make.

3. Humans And Their Measures

As well as being the basic measurers and engaging in measuring, humans make and devise measures. These measures are extensions of themselves, adaptations of themselves, interpretations of themselves, aspirations for themselves, conveniences for themselves. They are constructions emanating from earlier measures and constructions, interpretations of how external objects and phenomena impinge upon humans. They are selections about what really matters out of what there is in the world, what happens in the world, and what follows what in the world.

It happens, of course, that the measures which humans make can become distinct from humans themselves and from human life. Measures emanating from original human-directed measures, and higher order measures devised to pursue questions which the first set of meta-measures threw up – such developments are commonplace in the world of research. In one sense, these esoteric measures have some connection with the lives of those who employ them in their research programs; many researchers become intimately involved in their research. But never wholly at the expense of other aspects of life. Researchers such as these tend to live in two worlds, one exceedingly commonplace (surprisingly so in most cases), the other exclusively academic. Such lives are commonplace because their practitioners never manage to bring about interaction between the two parts of their lives.

Only the greatest scientists can make science a way of life that genuinely rises above the common round. Few researchers can invest the conversation of the marketplace and the parish pump with that peculiar magic which the occasional great person attains. In those rare cases, there is a kind of transference, at some unspeakable level, between realms of human living – a kind of dialectical interchange and imaginative interbreeding which is marvellously enriching. But those researchers who research in worlds apart, and lack a genius for living, tend to live two lives, which are soulless because neither gets enough time, nor receives enrichment from the other.

Esoteric measures may end up coming full circle, and revealing something that has bearing on human life. While rare, this is not surprising. For people cannot really cease to be themselves, no matter how far they may stray. Their researching must always have its directions being renewed – for new questions that research throws up are seen as questions because human interests are what they are. In addition, more questions usually arise than can be considered. This again makes it necessary for researchers to select, and such selections cannot be made purely on the basis of the research as it has transpired thus far.

It should be kept in mind that to the extent that science displaces humans from the centre of the universe – as it has tended to do for several centuries – science tends to become divorced from life. Humans do not bow out because science says they should. On the contrary, humans then treat science as an appendage. They are willing to take pickings from it, and willing to allow it to go on in its own way. But they are not willing that it should become the master, nor to allow it to dominate their own lives. (Science as discussed here is distinct from technology, which is considered in the chapter on machinery.)

That said, it is also true that science seems to be making some kind of takeover bid, and saying that humans are not ultimately the measure, and that the increasingly higher order measures which science itself devises are the true measures, that these are the ways really to get at reality.

It is peculiar – though not in terms of the analysis of religion offered earlier – that the displacement of the earth from the centre of the cosmos was regarded as posing a threat to religion. In a way, it should surely have been seen as a threat to humans rather than to God. But however that may be, the fact is that at that time humans did not allow themselves to be displaced from the centre except perhaps in some purely astronomical sense. Science spoke, but humans did not become humbler beings. It is impossible to say whether the present apparent threat from science to the supremacy of humans will fare any differently – but it is possible to outline the bases of the contest.

At base, it is a contest of nerves – and this is because science is itself a human activity, and because the conclusions of science are mediated to us by scientists – who are nothing more than humans. The essential claim of that science which challenges the supremacy of humans is that certain mysteries (as discussed in Chapters One and Four) can not only be persuaded to speak, but that when they speak they reveal a reality and coherence which is intrinsic to themselves, which reveals what humans really are, and by extension reveals what human life is all about.

If humans give way to this, they are really allowing the mysteries to dictate to them. For it is not science *per se* which says all this, but scientists. Science is really what scientists make of the world – and what anyone makes of the world is for others to take or leave. This is not to say that whether certain consequences will result from certain causes is a matter which depends on the decisions of individual people. It is not to say, for example, that people can decide for themselves whether they will die if they administer poison to themselves. It is rather to say that what one will take account of is one's own affair. Even in the extreme case just cited, a person may decide that death is of no concern to him or her. Science cannot say how important death is. Science *per se* cannot tell people which consequences they should take account of. Nor can it tell humans what they really are, unless they choose to accept some of the findings which scientists make.

The fact is that the mysteries cannot be made to declare themselves, and humans must beware of being over-impressed by mysterious invocations of scientists. This is not to belittle science, or what scientists can do for humanity. Scientists are embarked upon a way of life which has a profound impact on what people make of their lives. People do well to take great account of what science has to offer to them. But science does not speak *ex cathedra* – the scientific way of life is not itself fixed. This means that, apart from everything else that has been said, those who would give way to science *per se* and its truths would be committed to waiting until the end of time when science was washed up in every sense of the term. In its finality, its inerrancy would be the infallibility of the dead.

Meta-measures have value, but they must be related to the other more immediate measures that humans make. These substantive measures, as I would describe them, have their own relations to humans as measurers and as themselves the basic measure. A complex of relations is at work here. The measures that humans make reflect their conceptions of themselves, and they are also conducive to certain ways of life. But while they reflect humans' conceptions of themselves, they also end up reacting back upon these conceptions. And at the same time that they tend to lead people into certain ways of life, they also reflect people's ways of life.

The measures that humans make are essentially related to people's own concerns and interests, to their convenience, their ideas, their imagination, their feelings. The construction of measures is in the fullest sense a sympathetic activity. People must themselves enter in the measures they make. They cannot contemplate setting up measures of matters which they regard as having no import. The measures that people make and adopt become the codification of their ways of viewing the world, of interpreting their experience, of organising their affairs, of conducting their own lives. The measures that humans make are measures of the world in which they find themselves, of the lives that they want to construct for themselves, of the behaviour that they engage in, of the conceptions that they develop for themselves. The measures that humans make enter vitally into virtually every element of their being. People become in a vital sense dependent upon them. For once having begun to engage in measuring, there is no getting away from it, no going back upon it, no doing without it.

People make measures to help them decide both what to do and what to think. People's measures provide them with guidance at all stages of their living. In a way, their measures become their senses, helping them to find, and define both their way and their goals. Their measures help show people what they themselves are. Their measures become their guidelines, their standards, their preconceptions and assumptions, their categories and taxonomies. In a human life, in the way of life that people make for themselves, the measures that are employed become all important, all-embracing, and absolutely integral to everything that is and that is done.

The variety of measures that people make and work with is bewildering. And one might classify them in a variety of ways. One might talk of measures to understand the external physical world, measures to come to terms with one's fellow humans, measures to regulate one's own behaviour, measures to guide one's thinking about what essentially is and what matters, measures for regulating relationships between human beings, measures for coming to terms with the various aspects of human production. Whatever becomes of concern to a person is something about which that person might choose to establish a measure, and forthwith set about constructing.

In one sense, there are no limits on the kind of measures that humans can construct, or to the way in which they construct them. As soon as people get a conception of some particular aspect of things, they can go to work on it. They can begin to weigh it up, they can proceed to relate it to other aspects and to distinguish degrees within it. As they do this, and as they become increasingly regularised in the doing of it, humans develop a measure of the aspect of things that is in question. The extent to which the measures that particular persons construct for particular matters would be found useful by others, and the extent to which they serve to indicate the various consequences of natural events is an entirely separate question from whether they are genuine measures, from their authenticity as measures. People can and often do rely upon measures which give rise to expectations which are wildly astray from what actually happens. And they often continue to rely upon them even though they are misled; indeed, the very core of their lives is sometimes based upon such measures.

Some of the measures made by humans are highly idiosyncratic, others tend towards universality. In the first place, we may note that some types of measurement are made, in some form, by virtually everyone. It is virtually impossible to do without some measure of space and time, for example, and despite the variety of such measures, nobody (or virtually nobody) does so. There are people with no sense of time or distance; and we should admit that of these, some may have no relevant measures. Most people of whom we say they have no sense of these matters really do have such a sense, but are vague or irregular in their application of them. Some few people, of a mystical bent, however, may truly be oblivious of these matters – although possibly being able, if required, to grasp the sense which is attached to them by others.

It is to easy to presume that everyone must operate with, if not the very same measures as we ourselves use, then at least with measures of the same type. The lessons of cultural diversity are difficult to learn, and the lessons of individual diversity even harder. And of course it is not to be wondered at that we have difficulty in getting away from the measures which we ourselves use, and to conceive of people using different measures. The person with no sense of space or time may verge on being incomprehensible to those in whose understanding such measures are central and fundamental. We can surely be willing to allow that such things can be, and that there are such people, even though we may not really be able to grasp what it is to be like that.

There appears to be a substantial degree of exact comparability between the measures of matters such as space and time. Metres can be changed into yards, and metres or yards can be added together to make kilometres or miles. In the same way, it would seem, each day might be broken up into minutes and hours, or equally into any other set of units that might be chosen; and minutes or whatever, and days or whatever, will add up to years or whatever.

But this appearance of comparability is highly liable to be misleading. It is by no means clear that the historian who thinks in centuries has the same concept of time as the schoolchild who waits for the tuckshop to open, even though the units of time used by the former are compounds of those used by the latter. It is not even clear that the time until lunch is the same for the child who is hungry as for the child who is not. The problem raised by all this is the relationship between certain more of less universalised measures in their externalised form – abstracted from any particular person's use of them – and these same measures as used by particular people in particular contexts. In their externalised form, these measures may be regarded as purely descriptive. But nobody would ever actually use them in their own life in a purely descriptive way. The very fact that they call them in aid, in some particular moment, reveals that they will then necessarily be employed in relation to something else, and that they will therefore not be purely descriptive, but relational and in some way evocative, possibly suggestive for certain purposes, as well.

In view of all this, the universality of even such basic types of measures as these needs to be described with certain qualifications.

Everyone uses them – but possibly not quite everyone, and then some may use them under sufferance. In this connection, there are obviously some questions to be asked about educational practices. Society does consider whether the rulers we give to children should be marked in inches or centimetres; but society should perhaps also consider whether rulers should be given to children at all – or at least whether they should be given to all children.

Again, everyone – or nearly everyone – uses the same or transposable units for measuring space and time. But this must not blind us to the fact that the basic units within the range which are used by different people (e.g. centuries for the historian v. minutes for the schoolchild) may cause basic differences in orientation to these matters. Again, the same units, even when used on the same scale, even by the same person, and even possibly in relation to the same kind of matters, may have different meanings depending on the context. All this bespeaks diversity and individuality on a tremendous scale.

This discussion of the measures which humans make is not intended to be exhaustive, but to take proper account of some major measures. Space and time may be said to have something natural about them. It is hard to conceive of the possibility that these measures might never have been brought into being by humans. Certainly human history would have been unimaginably different without them. But there are other kinds of measures which seem in a sense artificial, yet also enjoy considerable universality. I shall discuss two of these, law and money.

Both are concerned primarily with interpersonal relations, although each may also become a kind of standard for an individual who so chooses. In addition, the range or scope of each is dependent upon factors external to itself. There are variations as between individuals and as between groups about what can be bought or sold for money; and there are variations about what matters can or will be regulated by law. Both are instruments of social control, both enable individuals to do things that would otherwise be impossible – and both make impossible certain activities which might otherwise be possible. Both allow some individuals to influence the activities of other individuals. And in the process of such control, the controlled may accept and be amenable to the measures no less than the controllers.

For good or ill, these measures seem almost to have a dynamic of their own. For example, in a milieu in which money can buy high status, virtually nobody is able to do much by way of dissociating the two entirely from each other. Or in a milieu in which law is a fundamental method of social control, the sway of law — i.e. the matters to which laws are addressed – seem or tend to widen and extend irresistibly.

In groupings in which law and money are major measures, it is possible to do without them only within quite severe limits. In the case of law, it is possible to live outside the law in relation to particular matters and particular ranges of matters, but hardly in relation to all. No criminal could defy every part even of the criminal law, much less of every branch of the law. And with regard to money, only the complete recluse — hardly a member of the society at all, having no contact with others — could do without it completely.

But all that said, it remains true that different people, even while accepting and employing and living by these two measures, may regard them differently. For some people, the accumulation of money is the very aim of life, while for others money is merely the means to attaining the essentials of life. The same is true in relation to law. For some law is a semi-sacred bond between humans, while for others it is just a means to material ends.

We are led from this discussion to two related questions. The first is whether any single measure could be viewed as the real key to human life. The second is about high order measures which relate day-to-day measures to each other. Can there be any supreme measure for human life, one whose own pronouncements cannot be gainsaid, and which puts all other measures in their place? Can humans devise a supreme, all-embracing and regulative measure? These questions require both a negative and a positive answer.

The negative answer is based on the point that humans remain the ultimate measure – no matter what they do.

Persons can become the servants and devotees of their own measures, especially their highest ones. They may in a sense forget themselves – even in a sense lose themselves – in their commitment to and their reliance on them. They may even become their virtual slaves, in the sense that they go along with them against their better judgment. But it makes no sense to say that these measures can enslave them. This can be seen from the really extreme case, where their measures take over from, and thus become their better judgment. For what happens here is that the measures become absorbed into the persons as in effect part of themselves. The persons remain the basic measure, and the measures they made at an earlier stage of their development have been absorbed into the person. This is not just a verbal or even just a conceptual point. For what it does is highlight the reality that humans are the measures, while at the same time taking account of the flexibility of humans, and revealing that what humans become is to some extent a product of their own doings and makings.

The singularity of each person's measurings carries with it the almost certain implication that no particular supreme measure would ever be adopted by everyone. There certainly have been times when authority has been strong, and when vast numbers of people have given credence to some particular set of standards or measures. But one has the strong sense that giving credence as supreme to a measure that is external (and in its essential character even unintelligible) does not mean in fact that such a measure actually exercises the supervisory role envisaged for it across the whole range of a person's life and activities. On the other hand, people's lives can more or less be split in two by measures which are supposedly supreme and foisted upon them.

Given some free rein, it is virtually certain that each human being would order the world in slightly different ways, and thus that supreme measures would vary as between different people. Furthermore, it is unlikely that everyone would in fact regard a supreme measure as an appropriate or useful thing either to have or to work with.

It is not incumbent on people to attempt to formalise or articulate the relationships between the various measures which they employ. Clashes between different measures, in the event that they occur, can easily be dealt with on an *ad hoc* basis. There is generally interaction and development as between the various measures with which people operate and in terms of which they organise their lives.

Indeed, one may even have some doubts about whether a supreme measure could actually perform the functions assigned to it. Those who have doubts on this score, and who accordingly keep clear of supreme measures, have a good case to make. Essentially, their case would be that nobody could in fact live by a single measure which they set up as supreme. There are two reasons why this would be so. The first is that nobody could ever be so relentless in the business of life as to subordinate everything to one particular measure. The other is that nobody could be so calculating as to do so even if they had the will – or so inventive as to be able to elaborate a measure which would serve the purpose.

This leads to the positive part of the answer to the questions about supreme measures. In contemporary parlance, people's values, and especially their highest values, may be thought of as their supreme measure, performing the function of both regulating the other measures with which they live, and of taking precedence over all other measures. The concept of values is in fact singularly apt as the description for a supreme measure.

Morality is not simply an earlier term for the same thing. For morality is a particular dimension of human life — distinct from the material dimension and from the physical dimension and even from the spiritual dimension. Morality takes its place in a certain context, but does not as conventionally understood spread its wings to absorb everything into itself.

Similarly, principles are distinct from values. Principles are a particular kind of value, and are characteristically to a considerable extent derived values, with considerable concreteness, and designed to have more or less direct application to particular situations. Principles are too strict, at least in their conception, to be regarded as supreme, or like the highest values that could be regarded as supreme measures. And at the point where they might imaginably become supreme, principles are inevitably too vague to be sufficiently directive. Principles are like school principals, whereas supreme measures would need to be like presidents or elevated and elevating heads of state.

Of course, the concept of values is not easy to elucidate, nor easy to cut sufficiently loose from its economic associations and overtones. But in the sense in which values might be supreme measures, they are broad and articulable orientations, attitudes, and approaches. They have the flavour of deductivism about them, and of somewhat mathematical calculation, and yet they are also bound to stand in need of a degree of interpretation. For nobody could believe that in the formulation of a set of top values, they could anticipate all the contingencies and variations of life, or what life holds for them. There is no question but that people do have values in this sense (some people do, anyway), that they attempt to stick to them and to live by them – to regulate their lives and their other measures by them. People with such values attempt to use them for their perspective on everything else, for their approach overall to the business of living and the construction of a way of life. Such ways of life perhaps lack a degree of flexibility, or spontaneity, or creativity. But they do exist; and the people who manifest them are keen to identify their values with themselves and themselves with their values.

In this sense, then, there can be supreme measures – but a qualification seems unavoidable. As previously discussed, supreme measures will stand in need of interpretation. They will also need to be developed. In the course of being applied to new circumstances and unanticipated contingencies, they will at the very least evolve. Even if expressed in the same words, and even if their upholder is not conscious of anything having happened to these words, changes will have occurred in the course of their use. The meaning and force will not be the same; the values concerned will have a different hue, a different character, a different tone, subtle though the differences may be and difficult to detect. Accordingly, the requisite qualification is that if the measures in question are mobile, then they are not supreme in quite the sense – implying immutability – that the term suggests.

Among the most noteworthy and interesting aspects of any measure or type of measure are the factors it treats as constants, and those it treats as variables. This general matter has more to do with compounded measures, such as are represented by academic disciplines. For its concern is with types of measure rather than particular measures. The essential point is that in the laying down and application of measures related to various kinds of matters, some factors are taken into account and others not. This matter is particularly illuminating in relation to Chapter Four, "Mystery and the Facts", but is also pertinent in the present connection. Its character can be illustrated by considering that in measuring wealth, for example, some measurers may take account only of financial or monetary assets, whereas others may also take account of assets in kind, or of quality. Similarly, some measurers of achievement would take account only of the end product whereas others would want to relate the starting point to the end product.

The person who takes no account of the starting point regards that as a constant; the person who takes no account of the degree of effort expended on an attainment regards that as a constant in connection with achievement. Or again, one person might regard the securing of daily necessities as having nothing to do with achievement, whereas another might think of them as being part of it.

The point here is that insofar as measurers take no account of an aspect but treat it as a constant, they really are ignoring it. Thus the detail of the measures which people use is of immense importance. For measurers to understand themselves and what they are about, and for outsiders to understand measurers, it is essential that there be understanding not only of the kind of things that, in broad, they measure, but also of what they take into account in doing so. The matters treated as fixed tend to indicate what is regarded as the limits of action and effective activity, while at the same time offering some definition of these matters. Nothing is more important in order to know others with insight, or to know oneself.

Humans cannot do without measures. They must make them, use them, and rely on them. Measures are the keys by which humans can open the world to their intervention, and themselves to their own potentialities. Humans make the keys – but pursuing the metaphor, humans cannot be wholly the masters of which doors will be opened by the keys that they make, nor the determiners of what they will find inside.

They will obtain a perspective on what is inside by virtue of having come in by the door to which they made the key. In this sense they have some kind of determining role. But this role is not complete mastery.

The measures that humans make tend to start them on a path of life, and lead into a way of life of whose character and ramifications they are not fully aware at the time of constructing the measures. Humans make them, but they may take their creators in unforeseen directions. This is not to say that they become people's masters, or that humans cease to be on their own when once they have begun to articulate the measures with which they are working, or that people do not really make their own ways of life. But it certainly amplifies some of the real dimensions of these central aspects of the human world.

A factor not to be underestimated is that the measures that humans make achieve a momentum of their own. As the makers of measures, people retain ultimate mastery over these measures. But as noted already, the ways they would want or choose to be able to exercise this mastery reflects to some extent the impact upon them of the measures with which they are currently operating. Furthermore, the momentum of measures already made, especially established ones, is strengthened by the way various items based upon them have developed.

The momentum of measures is partly a matter of the emergence of further measures based upon them and presupposing their development, but partly also of particular measures themselves becoming entrenched. They become entrenched by various processes of gathering worlds around themselves, by becoming foundations of ways of life, by being built into machines which people rely upon and hold onto, by inspiring the construction of other machines which rely on them, and which then become extremely hard to do without because they make things easy so that people come to be dependent on them.

3

MACHINERY

For better or worse, machinery is more the nature of humans than is art. The step from measuring to art or to pure thought is immense, great though it be when made. But the step from measuring to machinery is immediate. If it is an extraordinary thing in humans that they have the capacity to measure, it is no less extraordinary and remarkable that they have the capacity to make machines. And just as measuring has an impact upon the measurer, so do machines have an impact upon those who make and use them.

The impact of machinery on people has the most profound significance for them and their lives, and indeed has become a quite fundamental and integral part of the human world. This chapter is divided into three sections. In the first, the nature of machinery is discussed in general terms; in the second, the various types of machinery made by humans are examined; and in the third, the impact of machinery upon humankind is considered.

1. Machinery In General

Machinery was described or defined in Chapter One as the functional productions of human beings. It was said there that machinery, while distinct from pure art and pure thought, includes everything from aspirin to automobiles, coinage to constitutions, and drainage to drama. As used in this work, the term machinery has a very broad coverage indeed. For there are all kinds of human productions which would not commonly be thought of as machines, but which nevertheless do a job.

At their simplest from a conceptual point of view, there are machines which do jobs which can be done by humans without the machine. Such machines do little more than speed up processes which are able to be done anyway. But there are other machines which enable people to do things which they could not otherwise do at all. An example of the first type of machine is a roller to put under something to be dragged along – without the roller, one could still drag the item, although less rapidly and efficiently. An example of the second type of machine is a needle, without which it is not possible to sew, although it may be possible to join fabrics in a manner somewhat analogous to sewing.

The distinction between machines and consumables is not hard and fast. A machine is essentially functional, that is, it is to do a job that is in some sense beyond itself. Machines are essentially for use, consumables to be used up. But not merely can some consumables be put to use, and thus function as machines; and not merely are some machines burnt out before ever they do their job; there are some human productions which are designed to be used up in the doing of their job. And more than this, the distinction between using for a job and using up cannot easily be drawn or sustained in a number of cases. A Ferrari motor car is a machine, and yet it is not merely functional. It is not merely a provider of transport, and if we say it is a provider of luxury transport, then we are beginning to move in the direction of consumption rather than mere use. Plainly, there is a whole range of distinctions that might be employed in this connection, and endless articles might be written trying to make plain the distinction that is being got at, trying to pin down exactly what is meant by the concept of a machine.

It is unnecessary for present purposes to distinguish sharply between machines and consumables, for the subject is illuminated by the blurred edges of the concept. The word machinery is not being used in any narrow sense, and not with any presumption that machines are only or even characteristically confined to use in factories, or for the manipulation of material, i.e. physical, objects or materials. Humans invented the wheel, but they also invented government; they invented flying machines but also educational systems; they invented communication systems and monetary systems and law enforcement systems – all of which are machines in the sense under discussion.

Beginning with the nature of machinery in general, it is of the essence that machinery is a means to something else, and that it involves a particular method of operation and doing things. These two aspects go together, and a due understanding of both is vital to an adequate comprehension of the place of machinery in the human world. Any machine has its own mode of operation, which is fixed. Machines have no capacity of inventiveness or adaptiveness (apart from what may be built into them), and so they operate as constructed. Thus they do things 'in their own way' only in the most limited sense of this term.

Their extraordinary capacity to do things, to make things, to serve human ends, to increase the comforts and command of humans over other aspects of reality can easily be overestimated. Humans do themselves a great disservice if they presume to anthropomorphise machines, for they then inevitably impute to machines a kind of autonomy and good sense which they do not and cannot possess.

Machines are both instruments and slaves – and slaves in a double sense. They are instruments in that they exist for a set purpose, and more specifically in that they perform a set function. In isolation at least, machines do not set themselves in motion or continue in motion by themselves, but must be used by someone or something outside of themselves.

They are slaves to those who use them in the sense that they cannot take it upon themselves to defy those who give them certain 'instructions', or place any kind of selective interpretation upon 'instructions' given to them. They cannot rebel or 'jack up' or assert any independence. They are in this sense more slavish, perhaps, than human slaves, for they have no will of their own. But they are slaves in another sense as well; for while they have no will, no independence, no autonomy, they have a constitution (either physical or institutional) which is absolutely binding upon what they do. Machines are slaves to themselves – to what they are even more than to what they can become. Indeed, they cannot become anything except a 'worn out' what they are.

This reveals a paradox about machinery, which cuts to its foundations, and is profoundly significant in understanding its impact on the human world. For while machinery is always a means, it is equally no respecter of persons. Machines have to be productive, effective, efficient – they must do a job, and do it about as well as it can be done as well as a bit more quickly. That is why humans make machines, that is what machines are for.

Some devotees enslave themselves to their machines, loving

and cherishing them with no regard for how they do their job. For such people, a machine is at its best provided its operations are perfect, regardless of the job it is supposed to be doing. Such people are truly 'rude mechanicals', subordinating themselves to the service of the servants of humans. Yet they find a way of life in this, and a life dedicated to machinery is not without its own fulsomeness.

Apart from this human quirkiness, the *raison d'etre* of machinery is to produce something beyond itself, or achieve certain outcomes. The machine itself is never sacrosanct, but is the servant or implement for achieving the purposes for which people use it. If it will not do the job desired, people will stop using it, and either find or make a different one, let the job go, or do it by hand. A machine must make something or do something beyond itself and outside of itself. It is the servant of humans, of human purposes. If it does not do a job, or if it does not do that job as well as anything else that is available, or if the job it does is not wanted by anyone, or if what it does is not in demand, then it should surely lie idle. If it continues to be used when it is not serving people, then it is being misused, and the proper hierarchy in the relationship between humans and machines is being inverted.

But this hierarchy can be inverted. Like printing presses, machinery will roll when it is set in motion. Machinery can be misused, can be allowed to produce what is not wanted or even what is damaging. If machinery were conscious, and based its impression of itself upon the way in which it operates, it would regard itself and its operations as endowed with dignity and integrity and as possessing the supreme authority which goes with impartiality. Machines, *qua* machines, are incorruptible, they are impartial, they cannot be turned from their course, they are absolutely faithful to themselves and to those who, knowing how they will function, set them in motion. If people use machines by rote, or out of thoughtless habit, or because they are told to do so, then the machines will not gainsay them. If people use machines without greatly considering whether what they do or produce is worthwhile, the machines will not bid them pause.

Machines are quiet slaves, which simply get on with the job, and never consult or question the interests of those who design them, or those who use them, or those who are expected to benefit from their operation. Machinery cannot be depended upon, except to do what it does as determined by what it is. It is a means to ends which are fixed by its own constitution. It will not interpret that end, nor depart from it except by some malfunction.

The lines along which machines function are predetermined. It is their own constitution which determines how they will function, and how they will react if they are constructed with any capacity for reacting to people or events. Machines have a way of discounting characteristics or considerations which are extraneous so far as the machines themselves are concerned, ie. so far as the constitution of the machine is concerned.

The respect that a machine pays to a person has nothing to do with what the person would seek from the machine, nor does the treatment which individual persons receive at the hands of a machine depend in any way upon what they would seek from it or even on the kind of case that they might think relevant to it. The point here is not just that a chaff-cutter will slice off a finger that is put into the path of its blade; the point is also that persons appearing before a court of law will have no heed taken of any case they might wish to put unless they express that point in terms conformable to the ways in which courts of law operate. If they do not do this then it will be disregarded, and if they do do it then they may well have to compromise and distort utterly what they really want to say.

It makes good sense to talk of getting the feel of machines. One certainly needs to know how to work a machine in order to be master of it and get it to do what one wants. This truth modifies what was just said about machinery as no respecter of persons. Machines almost invariably have their own distinctive way of functioning. They not only have individual quirks and an optimal pace, but they are responsive to the inputs they receive, and react to how they are handled.

In the case of institutional machinery – such as the operations of courts of law – nobody would question for a moment that there is such a thing as a 'feel' for the way the machine works. But even with the most mechanical of machines, the same thing applies. Whether one is talking about the rhythm of someone who can handle a shovel, or the sloppy telephone dialler who is always getting wrong numbers, there is a certain touch to the operation and working of machinery. Machines with no room for 'feel' are rare, although it is fair to add that a certain class of machines which may be called public — such as telephones – are increasingly being constructed so as to be foolproof.

Different people are good with different types of machines. The person who can get the feel of a legal system is probably not going to be the sort of person who can get the feel of a motor engine. How far 'feel' is due to education and experience is difficult to say. Some people can get more out of machines than others, and some people are accident prone with machines they become involved with. This is not to say that the constitution of the machine does not determine the outcome without respect for the person, granted that a certain input is made. But it is to say that substantially different outcomes can result from virtually imperceptibly different inputs.

In order to understand this, to appreciate it – and perhaps to enable oneself to get the most out of machines — it may be well to anthropomorphise them. For by doing this, by imputing feelings and reactions to machines, one may be on the way to understanding the nuances of their operation – at least one is on the lookout for what is distinctive in their functioning. One gets the best out of machines by not forcing them, by adapting to their pace, their quirks, their *modus operandi*. Getting the best is partly getting what you want, but also largely getting in its finest form that which a machine produces or does.

This reveals the other side of the fact that there is a feel to the operation of machinery. In order to get the most out of machines, one has to be after what they do best. One must accommodate to them. The person who gets the feel of machines is typically the person who likes what the machine does partly because the machine does it – and who likes best what the machine does best because it is what the machine does best. Whatever a machine does best is certain to have some specific kind of perfection about it, so where there is a congruence between what the operator likes and this specific perfection – and the fact of its perfection in its own terms provides a basis for this liking – then there is the kind of harmony that may be nicely connected with the good working of the machine.

But to accommodate oneself to the machine, to begin to identify with what it does because it does it, is tantamount to viewing the machine not as a means to one's own ends, not as the slave to human purposes, but rather as the decider and arbiter of what one should be on about in life. The process is apt to be subtle, and may be thought insidious. It is not that one stops considering what one is after, but rather that in this consideration, what one can get looms very large, and one's assessment of what one can get is essentially determined by considerations of what is done and produced by current machines.

As soon as one's horizons are fixed in this way, one's world has been circumscribed by something whose proper role is to be subservient to the idealizing and constructing of one's way of life. To accommodate too much to what is possible, and to conceive of what is possible in terms of what can be produced and done by existing machinery, is to be realistic to the point of reaction, and to take no account of future potentialities or indeed of one's own constructive and generative capacities.

There is a further dimension to the potentially dominating influence which machinery can acquire, and to the way in which people can end up accommodating to it in ways that are detrimental to human supremacy. This is tied up with the fact that machinery is apt to acquire a momentum of its own. Just as people's options become defined and thus to an extent limited as they develop their own measures and relate them to each other, so does the range of possible future machinery tend to become defined and limited by the kinds of machinery that currently exist. The general point here is that humans cannot cut themselves off completely from the past, and the real issue concerns the extent to which they can retain or create room for manoeuvre.

Machinery, as already noted, does particular things and does them in particular ways. As soon as machinery has come to operate on a scale that is at all considerable, it requires a certain base for its operations, and it requires certain services to be provided. An infrastructure grows up alongside various machines. The dilemma that is likely to develop when deciding between possible new machines is that some would both complement the operations of existing machines and at the same time require at most certain modifications of a minor kind to the infrastructure, whereas others, which may be better calculated to generate new and desired points of departure in human affairs, would call not only for the abandonment of existing machines, but also for a new or at least substantially altered infrastructure.

In such situations, not only is the effort of making the break enormous – possibly greater than anyone would care to make or be able to carry through without enlisting widespread support and assistance which may not be forthcoming – but the established machinery and infrastructure is likely not only to have supporters, but to empower them in any ensuing contest.

Thus machinery is not, in its actual operations, simply a neutral servant, not simply something that gives humans unqualified support and help in the construction of their lives. As isolated machines grow into integrated systems – and such growth can seldom in reality be prevented – the system acquires both a momentum which will point towards one kind of development (and rule out other kinds), and at the same time generate around itself a degree of preservative power which is hard to overcome.

Related is the reality that machinery tends to impose a degree of regularity upon human life – it regularises, and then goes further by regulating. Machinery is characteristically a hard taskmaster. Not only must it be operated as dictated by its own constitution, but the other side of this coin is that those who use machinery must subject themselves to the discipline their machines impose.

The uniformity of machine-made products exacts a further conformity, for it is not easy not to use machine-made products, and they must necessarily be used as they are. Furthermore, as new systems of machinery come into being, with mutual relations and interconnections, it tends to become incumbent upon people to work in with the system, to adjust to it, to go along with the demands that it places upon them. The integration of the machinery that a society employs tends almost inescapably to result in the integration of the society itself. It is characteristic of machinery that it makes its demands on a more or less regular basis, that it is not amenable to calls for special efforts or anything of the kind, that it rises to no special heights or enthusiasms no matter what the situation might be, that it manifests no spontaneity of any kind whatever. And as human beings work their machines, a similar greyness is somewhat apt to come over them as well.

This is not to say that there is anything unnatural about machinery in the human world, or that humans should minimize their use of machinery if they are to retain mastery of themselves and their lives. Indeed, to the extent that people tie their stars to machines that they have themselves fashioned after their own desires, they are in a major sense relating themselves more intimately to nature than if they simply fall into relationships with the realities and mysteries which constitute the environment in which they find themselves. There is no basis for presuming that people are being natural or living naturally when there is nothing to mediate between them and the physical world in which they are located. People who are disposed to make and use machines are no less natural than people who steer clear of machines.

Indeed, it may be argued that there is more truth in the proposition that machinery is human nature than in the proposition that art is human nature. Machinery has no being apart from humans, or apart from the use that humans make of it. The third section of this chapter explores more fully the impact of machinery upon humanity. But it is hard to deny that machinery is one of the most basic, far-reaching and assertive responses that humans can make to the fact that they are on their own, and also one of the most crucial moves they can make in carving out for themselves a way of life.

But while machinery is not unnatural, it has its dangers for humans, for the life of humans, and for the human world. The fundamental danger relates to the retention by humans of mastery over their machines. The fact that systems of machinery acquire their own momentum is not of itself detrimental to humans or their world. Humans may well be able to ride on the back of this momentum. If people were truly farsighted, they would be able to anticipate and thus control the directions in which systems of machinery might move. There is always room for some manoeuvre (or people do themselves less than justice if they fail to make sure that there is) in guiding the development of machinery.

If it comes to a point, people can decide to jettison a whole system of machinery if they are unhappy about its tendencies. This may be desperate – and difficult – but attaining and maintaining human mastery is never easy. In simple terms, the stakes are higher when questions are at issue about the future development of systems of machinery, and the operations of established machines. Humans stand to gain or lose much, precisely because machines can do so much for them. And while it is the nature of machinery to attain its own momentum, it is not its nature to dominate people. That occurs only if people let it, or possibly if they are injudicious in the machinery they construct.

Humans also need to beware of machines and systems of machines simply growing up, and emerging without having been selected or established. The logic of particular lines of development for machinery can seem so convincing as to carry easily the day in ill-considered planning. In such development, one thing is allowed to lead to another without the interests of humankind being explicitly considered. To presume what human beings will want is the high road to some of the greatest delusions and obsessions of which humankind is capable.

Some human measures can easily be transmuted into machines. This is typically dangerous, for it means that something which should have a role in assessing the performance of machines has that capacity compromised. By the same token, however, the development of dangerously close relationships between some measures and their related machines is not only inevitable, but can actually be beneficial. The law provides a good example. For while law itself is a measure, the law becomes a machine in its administration. Those who administer the law, those that is who are the motive power of the machinery of the law, certainly have inside views on the quality of the measure with which they work, and these views must be accorded their due weight.

In one sense, those involved must be accorded a degree of dispassionateness, and the capacity to understand the real effectiveness of the measure. But by the same token, their position makes it difficult for them to distinguish between the worth of the measure and the effectiveness and appropriateness of the machinery by which it is administered. Insofar as this distinction is not satisfactorily sustained, and insofar as the measure and the machine are interacting in the minds of those who would wish to consider what I might call 'law reform' in the broadest sense, we are dealing with 'in-house' views. Such views, while conceivably disinterested, inevitably lack the detachment which is a necessary precondition of discerning fresh approaches. In summary, while the inside view may have something useful to say about the real worth of a new approach, that is all.

The final section of this chapter comments on the idea of the 'machine age'. But it is important, as a prelude to that, to examine more fully the matter of systems of machinery. Some reference has been made to this already, particularly in connection with the idea of infrastructure. But it is essential to the understanding of machinery in general that the ideas of integration, expansion and cumulation should be fully grasped. It is probably because machines can be so marvellous in doing a job, and because machinery has undoubtedly captured the imagination of humanity, that we allow and encourage – and indeed create – systems of machinery. A further reason relates to the fact that humans do not simply live snippets of life in isolation from each other, but live ways of life, in which the various parts have more or less integral relationships to each other.

A machine does a particular job or type of job, but a system of machines does an integrated series of jobs. A system of machines may well have a kind of integrated infrastructure, and possibly also an integrated mode of operation. But it is system at the level of functions performed that is of the greatest significance in connection with understanding the nature of machinery in general in connection with the human world.

A way of life would become jerky if it depended on the productions simply of a group of unco-ordinated machines — particularly as machines need to be used with a certain touch. As a simple illustration, carpenters using a mixture of hand tools and machine tools are not only likely to be working to different degrees of exactness, but their touch with the hand tools is likely to be adversely affected by the vibrations of their power tools. Further, the ease of work with the power tools will induce them both to get more power tools, and also to avoid procedures which can only be done with hand tools. Correspondingly, as machine tools become accepted, there will be attempts to design power tools to do more and more jobs.

Thus a system of machines not only tends to develop, which affects not only what is done and made, but the character of the ways of life of the people involved. It affects and at the same time works in with their ways of life. A system of machinery carries with it overtones of a confining and structuring impact upon those whom it draws into its ambit. Unquestionably, there are dangers for human mastery implicit in the creeping tentacles of a system of machines. But humans need not give way to these dangers, nor be overborne by them.

Machinery is one of the most characteristic of human productions. And it is one of the most remarkable things about humans that we are capable of producing machines. As a means of mastering, controlling, and using the world that we find around us, there is nothing more effective than machinery. For it is potent yet disciplined, determined yet biddable, rampant yet, in the end, controllable. Nothing could serve human purposes better. And our capacity to create it is a remarkable thing.

The definition of humans as toolmakers[15] suggests something extremely significant about us, namely that we can make things that can help us to do our own jobs. In that sense, humans not merely use what comes to hand, but fashion it as well – which is a remarkable thing in its own way.

But to think of humans as machine makers is a far greater thing. For machines not merely assist people to do their jobs, they do the job for them – at least sophisticated machines do so. Indeed, people can sometimes even fashion machines to do a particular job out of materials which formerly prevented them from doing that very thing.

Sophisticated machines are invented and made by very few people – but everyone uses machines, and most people use them in some sort of characteristic way. The range of available machines plainly increases the range of ways of life which people can effectively choose – provided that the range is real, and that it has not been flattened out in such a way that all available machines are more or less of a type and the differences between them trivial rather than substantive.

2. Types Of Machinery

The most important distinction is between machines that are wholly mechanistic and impersonal in their mode of operation, and those which bring some aspects of human interpretation into their operations. This interpretation may be a matter of understanding or assessing such matters as expectations, or it may be a matter of importing human feelings, in any sense of the term, into the operations of the machine. A legal system, for example, is a kind of machine, and it may allow discretion to judges on certain matters, and judges may, within the sphere of their discretion, give some rein to their sympathy in certain matters. By contrast, an electro-cardiograph or a parking meter functions in a purely mechanistic fashion.

Of course, it is possible to classify machinery in a large variety of ways, basing distinctions upon an almost illimitable variety of different factors which may be relevant for various purposes. In some contexts for example the distinction between wooden and steel machines would be relevant, although such distinctions have little relevance in the context of the present discussion. The distinction referred to in the previous paragraph is part of the distinction between what I call physical machines and non-physical machines. It is the major task of this part of this chapter to consider certain aspects of this distinction, to consider the characteristics of these types of machines, and to set forth their particular ways of functioning.

By way of preliminary, many of the distinctions considered in this discussion are not absolutely rigid. Depending particularly on the point at which one machine is thought to end and another begin, we can see overlaps between modes of operation and essential characteristics of various machines and types of machine. Only the very simplest types of essentially mechanistic machines really satisfy the strict criteria of necessarily functioning with absolutely no regard for persons. Less rigid physical machines – such as spades or wooden looms – have qualities which call for adaptation in use, which mean that they cannot do their job without a skilled operator (or at least, such that a non-skilled operator will do an absolutely different job from a skilled operator).

When we come to non-physical machines which function from the very centre through the conscious actions of human beings, they tend to find it difficult to operate with absolutely no regard for persons – although it should be added that such machines tend to develop a kind of stylized regard for persons. Their institutional momentum sets up within them syndrome-like modes of categorising individuals, and this heavily overlays and underscores the individual treatment that people might be able to draw upon themselves because of what they are or need or want as individuals.

Related to this is the fact that there is no rigid distinction between the general idea of a group of interacting machines, and a system of machines. Indeed, there is not always a clear distinction, especially in the sphere of human institutions, between what is and what is not a machine. With regard to the first distinction, consider the political and the economic systems which operate within a capitalist economy. Regarded as a pair of machines, they certainly interact, but whether they form a system is unclear and open to interpretation – no matter what the particular relations between them may be. Insofar as they work in with each other, insofar as the operations of the one are consciously slotted into the operations of the other, insofar as each relies upon the workings of the other for its own effectiveness – then they would tend to be a system rather than merely a group of machines. But none of these categories is clearcut, so the distinction between a system and a group remains loose.

The distinction itself is of real moment because it has a real bearing upon the view which one would have of the whole society. It may also have an impact upon the way in which the various machines themselves impinge upon each individual person and fashion their world. For example, if one thinks of a relatively homogeneous society with an established church, with only the wealthy enfranchised, and with an immobile social structure in which wealth and high social status go hand in hand, then it could hardly be denied that there was a system comprising the political, economic, moral and social machinery of society.

Insofar as this was the case, the world which individuals could contemplate creating for themselves – the ways of life they could contemplate creating – would be exceedingly narrowly circumscribed, largely because these machines formed a system. Not merely would they be effectively unable to think of anything different from that which went with their established stations, but they would be unable to do much about it, by way of carving out something different for themselves. This is because any break which they made in one area of life away from what was expected of them would inevitably have ramifications in other areas of life, and all such ramifications would go against them. As they ventured into unconventionality, they would cut themselves off from other people and from opportunities that would otherwise have been open to them, without really being in a position of being able to open up other opportunities to themselves.

Such a system of social machines inevitably becomes a tremendously dominating force within a society. And insofar as it begins to break down as a system, the individual tends to become able to make a break in one area without there being such immediate and undesirable ramifications in another.

It should also be noted that some machines can be more or less machine-like in their operations – without necessarily becoming less effective. Morality is one of the most significant examples in this connection, although the kind of effectiveness will certainly alter. When morality is a machine, it offers clear precepts rather than general principles, it contains established penalties for misdemeanours – established without being written down – it operates within a clearly circumscribed sphere, and its precise application to the affairs and circumstances of each individual person is more or less universally known.

A machinery morality is insensitive to the nuances of situations, to the inner meaning of events, to the thinking of the people to whom its precepts are rigorously applied. It is effective, for so long as it is a machine, in inculcating a certain tone in behaviour to which there are very few exceptions. Of course, such a morality need not touch the feelings of those who must comply with it. It functions through edicts, even though these edicts may not be trumpeted from housetops.

A less machine like morality would clearly be effective in different ways – it would be effective in terms of different criteria of effectiveness. There may well be far less strict conformity with the letter of the precepts of the morality – although this would not be entirely easy to measure, for principles rather than precepts would be the order of the day, and there would be room for interpretation on the question of whether a particular action counted as compliance or not. But in terms of entering into the thinking and feelings of the people subject to it – which is certainly arguably a criterion of the effectiveness of a morality – such a code may be far more effective than the machine one.

The most amazing machinery which humans create is in many ways the political, economic, social and religious/moral kind just referred to. It will be necessary to come back to it as utterly crucial. These machines can be tremendously mechanistic in their own way, but it is more illuminating to start with the characteristics of some inherently mechanistic machines.

The most vital kind of machine to consider in this connection, especially in our time, is the computer, which represents the ultimate in what humans have thus far devised in refined mechanisation. A purely mechanistic type of operation conjures up the notion of something rather crude and unsubtle, something that is incapable of adjusting itself to the vagaries of circumstance, the complexity of affairs, or the nuances, intricacies and subtleties of responses and interactions. Computers, as well as being utterly and precisely mechanistic, can be programmed to be remarkably sensitive – certainly to take account of more factors than many human beings would take account of, and potentially to take account of any number and combination of factors which can be computerised, and to take account of them in any way or range of ways that can be computerised.

All of this is very different from what one would tend to think of as characteristic of the operations of a thoroughly mechanistic machine. But the sensitivity must not be allowed to mask the essential rigidity of the computer's functioning nevertheless. Granted that a computer is programmed as it is, the only way to defy it is to deceive it. There is no getting around it, assuming that it is fully programmed to take account of any factors which one might bring into consideration – and it will take no account of factors which are extraneous to its programming.

When it is said that the computer is no respecter of persons, what is meant is not that it will not take any account of a person's characteristics, but rather that it will place an absolutely stereotyped and predetermined interpretation upon those characteristics: in short, it is a respecter of stereotypes of persons, not of persons themselves. (And of course, it becomes necessary to consider whether persons can respect persons in any other way than this.) A related comment that may be made about the way in which computers treat people is that they do so with complete impartiality: computers are not, we may say, affected by irrelevant characteristics, they have no feelings to come into play.

This point raises some questions about the concept of impartiality. For the whole question of whether partiality or impartiality is involved depends upon which considerations are deemed relevant in dealing with a matter. Insofar as a computer is programmed to take account, in some specified way, of certain considerations or characteristics but not of others, it is not impartial in the way in which a parking meter is which will register 'expired' when the money runs out regardless of whose car is parked there. A computer, insofar as it takes account of particular characteristics, may be programmed to take account of irrelevant ones as well as of relevant ones. The only difference then would be that the partiality of the computer would be mechanised and universal. Further, the way in which it took account of irrelevant considerations, or the extent to which it did so, would not be dependent upon its own condition (or 'feelings' as is the case with people) at the time in question. Thus there are some very substantial qualifications to be placed upon the notion of impartiality in connection with machines such as computers. A point that should be made in this connection concerns the characteristics of those who do the programming of computers. In one sense, it is true that what a computer will do is determined wholly by the way in which it is programmed.

But there are qualifications on this as well. In the first place, any particular computer will be capable of being programmed only in particular ways. And in the second place, the computer itself will inherently be of such a type that the way of programming it on matters on which it can be programmed will itself be stereotyped and predetermined, at least within certain limits. The point at issue here partly concerns technology, and partly also technologists and technocrats.

Generalisations in this connection are easy but inaccurate, so it is best to deal in possibilities rather than to attempt to state the way in which things are likely to go. And the point is that technologists may be unduly prone to presume that what the machine cannot take account of cannot be worth taking account of, or that what machines cannot be made to take account of (at the present stage of technology) cannot be worth bothering about. Further, it may be that the technologist is not really capable of taking account of ways of putting things unless they fit in with the machine's ways of doing them; or worse, that the only language in terms of which the technologist will be able to deal will be that of the machine – that the technologist becomes incapable of thinking in any other language, and thus unable to question the adequacy of the machine's way of dealing with things.

Indeed, it may be thought possible that the technologist could become so enmeshed in the machine's way of approaching and coming to terms with things – with the way in which the machine is actually used in order to do this – as possibly to lose a sense that the machine really does have some reserve potentiality which is not currently being used but could be tapped in order to do things in a different and more appropriate fashion. The possibility that comes to mind so far as the technocrat is concerned is more sinister – for the technocrat is concerned not merely with making the machine function within the jurisdiction that is laid down for it, but also to extend the sway of machines generally.

Putting it differently, the technocrat wishes people to conform to the image of the machine, to function in terms of the categories and approaches of which machines can be made cognisant and can be made to master. And the technocrat would be willing to enforce this stand by using the machine to delimit progressively the options which lie before people.

How far these apprehensions are likely to be warranted is, as noted, incapable of being generalised. But it can be said that the technocrat and the technologist are mechanistic machine people. The type of machine with which they are familiar is the one whose motions are determined with mechanical precision. And theirs tends to be the kind of mind which regards the machine's capacity to take account of particular factors as a kind of plaything. Such refinements and sensitivity in a machine are regarded with fascination rather than with any kind of awe or genuine respect – as something that is not really intrinsic, nor of central importance in the operations of the machine.

This discussion about technologists is of central importance to the discussion of the operations of mechanistic machines because it is always important to know something, not only about the way in which machines operate, but also about the way in which those who will operate them will proceed. Particular types of operation usually tend to attract a certain type of functionary – partly no doubt because of the dispositions previously attracted, and partly because of the character of the machinery.

Having attracted to itself a person with the disposition to serve its characteristics, a machine proceeds to draw the person further into its toils – or at least this is the typical stereotype – by embroiling the person in its way of functioning, and in the things and types of things that it does. In this way, the functioning of a machine, its general *modus operandi*, tends to become entrenched, to become almost reactionary. This is a major part of the reason why those who would set themselves to alter the workings of various kinds of machines have such a hard row to hoe, even assuming that they are capable of resisting the pressure to conform their own thinking to the way in which the machine has been accustomed to go.

Turning to non-mechanistic types of machines, the focus is on a political system or set of political institutions. Political institutions need not operate as machines, but they tend to do so.[16] They have a great tendency no sooner to be created and set up than to solidify in their ways, and thus to become machines of a somewhat unduly and unnecessarily mechanistic kind. Further, it is probably possible for political institutions to preserve a tolerably non-mechanistic operation in small and simple societies, in which there is little need for politics because of accepted or unquestioned traditions of behaviour. But even in political institutions which are personal rather than machine-like, there is always the chance – and frequently the actuality – of the personal role being not only subordinated to but shut out by the institutional role. Thus kings and queens have had to throw over old favourites, and cannot have favourites for ever.

What then can be said about the characteristics of those machines called political institutions, and what can be said about their particular ways of functioning? These machines are made by people, but the basic thing about them is that they are also made up of people – by people playing defined (or more or less defined) roles. A political machine does its job through the medium of human actions, not through the movement of cogs or wheels or programs.

The sense in which human agents are replaceable components of the machine is of the first importance here. For it carries the implication that these machines do not begin to wear out from the moment of their inception. What must be understood is that the function of the human components of such machines is not really at all to be understood as analogous to that of a cog or wheel or program in a mechanistic machine. To be sure, the human operative must play a particular role in the functioning of the machine, but it is the person who plays the role, and plays it not merely by virtue of his or her individual physical constitution (as does a cog), but by virtue in part at least of his or her own perceptions of what that role requires, and of the way he or she wishes to discharge it – and of what he or she wants to make of it.

So from the outset a machine of this type is not a decaying and dying thing, but a living one. What the machine really <u>is</u> depends in large measure on what it <u>becomes,</u> and what it becomes depends in large measure on what its human components make of it. They operate within limits of course, for there are things that they cannot do – the more so if they are well down the line in terms of power and authority within the political machine.

The nature of these limits depends partly on the constitution of the machine itself, and partly on the other institutions of the society with which it interacts. Sometimes, of course, components of such machines can grow old in their job, they can wear themselves down, they can do less than justice to their role, and they can set up a measure of friction or ossification within the machine through their own inefficiency.

Again, the fact that the components of political machines are human means that there is a chance of friction being deliberately set up: a political machine can have a flawless design, and yet be destroyed or made inefficient by the deliberate efforts of its components. Not all would be in the position to do this, and once a machine has become well and strongly established then no single component may be able to do it. But in the end there can be no guarantee that a political machine will not be pulled down from within.

If the fact that the components of political machines means that such machines are potentially destructible, it also means that they are potentially dynamic, and in addition potentially permanent. What the machine is depends, as has been said, on what it does and becomes. It does not simply perform some predetermined function in a predetermined way. There is a kind of openness about its functioning.

This is perhaps most evident in connection with the replaceability of the human components of political machines. In one sense, people can be indispensable in political institutions – and this is the sense that if they go, then their role will be performed differently by those who replace them. The notion of 'the new regime' is not nullified because political institutions have tended to become machines. But there is a more fundamental sense in which the human components of political machines are dispensable. For when one person goes, another will come along: and while the new person might very well perform the role differently, this does not of itself carry any implication of being damaging to the machine.

It may be, in an extreme case, that the impact on the machine of the way a particular person plays a given role would be damaging. But it may also be said that a political machine which did not evolve would be living on borrowed time from the very first. For if it performed its functions unchanged by methods unchanged, then it would quickly get out of touch with the affairs it had to deal with. A political machine, if it is to have any permanence, must above all other machines contain within itself the means of its own development, of its own evolution, of its own adaptation. And the essential means is its human components.

If humans could be replaced by cogs in the political machine, then a situation would be created in which it would eventually become necessary that the machine be overthrown. For it would continue its operations unaffected by what was going on outside of it so long as it was left to continue to do so. Its controllers could do something about it – decide upon appropriate changes to its *modus operandi* and the functions it performed – only if they were themselves the real political machine, and it merely their administrative machine. Any given human component of a political machine is likely to perform the role within it in a comparatively unchanged way no matter how long they may stay there, and regardless of what changes may occur in the circumstances in which the machine is operating.

But when any particular human component is replaced, then the machine has brought into it a new source of evolution and adaptation. The dispensability of the components of a political machine is in this sense the very condition of any permanence which it might hope to attain. Such a machine is a far more remarkable human construction than anything mechanistic. And of course, being comprised of human elements, such machines are not merely appendages or servants of the human world, but in principle at least, integral parts of it.

Being made up of people, political machines are not merely in one sense less mechanistic than machines such as computers, they may also be less sensitive and responsive as well – again in a particular sense. The relationships between the mechanistic and the sensitive are not pure contrariety, although neither are they at all easy to set out in full. Insofar as the human agent interprets and carves out what role to play, that agent's place in the operating of the machine is not mechanistic – such an agent is not functioning like a cog or a program. It may be added that insofar as moods and feeling and general conditions have a bearing on what such an agent does, a curious further variant of the unmechanistic is introduced – curious because while there is an irregularity about it, there may also be thought to be a quality of physiological or psychological determinism about it which would seem to be mechanistic in its own way – albeit very different from the mechanistic aberration introduced into a machine by a cog that is running hot.

But the human functionary, while not guilty of the insensitivity of sheerly mechanistic responses to issues that confront it, may take account of fewer particular factors relating to nuance and circumstance than a computer does. There may be many reasons for this. It may be a matter of insensitivity to or unawareness of factors which are obviously or arguably relevant, or of a rejection of them as relevant, or of laziness, or of an inability to do anything about them in the complex shapes in which they might appear. A person may be extremely rigorous and inflexible out of sheer policy, or out of nastiness or weakness. One may go further to note that sensitivity and responsiveness are not characteristic of politicians – which makes one wonder how far this quality could really be valuable, as distinct from superficially attractive in political affairs. A political machine can be too refined and highly tuned, and it would then become like a sophisticated aircraft on a bumpy tarmac.

But there are other characteristics besides sensitivity that need to be taken into account in considering political machines and the people who make them work. There are qualities such as strength and leadership, prudence and judgment, force and fury. These are surely, in the end, uniquely human qualities, because of the element of spontaneity and if not unpredictability then irrationality which enters into them. A computer could doubtless be programmed to be tough in specified circumstances, but the reaction of the subjects to such toughness would be like that of motorists to an advertised police blitz. Again, if a computer can possess judgement, or manifest leadership, or develop fury, then none of these qualities is what it has ever been thought to be. Perhaps none of them is – but if that be the case, and if it becomes accepted as such, then the qualitative impact of the political machine upon the subjects is certainly going to change from the way it has been known.

In a sense, these qualities are uncharacteristic of the political machine as such, even though they are not infrequently to be found there. One would tend to expect them to be qualified and compromised out of existence, and it is perhaps an amazing thing that they continue to surface in our time, and not only during crises. For it is an undoubted further characteristic of political institutional machines that they tend to become administrative by nature. Spontaneous responses and gestures have probably seldom been characteristic of political affairs, although they may have occurred quite frequently in times when government was to a considerable extent personal and authority based on traditional position in society. As is always the case, several factors go hand in hand, and the reduction of personalised government has gone along with a decline in traditional authority[17], and increase in population and in governmental functions, with a rise in egalitarian ideas of justice, and with an increase in the general impersonality of life.

The greater resort to an administrative approach is not simply a response to all of this, but part of it. Nevertheless, the fact is unquestionable, i.e. that political machines are increasingly administrative in their approach. And it may be said here that the same is true of most large, potentially large and growing organisations. Organisations are almost all in the business of having some sort of impact on other people, and they proceed in this by transforming themselves into machines and then, or in the process, go down the road of administration. This is doubtless why, or part of the reason why, economics has become such an influential practical science in our day. For it provides a very straightforward measure of effectiveness – so much so that it becomes a machine in its own right.

What is involved in this administrative approach? That it is central in the human world as we know it is unquestioned. That there has developed an elaborate technical terminology in terms of which to comprehend and analyse it is plain. The trouble is that the concepts which provide the greatest insight tend to be no sooner coined than they are made into slogans – witness bureaucratisation and routinisation. But the essence of the administrative approach is surely that people and affairs come to be treated by virtue of the way in which they fit – or slot – into some codified or written down category or formula. Ideally, these categories should be sufficiently exhaustive that no contingencies will ever arise which they do not accommodate, take account of and provide for.

Insofar as initiative is called for by the administrator – as distinct from the policy maker – then the administrative apparatus is itself in some way deficient. Whether it is possible for there ever to be an apparatus which is not in this way deficient is arguable, although in terms of this work's analysis of the human world it would be an impossibility. It should also be added that while an administrative apparatus would ideally eliminate initiative, it would leave a certain amount of room for interpretation – although it would be interpretation in a very limited sense, with categories formulated for using in the interpretation, and ambiguities, uncertainties and complexities covered so far as is possible.

In a sense, the policy maker – the programmer, as it were, of the administrative apparatus – is not personally an administrator – and yet in a more fundamental sense the policy maker probably cannot help being drawn into that mould. For an administrative atmosphere develops within an institutional political machine, and new points of departure – as distinct from those which may simply emerge from current practices – become difficult to conceive of much less to develop. The theory of cultural revolution is designed to overcome the kind of inertia which machines attain, but there is no reason to think that cultural revolution would not itself become yet another political machine in fact.[18]

This discussion of types of machine has concentrated on conveying the salient features of a couple of major types of machine which seem to be the most characteristic and influential of our time. I have not attempted to give anything like a full classification of every type of gadget and contrivance which human beings have devised for their own comfort, for their needs, and for giving themselves something – often too much – to do. It remains to consider the impact of machinery upon humans.

3. The Impact Of Machinery On Humans

Machinery makes it possible for humans to harness all the power that exists, and all the capacities and potencies to be effectual that there are. Machinery can do virtually nothing for pure thought or pure art. But it is otherwise the means to virtually all the potency that humans can muster. Thus machinery makes things possible for humanity: it is a principal means by which people — whose immediate physical potency is minimal by comparison with other parts of the world — are enabled to translate ideas into practice. In this sense, machinery does a great deal for humanity, and this section examines this matter in general terms.

But machinery also does things to humans: and not only to those who are, as it were, components of machines. It will be necessary to consider not only what happens to people who become parts of machines, but what happens to humans (and the ways of life they make) in a machine age, where technology has become to a considerable extent all in all. The issue here is that machinery, at the same time that it liberates and releases humans, can also enslave them. Machinery can enter into a way of life like iron into the soul, and the impact of machinery on ways of life is a major issue in connection with the human world. This leads to two further issues to be considered — first, control of machinery, secondly limits of the effectiveness of machinery.

In the first — the very first — instance, machinery releases and liberates humans from enslavement to the satisfaction of their immediate bodily needs. But we can now take the wheel and the plough for granted — albeit while not forgetting their fundamental impact upon human life. The next stage in the development of machinery was presumably that of taking the labouring out of production – and this stage is not yet fully worked through.

It is not fully worked through for two reasons. The first is that there are areas in which machines have not yet been devised to do the labouring – or have not been made sufficiently cheap to be worthwhile. So we are in the situation in which drudgery is still necessarily the fate of some people. But there seems no reason to doubt that the endless expansion of human wants and desires will keep throwing up new kinds of drudgery which machines are not going to be able to cope with. In short, the reactionary plea 'who is going to make the roads when everyone is educated' does not, *prima facie*, have substance.

Secondly, machinery as it has developed has tended to absorb certain activities and operations which had better been left for the exercise of craftsmanship. There is a clear imbalance in arrangements that put crafters out of work while leaving drudges in work — while also creating a new drudgery in the service of the machines which replace the craftsmen. Posing the issue in this way – that machines should not be used for jobs which humans would find satisfaction in doing themselves – immediately poses a range of questions about the control of machines. Several criteria appear to have determined the directions of machine development, including economic factors, but seldom this criterion of what individual humans do and do not wish to undertake themselves.

The third stage in the development of machinery is enabling outcomes that are not possible without machines. One level of this is material, the other something above it. Flying exemplifies the first of these. For this activity, perfectly impossible without machines, nevertheless calls for little imagination in its conception. From the very first, the only thing that would have kept humans back from flying would have been their own incapacity. All they lacked was a machine. The second level is concerned not with mere incapacity, but with the need for some kind of vision before one could contemplate the idea of a machine to translate it into practice. The idea of printing, for example, could hardly have been entertained without some kind of vision of knowledge as the prerogative not of a few, but of the human race more universally.

A fourth stage in the development of machinery is concerned with — and arises from — the fact of the prodigious mastery that is now in the hands of humanity. These machines enable people to make use of all the machinery that is available to them. The old classified telephone directory was one of the most useful of such machines. In one sense, early computers typified such machines, which were to a considerable extent used more to find the economically optimal solutions to various problems than for any other purpose. Again, the kinds of machines which this stage affords may be further developed. Life would be very different if all individuals had available to them access to the best way of achieving what they want, i.e. if machines to facilitate this were geared to the wants of each individual.

These various stages of machinery obviously overlap, and many machines could be said to belong to more than one category. One thing that the distinction between the stages helps with is to make plain the extent to which machinery really does liberate, release and free human beings. There can be no effective substitute for machinery at any of these stages. Without these machines, people would not only have to drudge physically, but would have little scope or opportunity to engage in pure thought or pure art. Furthermore, machinery of any sophistication is plainly dependent on humans being organised socially. In fact, the existence of machines, and systems of machines, itself provides a cement for the continuation of social arrangements.

It may be observed that political machines fall into both the third and the fourth stages of machinery. Their impact upon humans is of the most fundamental kind, because without them (whether fully developed or merely embryonic) people would not be able to organise themselves socially on any scale. This is the sense in which we must be as grateful to our countries as our parents.

But beyond this there is the political machine as the means for implementing human ideals, and as providing the framework within which people and peoples are enabled to make their ways of life. The first of these roles falls very much into the third stage of machinery, and the second into the fourth. At the same time, the loose fit of political machinery into both stages indicates clearly the need to interpret these categories in a broad way.

Without machinery, the fact that humans are on their own would make them incapable of making ways of life. Their ways of life would be dictated for them by their bodily needs, if indeed they could survive at all. But of course it is the potential to make ways of life that leads and enables humans to make machinery. The perception of an incapacity, and the desire for something, is an obvious stimulus to people to do something about their own resources, and thus to develop machinery. And the process feeds on itself, particularly at the technological level.

It is probably fair to say that the purely material machines which humans make have a more immediate attraction to people in general than do machines such as political institutions. For the advantages conferred by the material machines are immediate and unambiguously perceptible; whereas the advantages conferred by machines such as political institutions can easily be taken for granted and go unnoticed. They can at the same time be attended with extremely obvious costs which may easily seem to outweigh the advantages, at least on a superficial view.

In the broadest terms, it may be said that what machines do is enable humanity to extend itself. In the first instance, they are like extra arms and legs, which perform manual functions with a speed, strength and in some respects an efficiency which is denied to an individual's own limbs – and which can unquestionably do far more than can an individual's without assistance. They can extend the range and effectiveness of people's senses – we can construct machines to use as our own eyes and ears in certain spheres and for certain functions. With some machines of this kind, people can give an exactness and an effectiveness which they could not otherwise possess to measures which they create.

Machines can also, through what they have done, reveal and suggest to people certain things to do which they might not otherwise have imagined – machinery in this way becomes a stimulus to people, and makes them want to extend themselves, to broaden their perspectives on what is within their reach. On a different plane, machines may be viewed as entering into a dialectical relationship with humanity *per se*, insofar as they heighten human consciousness and self-confidence. Not only do they stimulate people to extend their horizons, but may indicate directions in which it may be worthwhile to proceed.

Nearly all the above are purely physical and material extensions of humans. It is also necessary to take account of the extensions to persons via the organisational entities which machinery makes possible. Machines make it possible for humans to organise – themselves and others – on an unprecedented scale. Such organisation in turn enables people to construct vastly more expansive material machines. Organisation – particularly social organisation – also seems a necessary condition of cultural life.

Pure thought and pure art are in one sense the antithesis of machinery, but in another sense they depend upon it being there and being efficient. Machinery has certainly become an essential means for the communication and transmission of ideas – and without machinery, cultural traditions as we know them could have no existence. Indeed, insofar as art and thought depend on being communicated for their very being, the characteristics of the available communications technology will have a bearing on both their form and their content. There are doubtless many reasons why books now tend to be shorter and paintings bigger than they used to be – but there is little doubt that the availability of materials and methods of reproduction and binding have something to do with it.

Thus machinery enables humanity to spread its wings and extend itself. The limits within which it does this are considered later. But before coming to that, it is necessary to consider what machinery does <u>to</u> humans as well as <u>for</u> them.

Several human characteristics – pervasive although not universal – are particularly relevant. People are susceptible to examples around them. Activities people spend time on influence their style. People accommodate themselves – their thinking, their preconceptions, their approach, their attitudes and their values – to the ways things happen around them, their circumstances and their general environment. Humans are of course initiators, and they make of things what they will. It may even be true that machinery has no intrinsic power over humans, that their inner life may (as a result of their own determination) be insulated from any effects or impact stemming from machinery. But this is deeply rare.

The effect that is more usual is profoundly central in its impact upon human life, although often not obvious. The most overt impact of machines upon humans – affecting them – is to be seen in those who work the machines. It is inescapable that operators must set their pace by that of the machine – especially where a system of machines is involved – and have in the forefront of their consciousness a sense of what the machine does and how it does it. Operators have a role to play, and can play it in their own way, but only within the limits it permits. Seldom do operators have any control over the nature of those limits. So while working the machine, operators must work to its time, in its way, as it dictates; and insofar as they can interpret, they are interpreting it, and are therefore quite unable to think freely, or to let their minds range. To some extent they may be able to 'switch off' and think of other things, but then their being is at best split.

In short, machines have a major regulatory effect upon their operators. The machine determines – and very likely confines – their activity, and their thinking. So much the better, of course, if things can be arranged in such a way that what it exacts of them is basically in line with their inclinations, and to some extent that tends to happen. But this is only within limits, and new points of departure are made difficult for them because the machine keeps them in the rut. They may be able to forget their involvement with the machine when they leave it behind and go to their leisure – but this calls for a rare detachment, at least in the long term. What one is to a very large extent is what one does, and it remains a major fact of life that what one does is one's occupation.

The impact of machinery upon humans is less overt when people are not considered as operatives – but in some ways this impact is nevertheless more profound. In a machine age, it is inescapable that people will tend to let their own hands and eyes and ears be replaced, (as distinct from merely being extended) by those of the machine. It then becomes equally inescapable that people should tend both to measure in the way that the existing systems of machines dictate, and also that their vision and imagination should tend to be dominated and overshadowed by the machine ethos and by the various systems of machines that surround them.

This is not to say that they will necessarily become supporters of the machine – they might equally react against it. But it will, either way, loom large in their thinking. It may be a nightmare looming over their shoulders, or a monster confronting them, or a comforter soothing them – but the very fact that machinery becomes an extension of humans means that it begins to hedge them in. For machines are in themselves slavish rather than free beings – they follow their own predetermined patterns.

So to the extent that they really do become extensions of people, they introduce a slavish and unfree quality into the very being of these people. And part of what is meant by a machine age is that machines – for all that they are built to be obsolescent – come to be taken for granted by humans. It probably cannot be otherwise, and people really have no effective standpoint from which they could mount a challenge to such a development. For granted they are themselves the measure, and that the machine mentality enters into their being, the circle closes.

The upshot of this is not precisely reactionary, for a system of machinery may embody a dynamic thrust which rushes on from one thing to a new thing. Humans in a machine age do not turn away from the future, and there is nothing more dead than a dead machine anyway. But while the world of machinery is not reactionary, and while it does not put its head into the sand, it has qualities which are akin. It is perhaps most illuminating to liken it to an underground boring machine, insofar that while it will not stop going forward, there is something confined and limited about the medium (though not the direction) in which it can make progress.

It is fair to say that the impact of machinery is in virtually every respect two edged. It liberates humans to an inconceivable degree, and enables them to do and be what previous generations could never have contemplated. This becomes particularly apparent in an age of accelerating technology. There is no reason to imagine that present generations can conceive of what future generations will be able to do. But at the same time, machinery imposes undoubted constraints upon humans and their world.

The more pervasive machinery becomes, the more limitations are put on individuals. The same goes even more strongly for groups. If machinery makes for a certain openness in the human world – as it does by dint of widening horizons and providing access to the sky – it also imposes some severe constraints. Each day does not dawn fresh, for its agenda is largely determined by what happened yesterday, and by the requirements which yesterday places upon today.

The openness which machinery creates is openness within a system. To break out of the system requires people to cut away a good deal of what has become integral to themselves. It tends to be the system which provides the dynamic and stimulus to take up the potential that exists within it. The extension to persons itself becomes the initiator, leaving the creatures of flesh and blood a little in the background. They need to tag along, and concentrate their efforts on securing the best elements of their hearts' desire, but only within the general framework of development that has itself gone somewhat beyond their own control. Thus people tend to lose or be deprived of their capacity to think seriously of creating their world *de novo*, unconfined and unconstrained by hitherto existing patterns of development.

This is a profound constriction. Yet in a sense, it is a capacity that never had much substance to it – the vision splendid and extended was always a fleeting and usually ill-conceived thing, and certainly one that was out of human grasp in any form which would be recognisable to the seer of the vision.[19] By the same token, the basic direction which any system of machinery imposes upon people not only focuses their attention, but at the same time brings within their reach means of the kind they would find necessary to attain what they will decide to want.

Thus the impact of machinery upon humans is of profound significance. The history that humans have made – and the people that humans make — define the shape of the history that we will go on to make – even though that shape is likely to be describable with accuracy only in retrospect. The human world becomes a more material thing than humans themselves, and the greatest challenge that faces humankind is increasingly to control what we have made – including ourselves in our extended shapes.

There is, however, a further dimension to all this, for humans have not yet come fully to terms with machines. We have had machines from the start, but we have not mastered them as far as we may. Humans in relation to machines are like *nouveau riche* who cannot handle the servants they buy, much less train up their own. If machinery becomes the manager of people, as to a large extent it has, then human life is very considerably demeaned, and the cost of the benefits is high.

One might say that humanity has been seduced by the machine in an age (as it has hitherto been) where we have not been able to get enough machinery. And we still live in a time where there is much drudgery in labour. More than this, the age when there are machines to manage machines, and to organise machines for the benefit of people, is only just beginning to appear. Up until now, people themselves have had the full task, and not merely the responsibility, for ensuring that machines do serve them.

To some extent, we have gone along with the machines and have therefore had success in this battle only at the cost of some submission: the cost of such mastery as we have attained has been a drop in human character, a kind of dilution of our central nature. And the machine age, while in one sense posing the greatest threats to human mastery of machines, also suggests the possibility of humans developing routinised procedures for controlling machines from an altogether superior position to anything hitherto enjoyed.

This leads to the question of the control of machinery. There is a tendency for machines to have a far wider impact on human beings and on human life than could be deduced from the specific functions which they are designed to perform. Not only are there by-products (which are essentially of the same genre as the machines themselves). but there are impacts on the whole style of life of individuals, groups and societies. The machines that an individual or group makes and uses become part of the whole environment of humanity, viewed from some other perspective. Everyone, therefore, has some sort of interest in them – and whether they be pollutant or not is in some respects a matter of opinion.

It is a very serious thing to contemplate placing restrictions on the kind of machines that persons might develop or use in the course of making their ways of life – just how serious is considered in the final chapter. But it must be said, in general terms, that insofar as machines do ramify in their effects, the question of what machines are to exist, and the uses to which they should be put, cannot be evaded. Insofar as a people's machines are extensions of themselves, it is not wholly unexpected that the social nature of humans would possibly mean that controls would be needed. The requisite controls are considered subsequently.

The related matter of planning machinery requires consideration in its own right. This is a more radical issue, for if there are long-term plans about the kind of machines that it would be good to develop, then we run quickly into a problem related to intolerable constraints upon the ways of life that people can contemplate making. It may be smoother that the need for *ex post facto* controls should be avoided by the development of forward planning, and people may find it easier to make their way in the world if this becomes the order of things.

But herein lies danger. It becomes too easy, and such planning – insofar as it is taken beyond the minimum necessary for the servicing of machines on the drawing board – comes to be a positive encouragement to people to take life as it comes to be made by forces outside of themselves rather than making their own ways of life. How far planning is unavoidable is doubtless incapable of definition, but as with all such issues it is approach and attitude rather than strict principle or formula that will yield the best outcome.

The final matter for consideration in this chapter concerns the limits of machinery. There is a sense in which machines make humans omnipotent in their world, or rather in the world in which they find themselves. By turning matter against itself – which is essentially what machines do – humans are able to overcome everything that stands in their way – assuming that the ways they have in mind pertain to the material and social world. For machinery does not enable humans to do anything in the realm of pure thought or pure art.

'Give me an idea for material progress, and I will make you a machine to implement it' is the motto of the true technologist. Every material proposal turns itself, on this argument, into a technical issue, susceptible in principle of technical solution. The only limitation, so far as the technologist is concerned, is posed by the limitations — or nature as we might say — of matter itself. And so far as the technologist and machine maker is concerned, one cannot seriously want to do anything that is outside of the bounds or scope of matter itself.

But humans can in a very real sense have wants that are outside the bounds of nature – on the one hand unrealistic or even unreal wants, on the other hand wants that have nothing to do with material things. More than this, the bounds of matter are far from clear; facts are incontrovertible and unassailable, but we do not always know where they begin or end, nor what they exactly are. The venture into the unknown has not always proved entirely fruitless, even if it serves to lay bare what is impossible more often than what is possible.

Machines can create some non-material things – political machines, for example, play a considerable part in creating values. But there is a most fundamental limitation here, for we can no sooner be convinced of this, i.e. of the machine origin of a value, than we would begin to distrust its authenticity because of its provenance. And again, as has been said, while machines can suggest directions of movement, they can do nothing about really creating anything like new points of departure, or grasping opportunities for fresh developments in relation to the human world. In short, machines are very much at their best in dealing with the hard world of facts, but they certainly stop short when it comes to dealing with and coming to terms with the mysteries.

4

MYSTERY AND THE FACTS

The greatness of human beings is profound, autonomous, illimitable. Humans are on their own. They are the measure of all things. They make ways of life, and the necessary machinery for them. Humans can not only think and decide and act for themselves: their thinking and deciding and acting have profound bearing on what they are. Their ideas about themselves bear upon what they decide and what they do. Their decisions about their lives bear upon what they think and how they act. Their actions take them beyond themselves, into the worlds they make for themselves.

Yet while humans are on their own, they are not alone in space and time; and the ways of life they make are not made in a void. Humans have their being in a world which has a certain existence apart from them. People must make their lives within this world. While they may adapt it (within limits) to their purposes, they depend upon it – for there is nothing else (apart from themselves) which they can call in aid. Humans may (within limits) manipulate the world in which they have their being. Yet their world is set within this other world. Humans cannot take no account of the world in which they (and their special worlds) have their being.

This chapter sets out, in broad terms, what account is to be taken of this other – external – world. It seeks to establish certain aspects of people's relationships to this world, particularly the nature of their dependence upon it. To some extent, the account due to this world varies as between each different person. For different ways of life call for taking account of this world in different ways and different respects. In a similar way, different individuals will relate themselves to this world in a variety of ways, and will be dependent upon it in a variety of ways. In certain respects, this world's impact on people is independent of people themselves – for example, gravity affects people regardless of the ways of life they have made for themselves (although humans can make machines to moderate the character of the effects gravity has on them). But in other respects, this world's impact on people is vitally dependent upon themselves, on what they take account of, notice, care about: for example, the weather may have almost no influence on some people, whereas for others, it is daily the first item for consideration.

In dealing with the account to be taken of this world by a person (and this world includes other people) a major consideration is that while people can take account of some factors, they cannot take account of others – even though it may have been useful if they could. What people can and cannot take account of is essentially concerned with the question of knowledge – although by the same token they may have knowledge about matters which they do not need to take into account. Knowledge is therefore dealt with, not wholly abstractly, but as a kind of mediator between the human world and the external world.

Underlying all this is the view, implicit in the heading of this chapter, that the two really fundamental features of the external world so far as people and their worlds are concerned are the presence in it of facts on the one hand and of mysteries on the other. Neither of these two concepts is to be interpreted narrowly; yet viewing the world as essentially comprised of these two provides the chapter's point of departure and orientation.

1. Facts and Mysteries

In many ways, the broad character of the world we inhabit is so familiar to us that to articulate its overall nature is far from easy. We are both more and less acquainted with it than we imagine, more and less at home in it than we feel, more and less in command of it than we think, more and less at its mercy than we dream. We take its essential character for granted without giving much thought to what it really is. Or rather, we tend to accept without question or thought some particular set of preconceptions about the quintessential character of the external world and of people's relationships to it.

Humans have their being in a world of space and time, and they share this world with non-human matter (including various forms of life) and their fellow humans. So much at least is a matter of fact. Whether humans share this world with anything else – any other type of mind, any other kinds of force, any superior beings — is one of the mysteries which confronts humans. This mystery (and it is really several mysteries rather than one) has not only perplexed and fascinated humans from time immemorial, but it has stimulated a good deal of mental activity as people have tried to remove it from the realm of mystery. Some people have attempted to allow for it in the ways of life they have made and adopted. Others have placed mystery at the centre of their lives, and attempted to live by it and for it – or for some accepted resolution of it.

But that which is plain to human beings – space and time,

matter and other people – is clearly the best starting point for amplifying the general idea of facts and mysteries. No hard and fast distinction is here laid down between them, nor is any exhaustive definition to be offered. Both terms are broad, encompassing, and indefinite at the edges. To narrow them to pinpoints is to douse their authentic light.

In general, a fact is an ascertained (or ascertainable) quality or characteristic, under given circumstances, of some particular part or parts of the world in which human beings find themselves. Thus, a fact is a constant, it can be held onto, it is reliable, and it can probably in some measure be built upon. By contrast, a mystery is essentially an influence or potential influence which alters (typically by thwarting) humans' dispositions of things. A mystery comes to human attention only *ex post facto* (although people may suspect its imminence), and humans' only access to mysteries is through their effects. Thus, while a mystery may have a constancy of its own, humans are unable to grasp it. Mysteries (either specifically or by the general fact of being known to be present) create imponderable uncertainties, and people do not know when they will next strike. They are like mosquitoes buzzing in the dark while one seeks to be settled, and which vanish when one tries to isolate and know them. They are not always malevolent, and their influence, while uncertain, sometimes is for the better. Again, we can sometimes see them but not be able to chart their movements – or not seeing, know that they are there, and know that they will move, but not know how.

Mysteries sometimes become facts, as people pursue research and other activities. In one sense, this is the summary of the history of science. But at the same time that science triumphs over perceived mysteries, it also reveals new ones – and by gaining an excess knowledge of facts, it can even turn old facts into new mysteries. There seems, in fact, always to be mystery at the edge of facts. We encounter mystery not only where we try to peer into impenetrable darkness, but also, often enough, when we try to relate plain facts to each other, or when we try to assess their significance. Facts seem usually to have certain non-factual dimensions surrounding them.

All of this becomes particularly evident, and in many ways destructive, in an age of specialization. Like the Platonic problem of the third person, there are no specialists to link specialisations to each other – and where there are, the linkers themselves become specialists, and thus themselves need to be linked. There is nothing more specialised in its method than the so-called interdisciplinary mind.

Plainly, it is easier to elaborate on facticity than on mysteriousness. The ascertained-ness of facts places facts before us, so that their quality and character can be passed in review with comparative ease. Equally, it is doubly difficult to theorize about the character of mysteriousness, or to detail its significance. Nevertheless, granted the impact of mystery upon humans, it is important to delve as best one can.

There are, at the least, two kinds of facts, although we are unduly apt in our scientific age to take account only of one. There are, supremely to contemporary consciousness, the facts of hard and technological science – the chemicals that cause concern, the fertilisers that increase yields, the materials which make safe aircraft. Such facts can be thoroughly pinned down – their nature stated, their dimensions measured, their functions quantified. More, what they are and what they do can be separated and treated in isolation from what has come to be called their evaluative dimension. In some ways the most useful and dominant of facts, these are also in some ways the least significant and momentous so far as the properly human dimension of life is concerned. A life which revolved around such facts – as distinct from being so organised as to take them for granted, while making due allowance for them — is as fit for plants and animals as it is for humans. Those humans who live by such facts, with nothing else in view, could become like zoological or botanical specimens.

The other type of fact is scientifically softer. These other facts are apt to defy precise specification, to refuse to be confined by the methods of pure empiricism. Such facts concern <u>humans.</u> For it is fact that humans love and hate certain other people, that they feel moral imperatives, that they have a sense of quality and freedom, that they are fascinated by mystery. The dimensions of facts such as these are immeasurable, and their functions defy quantification. Further, they seem on the face of it to be shot through with the evaluative dimension. Science tends to shy away from them because it can only deal with them lop-sidedly – and the limitations of science (its shortcomings if it is viewed as the sole road to real understanding) are nowhere more conspicuous than in its dealings with such facts.

For humans, both types of fact are crucial, and the human world will be confined and cramped insofar as people shy away from the softer type of fact. For as people address themselves exclusively to the first type, and as they rely increasingly upon that type and make it their only concern, they turn their backs on a side of the world which they can escape only by turning themselves into some type of specimen. To be sure, humans themselves are not the only proper study of humankind – but they are part of that study[20]. If humans study themselves only by methods which are appropriate to other matters but themselves, then they will distort not only their own reality but also their own understanding. When the study of human beings is governed by research methods rather than by the subject of the research – and especially when the research stops at the point where the method says that research can validly proceed no further (regardless of whether there are questions still popping up) then the research has gotten itself struck down by the paralysis of introversion.

By concentrating on hard facts, people not only turn their backs on the soft ones – they also turn their backs on the dimension of mystery. Pure empiricism can make some sort of study both of the starry heavens and of the moral law. But when it has done (and especially if nothing else is done) then the capacity of either to fill the mind with awe has gone.[21] Humans can – humans do – reduce both themselves and the world to a kind of machine. But when they have done so, the purposelessness of the whole edifice can hardly but dawn upon a mind, and make it wonder and turn again to a non-reductionist study.

This chapter does not aim to state the facts, or even (in a sense) the most important ones. For which facts are important is crucially bound up with the life that each individual is making for himself or herself. For one, the possibility of getting a machine to wash dishes will be vital, whereas for another the vital fact might be how much blackness can be bred into the petals of a rose. Of course, there are some facts which pass nobody by – the frailty and mortality of the flesh, the movement of time, the shrinking (in our time) of space. But these facts, while they impinge upon everyone, do so in different ways. The shrinking of space destroys the sense of local loyalty (which has been almost a way of life in itself). It is even making bold to destroy cosmopolitanism. But at the same time it gives the individual an unparalleled chance to go life alone, and make the fullest truth of their being on their own. It is the way in which a fact is important that provides its particular importance.

Yet while various facts are important for different ways of life, there are some facts which are worthy of being observed as vital in connection with both the idea of humans being on their own, and the idea that the fundamental point of understanding is that people make ways of life. The particular facts to focus on in this connection are curiously interlocked, for the most part. That the future has yet to become; that there is change in every condition of mind and of matter; that matter itself is manipulable; that there are some constants in most spheres of human organisation even though we can never be sure to have isolated them; that the world in which we find ourselves, as well as our very own world, is riddled with contrasts and oppositions. Such facts, complex and encompassing as each of them is, not merely interlock, but they all have long boundaries with many mysteries.

There has always been a great question about the underlying dynamics of human affairs. What is it that really makes humans tick; what determines what shall be; what is the key concept for understanding? The only truth worth bothering with in this connection is that the search for a clear, single, final solution is futile. The dynamics of human affairs are not clear, they are not single, and they are not final. Every single purported key that has ever gripped the imagination of mankind over the ages – and there have been many – has had to be stretched on a rack to have a hope of coping, and has been split asunder, darkened in meaning, and disintegrated to a fragmented residue. The concept of 'nature' had had its day by the time it meant just fifty different things, and the concept of production[22] has long been going down the same road.

Perhaps the present enterprise has the same fate in store – for it seems to rely on precious few ideas. Yet I press on because these ideas are presented as neither simple nor clear – not even, in a sense, as final. They are a summary of what is being argued, not the first premises of a deductive argument.

What is vital in this section of this chapter is not to list the important facts, or to draw attention to the major mysteries. What is vital is to draw attention to these twin features of the world in which humans find themselves, and to amplify the mixture of facticity and mysteriousness which characterises our world. The presence of both facts and mysteries is the reason why we inhabit a world which is both dependable and uncertain, both determinable and impenetrable, both unchangeable and manipulable; and also the reason why the extent to which it possesses or does not possess any of these characteristics is partly specifiable and partly obscure.

The facticity of the world provides a fulcrum and a focus. Were it not for the facts, humans could hardly begin to construct a machine, or contemplate making a way of life as distinct from merely hoping for the next meal. Further, without facts, without the solidity which they provide, humans could hardly do anything but merely beat about. It would, as it were, be their condition to be at sea – and nothing walks firm upon the water.

Pursuing the analogy, if all the world was fact, and there was no mystery, the human world would be all land, with neither sea nor air – no changes of atmosphere, no unexpected breath to blow upon people, and none of the endless challenge that endless bafflement creates. Humans live, surely, not only by bread and not only by science as well, not even only by these plus thought and art and love and beauty. Humans also live by the breath of the unknown playing upon their lives, disposing in ways they never envisaged (whether for better or worse), opening vistas and perspectives and possibilities which an exclusive world of fact would not contain.

In short, the uncertainty of the world about us is no less decisive to the human world than its reliability; its obscurity no less decisive than its clarity; its fogginess no less than its luminosity. Of course, little of this would matter if the human world was a world of pure thought, a world of endless plurality, a world of grace, a pursuit of nature, a chronicle of conflict and self-pursuit, a saga of pure spirit, a purely productive enterprise. But it is the most important thing about the world about us granted that humans are on their own and that their world is fundamentally made up of ways of life which they make for themselves.

Were it not that the mystery of the world is moderated by its facticity, humans would perhaps not bear to the degree that they can their condition of being on their own. Were it not that the facticity of the world is moderated by a degree of mysteriousness, it is hardly possible to contemplate humans having any imagination, or being able to contemplate breaking new ground: for facts are apt to be not only prosaic in themselves, but also in the minds of those who deal exclusively with them. Uncertainty poses a challenge, and gives unlikely projects and people a chance; obscurity gives a certain licence to boldness and gambling; fogginess to determination and even intransigence. Fact and mystery induce both hope and fear, both optimism and pessimism, both drive and passivity, both confidence and hesitancy: plus many other qualities and contrasts with which the world as we know it is imbued.

Humans cannot but try – and in certain ways and with varying effectiveness succeed – in coming to terms with the world in which they find themselves. Being the measure and being measurers, being makers and doers, being controllers and lacking given lives of their own, humans cannot simply take the world as it comes, or as it impinges upon them. They are not even just the kind of beings that merely react, in what may pass for an instinctive way, to that which happens to them. Not only are they not just leaves at the mercy of the sun, wind and rain; nor animals with predetermined ways of looking after themselves and living the lives that are their lot. They are beings of a kind that cannot but take steps to come to terms with the world in which they find themselves – to view it, interpret it, and even construct it in their own images.

Indeed, there is a sense in which the external world has no being for humans except through their own eyes. Facts become facts as they are ascertained or come within reach of being ascertained; and mysteries are mysteries insofar as they impinge upon humans without being ascertainable. These are truistic points: they go no further than stating that the categories in terms of which humans view the world are conceived of by humans, and employed by them (with no matter how much impetus and stimulation from outside of themselves). The accessibility of the world in which humans find themselves is its accessibility to humans. Further, the world does not take the initiative in revealing its nature and secrets to humans. On the contrary, humans themselves must work out the way in – how we wish to enter upon it, and how we can do so.

Humans not only make the approach and entry, but themselves give words and meaning to what they are. The words they give are, at base, belief and knowledge – bearing in mind that the meaning of these words is debatable. One human response to the discovery/decision that the world they inhabit is one of fact and mystery (the facts becoming such via extraction from the sphere of mystery) is to develop beliefs and pursue knowledge.

This is not to say that the first and only enterprise of humans is theoretical. For there is a sense in which many people, confronted with the world, are seized with the immediate impulse to 'get on with it', i.e. to act. It would distort the reality of this response to say that the action succeeds the conscious formulation of some belief about what is to be done. But it would equally distort its reality to say that the action is blind, and without any inbuilt or indwelling or accompanying or evolving conceptions directed to something further – some 'purpose' perhaps.

Action (except the most routinised) is internally experimental. What this means is that we learn from it. And we learn, not merely how to do something that is given for us in our minds, but we also gather beliefs and knowledge about what to do and what we want and what is what.

Theoretically, the distinction between knowledge and belief – together with the nature of each – has proved difficult to establish. So it is fortunate that a comparatively informal exposition of this subject is what the present discussion requires. Both, of course, have to do with matters of fact rather than mystery – mysteries are what they are because we can hardly begin to wrap words around them. Yet in a sense, the quintessential practical difference between knowledge and belief is that where we are aware we are operating with a mere belief, we are not satisfied that we are not still out of our own depth, and floundering in the realm of mystery. When we act on mere beliefs, and succeed in what we are about, we are by no means confident either that we have not been lucky, or that we could repeat the outcome.

All the knowledge we possess – at least in connection with making ways of life – has a kind of provisional quality about it. 'For practical purposes' (as we say) it may be infallible and need no development or evolutionary articulation. But this expression contains a special limitation of its own, for knowledge that is inadequate in itself may prove inadequate for practical purposes in the future. Such knowledge can be relied upon to work in no cases other than those in which it is known to have worked. But even 'knowledge' which seems to have a very sure foundation can sometimes be found wanting, and need either to be superseded or even scrapped completely. More significantly, it can often turn out to be inadequate or incomplete for a particular purpose.

In practical terms, the provisional nature of knowledge becomes intimately bound up with the dependence of knowledge on certain conditions or constants. It is virtually impossible to be certain about what all these conditions are, or about whether they will all be met in any new situation. Further, a new type of situation might reveal that the knowledge in question is subject to further unnoticed conditions.

Nevertheless, humans can successfully rely on their knowledge – and their beliefs – to an enormous extent. This is in effect another way of saying they can rely on their facts. For some humans, and in some pursuits, the comparative certainty of various bits of knowledge can be a delusion and a snare (e.g. those who live unduly by opinion polls in electioneering). And by the same token, some people (we tend to say they have earthy good sense) do better in their spheres of life with poorly formulated (or even wholly inarticulate) beliefs than they would ever be able to do with the best knowledge that might be available to them. There is a good deal to suggest that a dependence on formulated and rationally justifiable knowledge can deaden human beings to certain kinds of awareness of which they are capable.

Purely theoretical knowledge has all the virtues, all the beauty, and all the limitations of abstraction in whatever form it assumes. The pursuit of such knowledge – or its construction and deployment – is apt to become something of a way of life in itself. Such knowledge tends not to be related, at least directly, to facts: insofar as it is relevant to facts it has to do with the ways in which we formulate and organize our knowledge of them. But essentially, theories should be viewed as more like works of art, whose relevance to humans are defined by their non-intrinsic merit (or form).

Knowledge and belief are enormously encompassing in their variety, and diverse in their sources. Everything that humans do, and everything that happens to them, brings beliefs and a measure of knowledge in its train. The formal knowledge with which we are endowed by educational institutions is probably apt, in many cases, to receive an unduly leading role, as a kind of regulator. It becomes the exemplar and model of all knowledge, no matter how inappropriate or indefensible it may be. The years when the cast of mind of a person is formed, and when the ideas and impressions that go in are never forgotten, are obviously crucial – the fact that those years witness the making of such permanent marks upon a person, indeed, is the thing that would really make one wonder whether each person really is on his or her own, and capable of initiating a way of life. But one's confidence in that is re-affirmed by the realisation that this impressionability marks the difference between humans (who are part of history) and gods (who can act ex nihilo).

On the other hand, reinforcing the re-affirmation still further, while people are formed by the educational influence to which they are subject, each person also determines what those influences will in fact turn out to be. In this sense, the knowledge each person has is his or her own construction, part of the edifice which they make into themselves and by which they are made themselves. Perhaps nowhere more than in the nature and sources of human knowledge do we find one of the best definitions of what humans are – up to the point when they start to make ways of life.

Human beliefs and knowledge have their being at several intellectual and practical levels. For not only can thought range across a good many aspects of existence and living, but knowledge can cut in at many points of human consciousness and activity. The grasp of facts and the capacity to use and mould matter are particularly basic kinds of knowledge, and they are also closely interlocked. This is essentially an engineering kind of knowledge – essentially prosaic and practical, solid, not overreaching itself nor reaching out beyond its own kind of thing to anything higher. The only way it goes beyond itself in any sense would be in terms of a move towards a purely statistical generality. In short, it lays the foundation of a way of life that is successfully repetitious – all in the same key, all of the same kind, a life in which the end is not merely implicit in the beginning but is in fact identical with it.

Without this kind of knowledge humans are inescapably substantially stuck with an airy-fairy existence, dependent on others for most material comforts – they become suspended in the clouds, the reality of Aristophanes' Socrates[23], their common-sense friends their best hope of ease. But between the drifting clouds of theory and the efficient tarmac of facts there lie some other possibilities for knowledge, and there is room for other types with other ranges and scope.

Those with a flair for interpreting human experience, including what they have themselves done, are in the running for a kind of imaginative knowledge. The same goes for those who can make their education a springboard, rather than the paradigm, for their adventures in understanding. An imaginative knowledge involves a dynamic mixture of practicality and idealism, of concreteness and abstractness.

While humans can know a great deal, and while they can advance their knowledge in line with their interests, there is a sense in which they never have quite enough knowledge for their needs. At least, this is the case if what they want/need/desire has not become static and stultified. At its simplest, the point here is simply that humans are always in fact wanting to venture into the unknown. The real fact is not so much that resources are limited as that the interests which humans can conceive and develop for themselves are not subject to the confines of practical possibilities. But the shortcomings of human knowledge need not be a brake on their activities – indeed, granted what has been said about the impact of mystery, they can be a spur and a challenge.

Nevertheless, in making ways of life, humans can hardly be so rash as to be plunging absolutely blindly into the unknown. They could hardly survive, indeed, if they were in the position of needing to do this. They need a measure of knowledge, including knowledge of a kind that enables them to make some predictions.

2. The Need For Knowledge

In constructing ways of life, at least after some form of predetermined pattern, humans need to know what is ascertainable, what is fixed and immutable, what is hard and soft, what is manipulable, what is uncertain, and what is incomprehensible. These are tremendous needs, of course, even in the abstract, and they are never met. And if they were, the lives we could make for ourselves would be so congruent with our hearts' desire that on the one hand there would be nothing new about them, and on the other hand there would be nothing to stimulate the desires which our hearts form. Thus adventurous human beings – and all are adventurous at least to some extent and for some parts of their lives – typically leap in the making of their lives, without fully knowing what they are doing, without a full grasp of what they are on about.

But the adventurousness and imagination of humans, while not coterminous with current knowledge, are related to it and bounded by it. Humans could not contemplate interstellar travel before they knew that the stars exist in space, nor cooking before they knew of fire, nor telephonic communication before they knew a bit about technology. Science fiction (or some parts of it) may progressively become commonplace reality, but even the most extreme science fiction is a case of imagination working on — or taking off from — current knowledge.

Thus, at the same time that humans need further knowledge in order to make their lives according to their hearts' desires, these desires are also an outgrowth of existing knowledge. This is the great truth in the idea that human knowledge is cumulative. This truth is consistent with structures of knowledge collapsing, as the ways they developed fail to allow for imaginative development, thus calling for fresh construction from the ground up.

The cumulative character of human knowledge, in the sense explained, is equally consistent with the fact that various types of knowledge fall into disuse. Whole structures of knowledge end up on the junk-heap of history, as new ways of doing things take over. The most conspicuous examples of this are in the realm of practical knowledge – the rigging of ships, the dressing of stone, and suchlike dying or dead 'arts'. Theories which have had their day are either falsified by new methods of investigation, or else pass into limbo as the methodologies by which they stand or fall are bypassed and fall into desuetude.

The limitations placed on humans by existing knowledge both cast a shadow and at the same time extend a helping hand to the idea of humans as on their own. If nobody could take off from where previous generations had got to – i.e. if we were not educated in current knowledge while we were children – our being on our own would mean that we could never get far beyond basic food and basic boots. To have to work everything out for ourselves would mean individualism of the most unpleasantly rugged kind.

But in fact, while hitherto existing knowledge gives us no option about the foreground – perhaps even the horizons – of our imaginative and creative reach, and while in this respect we may well resent it, our induction into that knowledge gives us a start, gives us something to go on. It gives us not only the realization that there are horizons and aspirations and further possibilities; and not only – in a way sadly – a necessarily restricted conception of what these are, together with a kind of inability to conceive of them in any other terms than those we have. But it also provides us with the wherewithal to start moving towards them, and formulating our decisions about which of them are to be for us.

Thus humans need to exist in a situation of current knowledge to be able to do anything with (and even make anything of) their being on their own. And *a fortiori,* they need to be in this position in order to do anything really human (anything more than the most minimally basic satisfaction of bodily wants) about making a way of life.

In this sense, the past – human history – infuriating as it may sometimes seem, is not just a dead hand. It may be a hard hand, or an almost withered hand – but it is also a hand we can use like a brace, to push ourselves forward. If the human person is like an aircraft, the past is like the airstrip we need to take off from. Without it, without adapting ourselves and our aspirations to it, we shall lumber about in a desperately unsatisfactory and inconsequential way.

Current knowledge as a whole – comprising what is known widely rather than the esoterica at the frontiers of research – is in many ways to be viewed as a particular picture of what is fixed, immutable, manipulable, uncertain, and incomprehensible. Current knowledge is something like the collective conscience of mankind. It mediates between humans on their own and the world as it is in itself; between the facts and the way humans come to terms with them. It indicates the point where humans are – or where they were in the last generation – in coming to terms with the world around them. It is not precisely an index to human mastery of the world, although it functions indirectly in this way.

In order to make a way of life, humans need a certain mastery of the world of matter in which they have their being. Such mastery is unattainable without a degree of knowledge. They must be able to manipulate matter in order to live at all, and certainly in order to live well. In some cases, where individuals wrest their food from the ground, this manipulation is absolutely direct – in other cases, it is more or less indirect. Different ways of life call for different degrees of manipulation of matter. The carpenter is more involved with it than the philosopher, and in a sense the politician more than the priest.

The knowledge required for the manipulation of matter may or may not be consciously acquired, and by the same token may or may not exist independently of the manipulative skills that are in question. But there is no question about knowledge being required for effective manipulation of matter. In order to work it, one needs must know how it 'works'.

Humans also need, so far as their own lives are concerned, to be able to find their way around current knowledge. To a degree, current knowledge is something we all have a sense of, something in our minds without our being greatly aware of it. A danger of over-education (or a too technical education) is that people lose this overall grasp that is the particular heritage of their generation. People can find themselves in a kind of rootless situation where their minds, focussed exclusively on some fragments of knowledge more or less out on the frontiers, lack balance, perspective and proportion.

The current generation is always weaving the next generation's knowledge with and from that of the past generation. The current generation cannot live well entirely off the knowledge it generates, for that knowledge does not fully come to be – is not actually realised – until such time as this generation will have joined the past.

We humans need knowledge not only of matter, but of other people – for our lives are lived and made not only in the midst of others, but in conjunction with them. We need to know something about what others do, and why and how; we need to know something about their wants and hopes and aspirations; and in order to interact effectively with them, we need to know something of their feelings and reactions, their limits, their values and their sympathies.

Everyone also needs to become fairly well acquainted with themselves in their own way of life. People obviously need to know something of their bodily needs in order to be able to satisfy them – and we know enough about the degeneration of persons to be aware that people must take account of their own needs as persons (as something over and above mere physical bodies) in order to sustain their initiative and independent capacity.

But humans need to know not only their needs – they must also know their limits, their talents, their dispositions and their wants. And if they are going to construct a way of life with which they can be in harmony, they will need to know something about the cast of their own minds, about their personality and character, and about the style and general approach that is congruent with all of that. Nowhere is it clearer than with knowledge of these facets of oneself that knowledge is always both developing and incomplete, and that it feeds off and depends upon as well as nourishing the life and person with which it is associated.

Some people seek knowledge more or less for its own sake. In them the impulse to know can become a passion. Perhaps one should say 'can remain a passion', for the curiosity of children, and their satisfied dissatisfaction when the answer to one 'why' question enables them to ask another, seem in effect to suggest that curiosity and the impulse to know are original passions in human beings. Some of the knowledge sought for its own sake is factual, some explanatory, some abstract, some spiritual. The satisfaction provided by any of the many forms of human curiosity need not serve any purpose beyond itself.

But for some people, knowledge is a means and simply a means. Often, these people seek it as a means to the end of some kind of mastery – either of matter or other people. Such mastery may be an end in itself (as when dominance plays a part in a person's way of life), or it may be a means to the satisfaction of some further desire or interest. In all such cases, the knowledge is being acquired in a calculating and deliberate way – the intrinsic fascination which may attach to extraneous items would not prevent their being brushed aside.

Other people, as noted already, seem to acquire most of the knowledge they need more or less unconsciously, and without really heeding it. It exists, as it were, in use – and would die if the skills or practices with which it is associated were to disappear.

Insofar as a way of life involves anything more than mere being – that is, insofar as it involves either moulding or doing something as distinct from simply messing around or being instinctive – it is plain that some kind of knowledge or belief must be at the base of it. Ways of life become, to an enormous extent, not just persons doing certain things, but persons relating themselves to the world around them, or it to themselves. Insofar as they have a grasp of what they are out to achieve, the methods they use are virtually immediately reliant on their pertinent knowledge. One acts, in relation to a matter, in the light of the knowledge or beliefs that one has about it. But it must be borne in mind in this connection that people do not merely need knowledge, they need to be able to apply it.

Knowledge which simply 'sits', which people are unable to do anything with, is irrelevant or immaterial so far as ways of life are concerned – except insofar as it may be made applicable at some future time, perhaps because it reveals something else in a light that becomes relevant to ways of life. If the current state of human knowledge reveals the inner core of human potentiality, the current state of people's capacity to apply such knowledge may be regarded as a crucial indicator of the outer limits of what they can make.

Their imaginations may range further, but this would likely become a source of disillusionment and discontent. The capacity to apply knowledge depends to an extent on what the knowledge is – but there is so much practicality involved in knowledge at that level that to talk of it in this connection is misleading. It obscures the importance of skill, dexterity, flair and inventiveness.

Nowhere is human keenness to <u>know</u> more evident than in people's resistance to involvement with mysteries. Those who delve into the mysteries are always trying to take the mystery out of them. The priests and priestesses of the mysteries do not reveal their mastery, but use it as a power over others. Submission is to these priests and priestesses themselves rather than to the mysteries. These cranks apart, humans typically attempt to insulate themselves against mysteries – to build walls around them, or simply to keep clear. Indeed, they will pay huge premiums to insure themselves against the deleterious effects that the mysteries can have upon them.

The unknown and the uncertain continue to break in upon us in spite of all that we may do to provide against them. They are a kind of gadfly, and a spur to humans to develop themselves more. Despite that, there is no question but that humans are messed around by the mysteries. Where people are ignorant and uncertain, they mostly do not tread, for that which they are in the midst of constructing can too easily be ripped away from them. It is pointless to try to make something that you will in all likelihood lose, with no real chance of being able to retrieve the situation or be more successful next time.

The knowledge that keeps people clear of the mysteries (insofar as that is possible) is partly going to be a matter of science, and partly of sense. A codified knowledge, where one knows the ground one is on and the conditions of its holding good, is the basis of the constructive part of making a way of life. In general, there is a good deal of hard slog and long slogging in making a way of life. Things must be pieced together, fitted in, and made to function in a regular fashion. Science is the master of this kind of knowledge. A way of life that is not based upon it is inescapably the more fragile.

But by the same token, science – and the kind of knowledge we can gather by it – never takes us the full way. To plunge along with it and it exclusively is to run the risk of overlooking or being overtaken by some factor about which one should have been aware. To play out the idea of having a sense of things – particularly of what is relevant to the making of one's own way of life – is difficult. Indeed it is strictly impossible, for the expression is used to refer to a type of knowledge (or reliable belief) which we are unable to pin down. Whether it is genuinely intuitive or extra-sensory is impossible to say; whether the sense of proportion and/or the horse sense that seems central to it really *is*, we cannot tell because we are not able to pin down the meaning of these terms. But in talking about the knowledge which people need, the idea of a sense of things must on no account be overlooked. Nor must so ratiocinative an approach to education be adopted that people lose this sense, or come to distrust it.

The kind of knowledge that people need is not always precisely what they get. But this does not mean that what they get will be entirely fruitless. The knowledge people need, at base, is that which will enable them to make the kind of life they want. In part, this includes the knowledge they require actually to ascertain what it is that they want. This knowledge is itself a continuing and developing phenomenon. One may know at a given moment what one needs, but one cannot now know what tomorrow's need for knowledge will be.

It may be added that many people are quite unclear as to their particular needs for knowledge. Only if one is fairly clear about the way of life one is making will one be aware that one can do so only by actually gathering pertinent knowledge and acting upon it. It is those who are calculating and farsighted who realise their own need for knowledge – and who are prepared to work out, so far as possible, exactly what their need is.

But even calculating people can have their ideas and aspirations changed by what happens to them – specifically by certain bits of knowledge which they get. The most calculating persons will still have pieces of knowledge fall into their lap which they will decide they want to make something of – which in fact impact their wants, and thus both the ways of life they are making and the knowledge they need to make them. Further, even if a calculating person does not precisely want to use some piece of knowledge, its having come his or her way may have an impact on the being he or she is. It may broaden him or her, or indirectly impact what he or she comes to be or to want.

People who are not calculating in this way, and for whom the making of a way of life is partly made up of what happens to them, have the more need of the knowledge they get. For without what falls in their laps they are liable to get none. Whether what comes their way does so accidentally or in some kind of pattern is immaterial to the idea of their need for knowledge, although it plainly has the greatest bearing on the kind of life which they actually come to make.

It is important not to underrate the ways of life that are made without much planning. Not only are they the vast majority, but they can be exceedingly dynamic and interesting, seminal and influential, coherent and futuristic. To be really calculating involves taking charge not only of things outside, but of one's very self. And if one is one's own boss, then that is another way of saying that one's present (or even one's past) self is the boss of one's future self: which in turn is another way of saying that one is static, even finished. And if that is true of oneself, it will also be true of one's life, i.e. of the life one makes.

There is a good deal of waste – especially of talent – in those who make and take things as they come. Such people not only tend to be oblivious of graspable opportunities, but they also easily and often take easy, dull options. Yet even this turns up trumps often enough. There are also lively non-calculators – not only gamblers, but also canny adventurers, and those who like to heave themselves out of their rut from time to time. It is to be expected that such people will often make something of what knowledge they get even though they may not have needed it.

A good deal of knowledge, particularly theoretical and scientific knowledge, serves what may be called organizational rather than practical purposes. Types of *thought* particularly tend to be of this nature. Such knowledge organizes – that is, it renders intelligible and coherent – the experience and achievement of people in various spheres of life. Such knowledge is particularly important in connection with education: whole ranges of experience, of achievement, of activity can be taught in a tremendously effective way, albeit at second-hand.

This type of education, right across the face of the human past, is the basic requirement in the business of introducing each generation to what I have called current knowledge. People clearly need this kind of knowledge, not because they can do anything with it, but because they cannot really do anything without it. It is retrospective, but gives a standpoint from which humans can become both introspective and prospective.

There is an important sense in which human knowledge is relative – a human construct rather than something humans discover. Even that knowledge which people seek for its own sake has its perimeters largely defined by the interests and capacities, not to mention the pre-existing ideas of those pursuing it. They then formulate their 'discoveries' in their own terms – and the ways in which they have gone about making the discoveries very largely predetermine the conditions under which the knowledge holds good.

The bulk of human knowledge comes either in the course of attempting to get the knowledge that is needed for constructing ways of life, or as an outgrowth of forms of knowledge that have been built up either to satisfy previous needs, or in the course of attempts to make people's previous experience coherent. This organization of previous experience, insofar as it has no practical aim (such as learning lessons from history), is inherently bound up with the conceptions of coherence, importance and interest which are held by those doing the organizing. It is probably not unconnected with this that such organizations of human experience are apt to be taken over by more ideological types of people, and to a large extent used, almost as tools, for some kind of practical purpose.

Insofar as knowledge is in its very nature formulated with a view to the making of ways of life it is *ipso facto* relative. For it is conceived of in its very being and nature as standing in relationship to something else, rather than purely and simply in its own right. And the crucial points here are on the one hand that the knowledge itself would have come out in a different way if that to which it was related had been different, and on the other hand that the knowledge (insofar as it is formulated as it is) will turn the minds of people who gain comprehension of it in some directions rather than others when they set about relating it to other parts of their experience and to their aspirations. This relativity is not a defect in human knowledge, not something which a more perfect knowledge could evade. On the contrary, it is inevitable, and more than this it helps to make plain the real point of knowledge for humans.

Insofar as humans are the measure of all things, it can be misleading to say that knowledge is relative. For granted that what is called relativity means that knowledge really and essentially relates to humans, then the knowledge is related to the 'absolute' – except, of course (and this is why the term relativity is appropriate) that this absolute has very different qualities from what the term as it has come to be used would lead one to expect. For it is an absolute shot through with fluidity and dynamism, and also one within which there is an indefinitely large number of variations on the one theme.

Having dwelt on the relativity of knowledge, and its direct relationship to humans, it is important not to overlook another vital dimension, namely that humans need knowledge very largely for purposes of prediction. The point of knowledge (or a major point) is that people need to be able to foresee and predict certain eventualities, particularly the outcomes of activities which they themselves undertake. They will never be able to foresee every outcome of their actions, and they may in fact be unable ever to be completely certain, because of unforeseen factors.

But the very idea of making a way of life becomes senseless unless people can predict outcomes with reasonable reliability in a substantial proportion of their activity. Nowhere, perhaps, is this clearer than in connection with machinery: which simply could not be what it is unless there were regular and predictable patterns of operation. Knowledge would avail people nothing if it were altogether *ex post facto*. People could not in any sense be themselves (the makers of ways of life, with coherence and continuity) if they were not able to predict.

It is one thing to say that humans need knowledge. But the question of what knowledge it is that they need must also be faced. In one sense, and at one level, it is only possible to say that the knowledge they needs depends upon the characteristics of the way of life they are making, and upon what kind of persons they are – including their interests, capacities, perspectives, and personalities. Further, the knowledge people need depends on the knowledge they already have, and how this knowledge both does and does not measure up to their aspirations and pursuits. The fit and the gap are both unique in every case. But all of this relates to the need for particular pieces — and types — of knowledge.

At a more general level, it is possible to be more specific about what people need to know. Humans need to know something about the worth of things — and here, very obviously, (although the same is no less true in other areas of life), the character of the judgements involved in the knowledge will be intimately bound up with the particular ways of life of individuals.

Humans need to know something about the reliability of the materials with which they work and live, they need to know what is variable and what constant, they need to know what kinds of considerations will move those other people with whom they have to deal, they need to know who their friends and enemies are, and what kinds of materials they must master in order to make their own ways of life. All of this we can say that humans must know — although what it amounts to will vary as between cases, and how far it is attainable will also vary. Insofar as people lack necessary knowledge (as they inevitably will to some extent) they are the more limited, and dependent on factors outside themselves.

3. People's Dependence on the World

It must be understood that dependence does not necessarily mean limitation, and that it is not necessarily a bad thing for people. On the contrary, talk of the dependence of people on the world is to a considerable extent talk about factors which help define the being of individuals. Without the world about them, as it impinges upon them, humans could not make ways of life. Nor would their being on their own have any meaning in the sense of their being able to move, manipulate or master matter. Dependence has many nuances and aspects. The following paragraphs amplify these matters.

What is plain above all, in the life that humans create for themselves, is that there are certain things they must take into account — indeed, before which they must bow. There are people who may seem never to give way and yet succeed. But not only are they rare: they trim to the wind unnoticed, or with a kind of natural harmony. Not the most potent figure even can simply carve his or her way through life untouched. Everyone must stop or be stopped at a certain point; everyone must go on or be pulled forward once past a certain point; everyone must turn or be overturned when the wind changes while they are moving. People cannot isolate and insulate themselves completely — or not completely and retain what we would call a way of life, much less make one.

For some, it is probably better that they make their own allowances: that they calculate and trim and deflect and stop and start in line with their own perceptions of their options. The calculators, who watch and guard, while providing for and against every move, have already been referred to. But for others, the accidents pursuant on blundering and carelessness are not always unproductive. Some people can roll with the bumps, and move superbly at the end of another's coat tails. Matter is more intransigent than other people — the river will drown whoever throw themselves into its moving waters, whereas hitchhikers often travel far and fast.

The Human World, in its totality, is compounded of many ways of taking account of facts, of matter and humans, of mystery and change. We may say that the human world necessarily contains within itself a balance between those who wish to take due account and those who refuse, between those who adjust and those who take a chance. The most prudent allowance can be overridden by a mystery, just as the wildest miscalculation can lead to no disaster — or the most stubborn unyieldingness can (in the face of all the evidence) sometimes lead to release.

The relationship between people and their worlds — and other people – is one of the most amazing facts of nature. The magic of the butterfly's wings is nothing to it. For individuals in the midst of matter and other people, people as the measure and the measurer, people as making machines from matter to control matter and other people (and equally, machines from others to control both other people and matter): the human being in these lights must be viewed as having great mastery.

And yet, fundamentally, humans cannot be said to alter that which they measure and master and use. It remains itself, at one level, with its own basic nature and structure; it stands, transmuted perhaps but still unbroken and entire, when humans have gone. Yet in another light, these impervious intractable immortal materials upon which and with which humans work have their very being defined for them by humans. Humans must allow for them, and take them as they come. Yet at the same time humans define what they are and what they do to them — and at the same time again, can transform their nature and manipulate their workings.

The world both reins people in and lets them go — and its doing each is the condition of its doing the other. It imposes limits upon them, starting from the point that while people are themselves both measures and measurers, that which they are measuring restricts their measures and their measuring. Restricts, limits, delimits, defines, makes determinate: all of these terms are apt, and all their nuances have a certain applicability. Further, granted that different people are going to be wanting to use all manner of materials in different and indeed contradictory ways, something that limits one person may well, by the very same characteristic or operation, release another person.

Not merely is people's measuring limited by what they measure, but so, quite obviously, are their other activities limited insofar as they come up against various solid objects in the world. Yet at the same time, were there no matter to come up against, there would be no matter to manipulate or make something of either. It is only matter and mind (and perhaps some other passions) that people can make something of and do something with: only these from which they can in fact weave and make a way of life. Without them — and humans cannot make them — we would be nothing, wholly without divine qualities.

There is a dimension of human dependence on the world which requires early attention, and which is the obverse of people needing to allow for things: namely that there are some things which they cannot allow for. These are the mysteries. To a degree, humans can be aware of regions where mysteries might bear down upon them — but only to a degree. And even then, they cannot really make allowance in any rational way: they can at best go quickly and evasively, and it would be more accurate to say that they are crippled or paralysed than that they are really making allowances.

Their other option is to try to keep clear of regions of knowably potential mystery. But this is not making allowance: it is ducking something, by not being willing to venture into such regions even though one would like to, because risks are attendant upon doing so. Without suggesting there is anything wrong with this response, it is fair to say that insofar as mysteries can have such an impact, they do subject humans to significant <u>constraints</u>.

Another respect in which the mysteries limit humans is that they sometimes burst in when totally unexpected and unpredictable. The people who are fearful on this score are those who are alive to the fact that this is the way of things, that there are some influences which cannot be foreseen, much less provided against, and which therefore place humans in a position of potentially unpleasant uncertainty. People who take this fact for granted are possibly, in some sense, a happier breed.

Another of the less likeable aspects of human dependence on the world — on our own worlds, in a sense — derives from the fact that we cannot always control what we set in motion. Not only may it react adversely back upon us, but we ourselves may become caught up in it, and find ourselves swept off our feet. This happens in many spheres. Once radio and various telecommunications were launched, there was really no chance of avoiding the impacts they have had upon humanity. Humans could launch television but could not then decide what effect it would have upon their children.

Humans could generate mass political parties, but could not then control how they would function. Humans could decide that every person has a right to pursue their own happiness, but could not then prevent money from becoming a virtually all-embracing value.

In a very immediate and pervasive sense, then, humans become dependent upon the human world – on this world as it was, as it has become, as it is becoming and as it will become. This dependence serves to define the vast majority of people in any given place and time – and it is partly because this great majority goes along with what is going that that is the going thing.

Other factors which make it a going thing are tied up with power; with the intermeeting and 'fit' between something like radio and other aspects of the human world as it had come to be; with the indispensibility and superiority of the item for doing its own job. Perhaps there is also something – possibly best described as 'momentum' – which is real but not easy to pin down.

Not everyone wants to go along with the general line of development of the human world. For some, the changes destroy the real values of life, and these people are liable either to try to put back the clock, or else isolate themselves. Without some heads in the sand, people's perspectives on their lives would certainly be more limited than they are. This phenomenon makes for much variety in human life at any given time. It is not simply resistance to the inevitable, for part of inevitability in the human world is that some people will hang onto things they find desirable for as long as possible. For other people, progress is always too slow. These people are put out by the fact that the generality of people take too long to adjust to change. These people would be happier if the pace could be forced – as indeed it tends to be in technological times. This is partly because technology has the power to set its own pace, and partly because technology can itself be used to induce people to accept a faster pace of change. For some people, sheer change and development is itself something of a way of life, and they want more and more of it. There is an interesting question to ask about what would happen to humanity if the bulk of people moved into the camp of those who love incessant change.

For it is perfectly plain that humans are dependent, not only on the world of space and time and matter, and not only on the machinery which they make from this matter. They are also dependent in a profound way on others. This is in many ways the most many-splendored, the most complex, the most constructive and the most destructive of human dependencies. It requires subtlety in its amplification, since the very same dependence will be nectar to one person and anathema to another: cf. the way one person treasures intense family involvement, and another (possibly in the very same family) not only dislikes it but is destroyed by it.

We are all dependent on other people by virtue of the division of labour, especially at a time when needs are increasing and diversifying. All services are perhaps on the way to becoming essential. But we are also dependent on other people for all kinds of stimulation from the most abstract and theoretical and artistic to the most concrete and prosaic. We depend on our fellow humans for support and help, for education in both current knowledge and techniques, for sympathy, for our material mode of existence, for a standpoint and point of departure on which we can proceed to make a way of life.

Others both enable us to do most of what we can do, and seek to limit us in much that we want to do. The human world is a composite of lives and ways of life; a kind of amalgam as well, granted that ways of life both overlap, interlock, interfuse and interfere. All people make their own ways of life, but they could not do so (nor would anything that they might do have any effectiveness or meaning) were it not that there are other lives around them, and also were it not that these other lives react upon and interact with their own. So this dependence — which is presumably the more fruitful as those who are enmeshed in it are able to make the most of their interaction with others as a consequence of knowing them – is enormously varied, comprehensive and profound for each way of life and thus for the general movement and development of the human world itself.

Another dependence of profound significance comes by way of machines. Machines are, as has been said, among the great liberators of human beings, and a profound means by which humans become masters of their surrounds and makers of their ways of life. But the nature of things — of matter and our fellow humans — determines the nature of the machines that we can make. Ultimately, people must use the materials that are to hand when they make machines. And the nature of these materials makes the machine what it is no less than the design that the human maker imposes on them in making the machine.

With machines, humans can mould the world to their will — but their will must be such that items in the world can be fashioned into such machines as are capable of moulding the world in the way that is desired. Human beings do tilt at windmills[24] — and while those who do so do indeed make their own ways of life, these ways of life measure up to their maker's wills only insofar as delusion bridges the gap between reality and will. Humans can make anything – provided it can be made; and do anything – provided it can be done.

The question thus posed is the relationship between what can be made and done on the one hand, and what can be thought on the other. In one sense the human mind is unbounded – people can think of anything, and will it, and want to weave it into the way of life that they are engaged in making. But to leave it at that is to subject oneself to delusion. Human thinking is not unbounded as we imagine that God's thinking might have been when God was omnipotent, when the world was not made, and when consequently there was no application for that omniscience.

For one thing, humans are incapable of thinking in any concrete sense about the mysteries: they are, by their nature as mysteries, beyond human comprehension. People cannot address their minds to them, or think anything of them, or dream of doing anything with or about them, precisely because we cannot begin even to identify them. Humans are also unable to conceive of things that are beyond the concepts or conceptual connections with which they are familiar; or at least any conceptual developments they devise must be drawn from their own concepts (in some sense). But there is a better, if in a way more constricting dependence as well as this: insofar as one starts from current knowledge and ideas when one embarks upon discovering one's will, one has some relatively definite boundaries of potentiality already sketched in.

Those who transcend their background may always have the highest flights of their thinking linked back with their starting point. This is not to belittle the achievement of transcending thinkers, but only to see their thought for what it really is. The one thing, perhaps, that is really clear (if one is inclined to think that current knowledge is a constraint on creative imagination) is that a mind that was cleared of what had gone before would be a void from which very little would come. It would be a blank sheet of the most confined possibility imaginable.

The situation in which humans are placed by the known fact that there is an active realm of mystery is curiously complex. The most debilitating mysteries do not precisely function like chains and gaols, precisely because they function mysteriously. They impinge on humans, in fact, more like trip wires and sudden weather changes. They confine us, catch us out, and bring us up short. They limit us, but we are not, because of them, in a limited condition: for they are too elusive in their operation to be regarded as creating a condition. Humans do well to be watchful, however, and to be ready to react to them. If we cannot provide against them, we can be ready to make the most of them.

It is possible for people to develop an attitude which regards the intrusion of the unknown as a challenge rather than a constraint. When something goes awry, one can view the situation not as the end but rather as a new point of departure. And if one wonders what can best be done with the apparent wreckage that mystery leaves in one's hands, then one is perhaps on the way to something rather more in one's real line than one would ever have dreamt of. It is impossible to be wholly indifferent to the intrusions of mystery into human life. Those who simply shrug and start again not merely manifest a treadmill attitude to life, but they also inevitably become a little soured, negative and downward looking. Many people either curse or rave. To do either excessively is foolish, and both can give a dynamic impulse to something further. Were it not for mysteries, humans would never get that kick in the pants which they so often need — and this is a kind of dependence of its own.

Mention should not be omitted of that dependence to which error gives rise, for it differs in some respects from that related to mysteries. Where one's own mistakes catch one out, one has a very clear spur to do better and get that knowledge upon which not being so caught out depends. Of course, people can be depressed by their mistakes, and they can also simply go from one mistake to another. But from a more positive perspective, mistakes (and the possibility thereof) can keep people on their toes.

In a sense, the need to be on the watch for error brings an inefficiency into human functioning. If we were infallible (without being omniscient), then we would not need to consume energy covering our tracks. But by the same token, if we were always looking forward and never had to look back when once we had discerned the way, the sweep of our gaze would be greatly narrowed – and we would not only fail to discern exciting possibilities, but would quite likely also lose something of our fullest attainable sense of everything that is going on, and of as much that is pertinent to our own ways of life as we may conceivably take note of.

The essential claim and argument of this chapter is that human dependence, in the most general and specific senses of this term, is best and most comprehensively understood as dependence upon what have been called facts and mysteries. For example, what matters most about other people for each person is the actions or reactions, the attitudes and values of those others as facts (or possibly in some cases as mysteries). In a vital sense, we depend upon others less as people than as facts and as mysteries. The same thing goes — albeit more strongly — for outside matter as it does for other people. It is not matter or space or time as such upon which we are dependent. It is the facts about matter that give us (or subject us to) dependence. Having said that, it must also be said that facts need not be regarded simply as totally overt kinds of phenomena. To say that we react with and depend upon others as facts and as mysteries is not to say that the relationship between humans and the world is operative at only one level, or indeed that there is no fundamental variety to be found in human life. For facts, no less than mysteries, are themselves extremely varied and many-sided in their essential character.

One particular advantage of viewing the externality of each person in this light is that it allows for a more precise understanding of human dependence than would otherwise be possible. When we talk about the world as it impinges itself upon humans, we are not just talking about the world in general, or about knowledge or ignorance in the abstract. On the contrary, we can and should concentrate attention on the impact of all this upon humans as makers of ways of life for themselves. In this perspective, what really matters is what people know and do not know about external reality as it bears upon those lives, both actual and prospective.

One of the greatest truths, and the most important, is that the matters upon which humans are dependent are determined almost wholly by (i.e. are themselves almost wholly dependent upon) the particular character of the way of life which they themselves are contemplating and making. In a vital sense, the crucial qualification to be made to this is its converse – more or less, (as already noted) that the way of life that people can envisage is tremendously dependent upon what they know, and upon the range of their visions of reality and of possibility. In this context it is worth noting that the limits of people's knowledge are defined (and determined) much less by their methods of research than by their industriousness in the first place, and in the second by their vision and their imaginativeness.

A further vital matter, also already mentioned, is that humans can do something about facts which they know. They are not of course able to get around everything (more particularly their own mortality, frailty and fallibility, although even with these they can take protective measures). Not all facts are manipulable, and many that are manipulable are so within closely or specifically defined limits. Nevertheless, people can adapt the world to their own plans, in the light of their own knowledge about it.

Humans can also adapt themselves — and this in the light of both their knowledge of the facts and their perceptions of mysteries. The extent to which individuals can do this varies along with their personality, their age, and similar factors over which they have little control.

Will also comes into it. Will is more likely to be exercised in this connection to the extent that there is knowledge. People are more likely to adapt themselves when they are aware of the impossibility of attaining something, or where they perceive the incompatibility of two desires. This has intimate connections with the most basic point of all, that it is in the world as they find it that people must find their happiness;[25] that it is with the world as they know it and as it impinges upon them that they must come to terms; that it is this world which they must adapt to the designs of the way of life which they design for themselves. It is within this external world, and against their own perceptions of it, that humans make their own individual worlds, and the human world at large.

5

THE PEOPLE

Now for the human world as such! The preceding chapters have explored its basis — its conditions and preconditions, its presuppositions and foundations, the concepts with which to conceive and think about it. The following chapters explore the integral quality and character of human life.

The previous chapters have not been underground foundations. They deal with matters that are continually prominent, continually asserting themselves at the core of the human world. But these next four chapters deal not so exclusively with the 'why' and 'how' of making ways of life as do the earlier chapters. On the contrary, we are now moving as well into the integral quality and character of human life as such: we are moving into the sphere of living ways of life as well as that of making them. The previous chapters have portrayed some of the major dimensions in terms of which life is lived and may be understood: and the following chapters fill the picture out. Putting it differently again, the previous chapters analyse the seed from which the human world grows, and the frame around which it grows: whereas the following chapters are more concerned with the plant itself, in the full character and richness of its being, in its dimensions and its ramifications and its interrelationships.

The heading of this chapter, 'The People', should not be

interpreted too narrowly. The chapter deals, not exclusively or even predominantly, with the people as a kind of single universal collectivity. To be sure, it has a good deal to say about this particular concept and the group to which it refers. And the chapter talks not only about the nature and constitution of this group, but also about its articulateness, its workings, its effectiveness and its authority. The point of the chapter, in general, is to consider humans as group beings as well as individual beings. Accordingly, attention is given to the various kinds of groups and groupings in which human beings arrange themselves — and find themselves arranged. More specifically, the chapter is divided into three sections. The first deals broadly with the relationships between groups and individuals; the second with the characteristics and dynamics of groups; and the third with the effectiveness and authority of groups. This third section intimates the major reason for the heading of this chapter – for 'the people' is not simply one group chosen at random from all other human groups. It is, on the contrary, that one group which is and seems always to have been accorded some peculiarly divine status and authority. It has meant different things at different times (once it did not include slaves, and often, it has only included landholders); and the status attributed to it has also meant very different things, both concretely and theoretically, at different times and in different situations. But it is eminently appropriate in dealing with groups in general, to have clearly in mind that particular type of grouping which has always been accorded a kind of supreme status.

In broad terms, this chapter is concerned with humans in their collective capacity – and as collective beings. Hitherto – as is discussed more fully below – 'humans' have been talked of without differentiating the individual from the group, or the isolate from society. And it will often not have been clear (to those whom the issue bothers) whether various references have been to people as individuals or in groups. But my concern has been, not so much not to tie together all the ends, but more to spin the threads whose ends need to be tied. And the ties are not all made in this chapter either — they continue to be made in later chapters as well.

Of course, this chapter deals not just with individuals and groups – underlying this treatment is the continuing exploration and elucidation of the two central propositions that humans are on their own and that humans make ways of life. These two propositions themselves clearly need to be considered in both a collective and an individual point of view. Ways of life are, as discussed in the Introduction, group phenomena as well as individual phenomena. The human world is a group (or collective) as well as an individual world — that is, not only are there many worlds of humans, but a good many levels of worlds of humans as well. And this chapter is also concerned with the way in which the group angle on 'humanity' ties up with and impinges upon the issues dealt with in each of the first three chapters — for each of these issues (and each of the treatments offered for these) is plainly susceptible to a kind of collective as well as individual interpretation. We must indeed go further and say that each is not only susceptible to such treatment, but demands it.

Insofar as this chapter is about groups in general in their bearing on (and intimacy and integral relationships with) the lives of humans, it is inevitable and proper that a good many of these references have application beyond themselves. It is also fair to say that examples are selected with a view to their own importance.

This chapter also introduces a hitherto submerged, yet increasingly pervasive dimension to the discussion of the human world. Humans live not only in a world of facts and mysteries: they also live in a world in which there always are, and in which there seem inevitably to be, controls and regulations. The existence of these factors is part of the human world, part of the ways of life that humans make, a dimension of humans on their own – and intimately bound up with humans as being both individual and group beings. The significance for humans of controls and regulations is plainly profound, plainly varied, plainly ambiguous. Controls and regulations inhibit and constrain people, they limit people, they often bear people down or at least weigh heavily upon them. But at the same time they also enable and empower people, they give people scope and capacity, they allow people in a very major way to know where they stand.

This chapter does not attempt to lay down a comprehensive position with respect to controls and regulations. For that position is integral to the full discussion of the ensuing chapters. But this chapter does attempt to open up the essential issues concerning the criteria of control, the ends to which it must be directed, and the people by whom it is to be exercised. This chapter also attempts to make the basic case that there is no basis for groups (whether collectivities, peoples or masses) overriding individuals in any general way. In various cases and types of cases, of course, the group must have the final say (although precisely which group is hard to say, yet needs to be said.) But never universally, or even as a general rule. For one of the most important things to be said in this connection is that there are no general rules.

The starting point for all the concerns aired in these introductory paragraphs is a discussion of the relationships between groups and individuals.

1. Individuals and Groups

When it is said that people are on their own and that they make ways of life, the subject, 'people' is a collective noun. It refers to the individual, but also to humankind, to nations and groups within nations, and indeed to any group or collectivity which crosses any national or other group boundary. For 'people' — or 'humans', or other such terms as indicated by the context — we may read this, that and the other individual, along with this, that and any other group or collectivity. The author is on his own, and so is the reader; the author makes his own way of life, and so does the reader. But equally, humankind is on its own, and makes its own way of life. Physicists, tall women's associations, churches, nations, families, classes, races, peoples — all of these are on their own, and make their own ways of life. Some of these, such as 'nations' and 'families', are themselves collective nouns, referring both to each individual nation and also to nations in general and as a whole. It must also be said in parenthesis that the 'groups' referred to — or some of them - may not properly be regarded as 'groups' in the sense to be elaborated particularly in the second section of this chapter - in which case the claim that they are on their own and make their own ways of life would not be able to be sustained.

This complexity, variety, hierarchy and collectivity of humans — as on their own and makers of ways of life – is what is being asserted in this chapter and this whole work. And the question which may be asked is - how can it all be true? The answer to that question is that they all moderate and interfuse each other. None is true, in any very full sense, apart from the others. In isolation, all are true to an extent and yet each is a considerable distortion. Each makes real sense and has real weight only insofar as it is viewed in relation to the others, as being linked and intertwined with them. Thus it is plainly misleading to the highest degree to say that all individuals are on their own, and that on their own they make their own ways of life amidst the facts and the mysteries. If any individuals were on their own in the plain and straightforward sense of these words, then they would obviously be overborne and die or be killed virtually immediately. It is equally, although differently misleading to say that humankind as a collective whole is on its own and that on its own it makes its way of life amidst the facts and the mysteries. For it is unintelligible to think of the collective totality to which we apply the shorthand term 'humankind' as a single actor or agent, doing this, that and the other thing. Humankind is an abstraction — which is completely ungraspable unless we think of it as an abstract shorthand which encompasses a variety of discrete and interrelating parts, i.e. individual people, small and large groups, the past, present and coming generations, and so on.

Of course, simply to assert the truth of all that has been asserted is fairly inconsequential. Furthermore, to attempt to prove it — to offer an argument and say Q.E.D. at the end — is not merely inconsequential and doubtless impossible but also futile. And it would be futile as well as all the other things to attempt to prove the foregoing contentions. What must be done is to elaborate and set out in full (not in detail, but in plan and elevation, with some sections and sketches as well) what is being asserted. And if the account is coherent and intelligible, if it is convincing and persuasive in its own terms, if it can be coherently linked with human affairs and ways of life as we experience and find them to be, then it is as good as it can be. The amplification and elaboration, of course, will relate not only to the concept of 'human', in all its ramifications, but also to the life of humans — to their ways of life as they find and make and live them, and also to their being on their own as they strike that condition and make their ways through it.

And so the place at which it is necessary to start this discussion of individuals and groups is with humans themselves. It has sometimes been said that humans are social beings, and sometimes that they are political beings; and both of these statements are true: furthermore, as amplified by some of their major proponents, both these statements are profound. They contain within them much more than appears on the surface, and they may be made to incorporate much that is important about humans. But they are still too narrow as a starting point — they point thought, not in the wrong direction, but rather in not enough of the right direction. The broader and more adequate thing to be said about humans is that they are individual within collectivities, and collectively disposed over, above and in the midst of their individuality.

There are many dimensions to this proposition. It plainly has a profoundly dialectical dimension, although it is the dialectic of development rather than contradiction, of complementarity rather than synthesis, of tremendous interplay, interpretation and mutual absorption. The truth of the statement can best be seen, perhaps, through the idea of imperviousness. No group is impervious to the individual, and no individual is impervious to the group. Whenever a group is joined by a new member, the possibility that this person will transform the group utterly is immediately created. New members are usually absorbed, but there can never be any such certainty. No matter how painstaking or efficient the routines may be for ensuring that the new member will fit in or be ejected or contained, we know that these routines may not work. And the reason they may not work is evident, namely that they cannot be certain of encompassing the individuality of every individual. Equally obviously, it is irrelevant whether this impossibility of imperviousness is good or bad: it is: it means death for some good groups, of course, but it supports optimism as well as pessimism. If nothing good is safe, equally nothing bad is unshakeable. Nor is anything moribund necessarily timeless, nor anything fundamentally sound incapable of renewal. In short, we cannot imagine what human affairs would be like — or what they would become — if groups could be impervious to individuals.

But equally, individuals are not impervious to groups either. From the earliest moments of childhood there is no full telling what may happen to an individual human being upon his or her entrance into some group. Their beliefs and perspectives and attitudes — and anything else whatever about them — may equally be transformed as may a group by an individual. There can never be any certainty about what may melt any determination, or subvert the most fixed idea. The impact of most groups upon most individuals is of course minimal – but by the same token few individuals are unaffected by any groups at all. This characteristic of the individual is again neither good nor bad, but simply something with many annoying and pleasing aspects but above all one without which we can hardly imagine what human affairs would be like or would become.

The integration of the individual into the collectivity, and the dependence of the collectivity upon the individual, may be viewed from another useful vantage point as well. Distinctions are often drawn between what we may call public and private in relation to the individual and also in relation to various organizations (which are a type of group). Such distinctions may be very well in their way, and enlightening at a theoretical type of level. But they always seem incapable of bearing any weight. When a concrete issue presents itself — usually concerning some kind of control or regulation — and when it would seem that such distinctions should be pertinent (if they are to be more than purely conceptual), they never seem to help. The person or aspect in question is always (i.e. in every case where something real hangs upon it) in one sense private and therefore not to be controlled and in another sense public and therefore to be controlled. And when it reaches this point, the distinction has no power of itself to rule on whether the public or the private side is overriding. Nor can anything rule on this, for the question is wrongly put yet again: the point being that the public and the private are shot through with each other — as the statement under consideration makes plain.

A kind of group conjunction is involved at every stage of the individual's being and development — and individual activity, distinctive and unique, at every stage of every group's being and development. It is of the last importance in human affairs and human thinking that groups and individuals should not be set over against each other. When we write about humans, we must always be writing about both even if one is in the major and the other in the minor key. And it must be said here that it is deeply deceptive to suppose that it is impossible to talk of one without the other. For just as certain sounds that are not music at all can draw an audience, so thinking about humans that is totally wrong and misconceived can draw to itself a kind of mind which cannot encompass reality. As soon as the group, *per se*, is set over against the individual, or the individual against the group, we immediately are trying to make progress with square wheels. And this means that neither is pre-eminent. And the reason why this is true (and why it is equally true that neither is fundamental or basic or anything similar) is that each is a delusive abstraction when divorced from the other. We cannot work up to the group from the individual, nor to the individual from the group. If we would comprehend the human world, we must be comprehending both group and individual — i.e. humanity — at every stage of the way.

In connection with this, we may turn to the issue of humans knowing themselves, finding themselves, and in a way organizing themselves. To begin with, even though humans are the measure — and each their own measure — humans tend to define themselves against other humans. This defining process includes the articulation of the measure that they are and are to be, it includes their conceptions of what their existence is all about — and to an extent it flows over into what they want to make of that existence, and what they want it to be. Other people provide an essential point of contrast, and thus a point of departure: and essentially, in order to provide a genuine contrast, a person must have some knowledge of them, which means that there must be some sort of association with them. That is, humans tend to define themselves (as individuals) against the group or groups to which they belong — and this may well explain why people who are cut off from groups tend to lack a sense of themselves.[26]

In addition to that, the process of self-definition commits individual people to using the language and usually the mode of thinking of their group or groups. They must use them, even if they take them beyond themselves (as they are likely to do if originality is in them) and even if they go away from them or use them against themselves. These factors are of great significance. The language and mode of thinking do not precisely determine the thought itself, but they have a direct bearing on its form and shape, and so indirectly on its content. Each individual is thus enmeshed in groups in this respect. They are also bound to draw very largely on the knowledge which these groups possess — or if at some time they want to turn away from that knowledge, they are committed to approaching other groups for the understanding and use of their knowledge. Of course, being in a group or having entered into one, and having drawn upon its knowledge, they then become able to make their own contribution, and will normally be in some sort of position to do this. Thus to say that humans are enmeshed in one or several groups does not mean that each is simply a kind of groupie. All the other members of the group are in the same position – both drawing upon it and contributing to it — in a sense helping to define it as much as it helps to define them. And all levels of groups are involved in this, from the smallest to the largest, from the most egalitarian to the most hierarchical, from the most to the least specialized. It is not precisely right to say that individuals will be more roundly and fully defined in proportion to the number of groups they belong to — for there are limits, and there is appropriateness, balance and coherence. But it is hard not to suppose that a broad range is more helpful — especially as definitions of persons spill over into their constitutions and determinations.

Defining, knowing, finding, determining and organizing oneself all run over into each other — and if knowing and defining are theoretically the most foundational, and determining and organizing the most concrete, finding is perhaps the most comprehensive and all-inclusive. In finding themselves, humans do not merely define or even know themselves (those both being, as it were, at one remove from themselves, as by themselves detached). In finding themselves, humans relate their knowledge of themselves to their perceptions of themselves, and both, in an absolutely integral way, to their lives — and thus to their determination and organization of themselves. The knowledge or perception need not be particularly overt, nor given much weight in their overall perspective — nor indeed need the finding itself be particularly conscious. In many cases, non-awareness of having found oneself may make for a fuller and deeper — if more complacent — finding. But regardless of that, the finding of oneself is not an isolationist achievement, for it involves not merely relating oneself to one's life and vice versa, but positioning oneself in the world — and this means relating oneself to other people, especially to groups. It means finding a place in some groups, distancing oneself from others, and achieving various degrees of involvement and detachment vis-a-vis the whole range of groups within whose milieu and sphere one has one's being.

In this connection, we may see that there is a major truth in the proposition that individual human beings belong much less to the human race than to smaller and more specific groups. It is effectively inconceivable that the human race will ever be able to give itself any kind of organizational coherence or genuine unity or sympathy or interaction. 'Humankind' has its uses as a biological term on the one hand, and as a term for moral theory on the other. But insofar as it embraces everything — all humans, with all their knowledges, all their sets of attitudes and feelings, all their historical traditions and their geographies, all their activities and perspectives; and not merely all people now with all this, but all people in every generation — insofar as the term embraces all this, it focuses on nothing, it encapsulates nothing. It may help differentiate humans from everything else, from the rest of matter, but it is completely unhelpful in connection with the analysis or organization of the human world. World organization, no matter how federal, would be inherently less consensual than any other that is imaginable. Hardly any group organization can be entirely consensual, but a consensus of mankind is strictly unintelligible — differences of language and meaning would be too great apart from anything else. So world organization necessarily becomes a case of domination — which might have some worth, of course, in relation to some specific problem, despite the awesomely terrifying associations evoked by the idea of a majority of mankind.

In a way, the concept of humankind is the limiting case of human groups. And it has a role in separating humans from all else, and as a shorthand for including everything that comes within the world of humankind — though for that very reason any idea that one can do anything with it in terms of defining oneself is a delusion. As the limiting case, however, it highlights several factors about individuals and groups. People who profess to be members of no group but the human race thereby declare their ignorance, their incapacity to be anything or make anything of themselves, and their refusal to become in any way determined: although no such people really exist, they only delude themselves in saying that they do. More than this, however, there is a key sense in which the groups which are really decisive to humans are such by the intimacy of their involvement with them. It is not just a question of size, although that often helps; nor of harmony, for that can be too bland; nor of immediacy, which can cause delusions which lack any permanence. The groups to which people really belong, in and through which they find and make themselves, are those in which they become bound up; in which they work or play, or act; with whom they enter into some kind of real communion. If the group is large and wide-ranging — like a nation, or like catholicism — then they will be involved with only some of its facets But mere size is not a barrier to full involvement in every aspect — freemasonry numbers many millions, but its character would allow a member to be bound up with every element of it. Similarly, a person may belong to a very small group, yet through slight involvement with it be only marginally defined thereby. There are some groups — families, churches, occupations — which are important in the development of huge numbers of individuals; and other groups — political parties, special interest associations — which seem important in the development of comparatively few. There is probably no generalizing, however, about which groups or types of groups are crucial to various individuals. People find themselves in some groups, and very likely find their way into others. And in those various groups, by processes of reaction, contrast, osmosis, activity, learning, following, imitating, involvement, rejection, withdrawal — and much else as well — people find themselves and make themselves. And at the same time they partake in and contribute to the making of the group and its life.

It is important to realize that just as 'human' is groups as well as individuals, so 'ways of life' are made by groups as well as by singles or couples. In a sense, group ways of life are both composites of portions of individuals' ways of life, and at the same time they have a genuinely collective unity and integrity of their own. The relationships between the elements of individuals' ways of life which comprise group ways of life have a certain capacity, in many cases, to coalesce, as it were, to interfuse. The case is perhaps clearest when we are considering the life of a person who is deeply involved in, and devoted to a particular group. What is apt to happen is that the relationships between certain elements of that person's life (and of others' lives) themselves become more central to that life than the elements between which these relationships exist — and certainly more central than the other elements of that life. And when this sort of thing begins to happen — the most characteristic terms for it are loyalty, devotion, involvement, immersion and the like — then a group life as something in its own right has, as it were, taken off. This must be called the highest form of group life from one point of view, yet also the most ambiguous. It has a curious quality of corporateness about it; for there is in it an odd mixture of self-sufficiency and of mutual cannibalising. The group lives through its members feeding on (or off) each other. As a way of life it is apt to be extremely self-protective, and extremely supportive of the extraneous activities of its members. So where such a group way of life is not all-consuming, it can be the source and inspiration of some most valuable works. For the individual becoming involved in it, there is a process perhaps best called death and rebirth. Some individuals find a kind of permanent centre for their own life in their involvement with such a group life, even though they may only be at the edge of it. Some individuals become lost in it — some lose (and really demean) themselves in serving it, others are eaten out by it. And again, some individuals dive into it for a while, and bask or wallow or get frantic in it — and then they climb out and go beyond it to something else.

This highest form of group life has an intense quality to it. It is all or nothing in its proper form, and there can hardly be any hangers-on. It easily becomes dangerous in its intensity, passionateness and single-mindedness. For it really has no perspective on the rest of life or on other parts of life. It is perhaps most characteristically found in the cloister, and sometimes in the academic common room; it is fostered by some organizations, and often found oddly enough in the lower echelons of political parties. If comparatively few people can really enter upon it, and even fewer except as a sideline to the major business of life, it is equally true that people who have neither experienced nor properly perceived it have so much narrower a conception of human life and the human world.

Group ways of life that are less high tend to have a qualitatively different character. For all the reasons noted already they do not actually leave their members intact. Nor need their members' involvement be less demanding, or less all embracing. What is absent – for better or worse — is the immersion of self. The cannibalism, insofar as it is present, is not designed to be mutual. The life of politics, at the higher levels, is perhaps one of the best examples of this. One person may want to consume the other, but one could not wish to be consumed oneself. One may throw oneself into the life, but it is not self-sufficient since it is entered into and needed for one's purposes. It is not something in itself, but on the contrary it is for something else — even though that other thing may never be realized, and even be lost in the very pursuit of the life of politics.

And then there are much more relaxed and free group ways of life. Families are often such (although they can be intense and demanding) — and when they are, then the relationships set up reflect as well as develop individual ways: they are very friendly sounding boards. But to give this example (and then amplify it in only this one way) reveals how varied may be the ways of life of groups. For not only might groups vastly different from the family have been mentioned — but vastly different perspectives on the family might have been offered. Group ways of life are as various, as rnultitudinous, as transient, as developing, as transforming and transformable as groups themselves.

Before moving on, there is one more point to be raised, namely the mysterious quality and elusive reality of some group ways of life. One wonders what their mainsprings are, and how they are constituted; one wonders whether phenomena that seem like relevant relationships really are such; one wonders whether one is not merely getting hold of figments of imagination, and simply dealing with constructs of the alleged obsessor's mind. The kind of examples that spring to mind are epitomized by the idea of 'national characteristics'. They seem so real, so distinct, so unmistakeable, so unavoidable – and yet they are at a level of generality that defies analysis or quantification or even convincing falsifiability much less verifiability. Insofar as all this really is the reality of the case, the appropriate response is surely not to tread warily in trying to say anything, not to try to demonstrate the defensibility or validity of every item mentioned. The appropriate response is rather to sketch out boldly whatever seems to be right, not bothering too much about how demonstrable it may be: and then, when one has given such a sketch, and filled out a picture, to adhere to it with an appropriate degree of scepticism, invoke it with appropriate hesitation and reserve, and prevent other constructs from depending upon it. Restraint for lack of evidence in trying to get a grasp of some aspect of the human world is nothing but a delaying tactic — but restraint in assessing the credibility of the picture one devises is almost the beginning of wisdom.

Group ways of life are thus integral to the human world and to the understanding of human life — just as groups are an integral part or component of humanity as such. But they also serve humans — in general, their ways of life go beyond simply being something in themselves, for they can do something for people. And what they do, above all else that is done for people (or that people can do or make for themselves) is to enable humans. Groups enable not only individuals, but other groups as well. And they do not merely create the means of doing things, making things, being things — they create things to do, make and be as well. They create scope, possibility, potentiality, opportunity and options. And by doing and making more than they themselves can use or consume, they divide labour in a most liberating fashion. For what they do and make can be used as well as aspired to by others, and can be made the basis of something else as well.

To a degree, of course, individuals can create for themselves opportunities, options, possibilities, potentialities, capabilities and aspirations. But the degree is slight and limited in the vast majority of cases. It is not only that most individuals lack the vision and creativeness to look so far beyond their noses, or to conceive of fresh alternatives. The equally telling fact is that even where there is vision, there is seldom the means to implement it. The material resources to actualize a significant option for oneself — much less for others — are commanded by few individuals. Groups, by contrast, do command such resources, and can create opportunities and options — for themselves and their members, for other groups, and indeed for all individuals. Herein lies the greatest thing that groups can do for humans.

It is part of the nature of group operations to generate new options and opportunities. Whatever is done, especially at group levels, not only opens perspectives and reveals new things that might be done. It also increases the general stock of resources and capabilities of which humanity (in the most general sense) is possessed. So with a will, groups can go much further, especially groups which combine responsibility to others with a command of material resources. Groups can set themselves deliberately to the task of enabling and facilitating, to the creation of new options and opportunities. Quite plainly, people are making much less than the most of themselves and their capacities if they exercise no control or deliberation and play no constructive role in the formation of the opportunities and options which are available to them. Their capacity to make their own ways of life is enhanced by massive geometric progression if the available options and opportunities are right and good — if they do not have to make the best of a bad lot, or consume their energies creating their own options after they have worked out what they would like them to be.

Herein lies a doctrine to be called quality of opportunity. When we talk of a good and great society, we certainly are talking of one in which misery and suffering are minimized, in which there is tolerance and justice and freedom and respect, and all manner of similar virtues and values, along, no doubt with an adequate and universally distributed material competence. But none of this is enough. The good society is pre-eminently characterized by the fact that it has on offer all those options and opportunities to which people would aspire (and not merely those with which they would be content, much less those for which they would greedily settle).

The range of options involved is as far above the idea of a highest common factor as it is above that of the lowest common denominator: for the factors most appropriate to everyone must all be there, at least ideally. And insofar as a society has these options available, it breeds all manner of cultivation. In particular, it may expect to generate in both individuals and groups the presumption and disposition of naturally going for what seems qualitatively best. There need be no aping of fashion when goals of all descriptions are made to Bond Street standards. Of course, goods that cannot be made to this standard would go not only from fashion, but from production. There need be no shame then in choosing as one wishes, no envy or compunction.

But while groups can do much — indeed the greatest imaginable things — for people, they can also do much to people. And without setting individuals against groups or vice versa, it is necessary to look at the evil that groups can do and the damage of which they are capable. The capacity of humans to make the most (and perhaps the best) of themselves is probably rivalled only by their equal capacity to make the least (and possibly the worst) of themselves. Both collectively and individually, people can be lazy, unenterprising, conformist, complacent, static and stultified. When the group makes itself a prop on which people can – or do — simply lean; when it offers nothing but comfort together with insurance thereof; when it merely cossets and thereby benumbs; when its embrace smothers no matter with what goodies — then it does to people no less damage than the good which it could otherwise be doing for them.

Groups can also do damage to people when they become overbearing, all-embracing, or dominating. Certain groups seem to be shot through with monopolistic tendencies. It is not that they simply proceed to develop a life of their own, but rather that they place their hand on (or stick their fingers into) other ways of life. Some groups are apt to be busy-bodies, in short. And they can then thwart, impede, harm, nullify and indeed destroy the lives and ways of life that individuals in particular have striven for. For groups in general have available to them the resources to overpower individuals. Groups can thus destroy initiative, sap persistence, and in general set about stopping others from making their own ways of life. And insofar as groups do take this kind of road, the damage they can do has the most profound consequences. For it really is a case of their destroying one layer of a system which relies for its proper working on mutual interaction between all its layers — like interfering with an ecosystem in such a way that it becomes impossible to know what kind of metamorphosis may ensue.

Of course individuals can attain a degree of power that enables them to damage groups — especially if they have some authoritative position as well. Small groups in particular are apt to be vulnerable both to large groups and to powerful individuals. So the possibility of damage is not a one way street, although in our day all the evidence seems to point to damage to the individual. What is important is that humanity — humans — should flourish. In the end, groups both big and small, and individuals both powerful and private, depend upon this, and benefit from it. The diminishment of humans, especially within national societies as we know them, can come about with alarming ease — and somehow or other, it is necessary that continual attention and support should be given to the business of maintaining proper spacings, cultivating what needs some support, coaxing the weak, pacifying the strong, and containing the expansionary and over-zealous.

It is perhaps worth going on to ask why humans are group beings. For the notion that people cannot survive alone and in isolation, while doubtless true, seems to be an inadequate answer to the question. There is surely a far more deeply diffused sociability, interdependence, and combining tendency in people than this. At one level, people have their reasons for combining — certain groups are formed to enable certain goals to be achieved — and these goals may be purely material (like companies forming a consortium to undertake a huge project while minimizing the risk to any one of them), or goals of convenience (like people forming a club to provide them with comfortable lunches). There are also cultural and spiritual goals which are, on occasion, consciously pursued by the formation of particular groups. But only if humans were already group beings could any of these functional groups be a possibility.

The deepest answer to the question of why humans are group beings really seems to lie in the statement that it is human nature to be a group being as well as an individual. This proposition must then be amplified in several directions, by considering what humans are and do. Thus, it is surely human nature to use language, to have emotion, to form values, to think, to idealize, and so on. If notions such as these are the real key leading to our understanding of what humans are, then a group dimension is already present in their nature. To contemplate purely as an individual, as an isolate, is not to contemplate <u>humanity</u> at all, or certainly far less than the totality of humanity. Putting it differently, the grouping tendency is not something which arises out of human nature, but rather an aspect of this nature — and of course when one realizes that this is so, one needs to be very wary of the question 'why are humans group beings' insofar that it is asking, in part, 'why is human nature what it is?'

So we come back to the point that in talking about groups, we are talking about humans. And it must be stressed that people are the proper theme, the only subject proper to be focussed upon in trying to give substance and amplitude to the general idea of the human world. There is no need to deal with structures or systems, with modes of production or abstract dialectics. People themselves, in their various dimensions, are the beginning and the end and the middle of their own — the human — world. Other ideas and factors, while clearly not irrelevant to understanding humans, are not at the centre. But it must always and fundamentally be borne in mind that humans make them and gives them their measure — and that humans must also control them. The assertion that humans are controlled by such factors has often been useful as a sort of spur to make people reassert their mastery over them when it is flagging. And it will be necessary to return in later chapters to the question that was posed in the Introduction concerning the possible capacity of humans to make what humans will become unable to control.

In concluding this section, I repeat that groups must not be set against individuals, nor individuals against groups. Collectivist theories and individualist theories have both had their day. They are equally inadequate and roughly equally partial in their comprehension of the truth. But if group is not to be set above individual, nor individual above group, a fresh start and approach will be required with the question of authority. Controls and regulations — and we might also hope decisions about which options are to be available — are required: nothing that has been said about groups and individuals suggests in any way that their mutual relations will be wholly harmonious. But without either a collectivist or an individualist theory, (and without something that either tries to go down the middle or tries to include both ends as well as the middle) there looms a problem about who is to be entitled to control: which individuals, which groups, which combinations and/or consortiums. The third section of this chapter will make some approaches to this huge issue. But before that, it is well to look more closely at certain characteristics of groups — at what they are and do, and at how they function.

2. *The Dynamics Of Groups*

To get at this issue, it is necessary to go behind and around it. The starting point is a question which, while somewhat misleading, poses some major issues — namely, 'how do groups come to be?' While this question is not a call for a sociological encyclopaedia, it does turn the mind in the direction of really profound variety. It will lead us to pose the question 'what really is a group', and also 'what kinds of groups are there' which in turn will lead us to pose the question of the functioning of groups. The word 'dynamics' can properly be used to encompass all these concerns and questions.

Some groups are obviously consciously set up — political parties, national trusts, bridge clubs, and the like. These groups were not previously in existence — indeed nothing like them may even have been in existence. And yet rarely is a group established simply because someone has a bright idea from the blue about what would be good. Those who form groups in this way seldom construct the plug hole as well as the plug: they normally perceive the hole, and devise a plug which would suit it — and then draw together what has previously dripped inconsequentially down the hole. Sometimes the hole is a need, but by no means always — it can be an implicit desire, or a yearning, or something that will be seen as convenient and useful.

But consciously set up groups seem, in the first place to be inherently comparatively few (except that they can be endlessly multiplied in diverse and leisured societies) and in the second, comparatively ephemeral. In general terms, it would seem that far and away the most crucial and important groups and groupings both are and must be always there, in some form or other. They seem, in effect, to be part of the constitution of humanity. Thus there is the family, and there are geographical groupings for purposes of the division of labour and of defence. There is always government, and a certain number of basic occupational groups of one kind or another. There are always priests (whether clerics, holy persons, experts or whatever) and their various flocks. These groupings, and a few others of their ilk, are not actually <u>set up</u>, although they may consciously be given some specific form. On the contrary, these groupings 'you have always with you' with far more certainty than you have always the truly poor. And it is not just that humans could not exist without them — they come to be as the result of a whole range of factors: people's safety, to be sure, but also their sociability, their spirituality, their emotions and feelings, their loyalty, their ambition, their desires for scope and comfort and challenge and companionship. And doubtless a good deal else as well. Of course, these factors could not exist without the groupings — in a sense. But neither could the groupings exist without these factors. And all history, together with all prehistory, involves both these factors and the reality of groupings. One may be able to explain, in terms of at least half independent 'causes', how one or other of them came to assume a particular form at a particular time. But to attempt to explain how such groups come to be, as an intellectual exercise in isolation, involves a misconception. For their being is an absolutely integral part of the being of humans, and cannot be treated or even thought about in isolation from that. And of course it is groups of this order — rather than bridge clubs and the like — with which it is really important to come to terms.

It should be added to the foregoing, as an implication of it, that classifications of various kinds of groups are, at base, disconcerting undertakings. The following classificatory terms, which have enjoyed some currency (explicitly or implicitly) with regard to groups, bear some examination in order to illustrate this disconcerting character: natural, contrived, authentic, voluntary. If one considers the following 'groups' — the family, society, the priesthood, the government, and the faithful — there are respects in which all of them can properly be included within each of the classifications mentioned.

The term natural is notoriously ambiguous — yet it can hardly be dispensed with, for it seems to do far more justice to these groups than do any of the other terms. Ambiguities aside, however, none of these groups is wholly natural, for all of them will always in fact be such as to contain within themselves certain contrived elements. They can all (and all do) make themselves artificial, and can assume all manner of peculiarities. As for authenticity — which hovers between realism and legitimacy, artificiality and sincerity: each of them is that — yet all of them can also be invested with elements of spuriousness, and all can be distorted. Such spuriousness is not always just a case of overlays on the real thing — for overlays can be stripped away. Where any of these groupings is concerned, the case is that if one would really get at the thing itself, then one must recognize on the one hand that the overlays penetrate through to the core of the thing as it then is, and on the other that one does not really have the thing as it then is when one strips off the overlays. The Thames cleaned up is not the Thames that was, any more than the British Museum without the Elgin Marbles would be the British Museum as it is. Voluntariness is not dissimilar: the family is both a voluntary and an involuntary group. It cannot be dispensed with altogether, even though youths and rebels can reject and turn away from it. But if we talk of the tendency for people to be drawn to their own blood as they grow older, and ask whether that is a voluntary phenomenon, we are obviously talking in terms that are inadequate to the reality in view.

To classify groups, then, by putting them into 'boxes', is a futile and distorting pursuit. Yet groups are not to be regarded as unique and nothing more. There are similarities and differences, congruences and discontinuities. And what really seems to be necessary is to get at their relationships, if we are to understand them for what they are and thus to get a sense of what they do and how they work.

But first, what are they? What are the characteristics of groups, what is their essential quality, their governing principle? To attempt a definition is not my aim, for that would be too bland and too impossible. And likely to turn one from the heart of the matter. And the heart of it is — some kind of unity. Hardly pure oneness, for that would involve such uniformity as would give a mass rather than a group. It is unity in some kind of association with diversity that is involved — and it is likely that there is room for diversity in the kinds of unity that are to be found among various groups. Let it also be said that while the idea of unity is at the heart of the matter, to use this term, with all the obscurity associated with it, puts one on the right track rather than putting the solution to the question squarely into one's hands.

What kind or kinds of unity? Doubtless almost as many kinds as there can be among humans is the answer. But not coalescence as with welding, not continuing identity as with ships or axes through their repairs, and not mere contiguity either. 'The unity that can be among humans' — we have, of course, a circle here, but it is the right circle, for the subject entire and overall is humanity. There can be unity of view, of interest, of feeling or sentiment, of attitude, of approach and so on. And these varieties of unity are all pertinent and applicable in connection with groups — though not all of them with every group.

Most of those types of unity are not easy to analyse, and have some interesting overtones. Unity of view is an obvious case — in many groups (such, perhaps, as the Anglican Church) this unity would be on something of a par with a general will so far as being discoverable is concerned.[27] There doubtless is some kind of consensus, and in part it would be a consensus in the realm of view or belief (although it would also be partly in the realm of attitude and approach). But so general and so elusive would it seem to be that one strongly doubts it would be formulated — and one is certain it could not be formulated in terms which mean the same to everyone.

Even more elusive, however, is the concept of unity itself in its role as elucidating the heart of what makes a group. The notion itself probably varies as between different types of unity — and this compounds the problem. The best thing to be said is that it is unity in the sense of some mutual engagement of human capacities and characteristics and qualities. Some aspects of something in or about those in the group must engage, must harmonize or be in mutual accord. What this amounts to concretely is a matter to be determined in particular cases or groups of cases. Groups are not mere concatenations of people, not mere gatherings, not mere mailing lists. For those 'bringings together' need not involve any of that unity that can be amongst humans — and especially not any distinctively human unity. Something more is necessary, and whether it is present in any given case must simply be said to depend. A crowd awaiting a train may be a group, although it is unlikely to be; the regulars at a pub are likely to constitute a group, although they may not.

A club, that paradigm of groups, may become too large and too dominated by its committee, to remain a group; but a mass can become a mob under some galvanic influence. Great numbers tend inevitably, it would seem, to militate against the identity which is characteristic of a group. A group comprising millions must be held together by something big indeed in order to remain a group. But big unifying forces do exist — common languages, homelands, ways of life, and sometimes even symbols. Whether manufactured unity is spurious is a question on which it seems impossible to generalize. When a patriot rises to eminence and indoctrinates his or her formerly fragmented people so that they will all shout in unison and act in harmony — who is to say that there is not a group here, even in the most intimate sense.

Whether or not any problematic collection of human beings is a group in the proper sense is a matter that must be determined in the particular case. It is always a matter for interpretation, since the criteria which are relevant are not hard and fast, not empirically factual, but are rather shot through with human elusiveness. And the issue can matter. The classificatory issue is not arbitrary, in the sense that nothing hangs upon it but itself. For collections of people that are not groups are, some of them, capable of being mobilised or manipulated in ways that pose threats and dangers to the human world. This is treacherous ground, for generalizations can foster great conceptions. But is it not possible for a large collection of humans — we may say that those in it are anomic and alienated — to be welded into an instrument, a contrivance, a powerful club or gang which may be used to batter down and destroy even some citadels of the human world? An army which had no traditions but of war and obedience, and whose members had no conception of any other life but that of 'obey and destroy', might fall into this category — and hardly any greater threat to the human world is imaginable, more particularly if the army is owned and controlled by some variety of megalomaniac. Such an instrument destroys not only the human world of its members — for their capacity to make a way of life of their own is certainly nullified. But it also destroys other people, other ways of life, other facilities and potentialities for making ways of life.

Even here there are complications — for free people, making

their own ways of life, but thwarted by others, may need to compare themselves and subdue themselves in order to defend themselves. They may not be able themselves to afford the luxury of being greatly human 'for the duration'. And they must trust their leaders — also their underlying humanness if their leaders end up getting out of hand — to ensure that the 'duration' actually stops when it has really ended.

The life and being of groups as such can be tremendously wide-ranging. Groups can be active or contemplative, dormant or zealous, loose or tight, aspiring or complacent, decisive or drifting, harmonious or embattled, consistent or zany, coherent or diffuse, perceptive or foolish. Many additional contrasts might be added. And all such contrasts, and the characteristics which are at their base, add a further dimension to the variousness of human groups, and thus add greater richness and depth of character to the human world. Thus diversities cater to different interests of different individuals, and often to divergent interests within a single individual.

To presume that all groups should be efficient; to work on the assumption that unless a group defines its aims and sets about them then it is worthless (and unworthy of support); to presume that a group will always be the better for having a businesslike approach to its activities, a fair basis for admitting members, and a willingness to move with the times — all of this reeks of a unidimensional grasp and approach to the human world. It wishes to see everything in a single image, to bring everything under a single rubric. A single image of this type is plainly narrow, and it has a compressing impact — yet it is not easy to avoid. It is particularly difficult to avoid when groups acquire status and require money. For as money becomes an increasingly universal currency, the questions appropriate to it — am I getting correct value? — tend to insert themselves into places where they have no business. This tendency is exacerbated when the groups in question are invaded by status seekers, or when their own members begin to take account of status.

The only image in which groups should properly be seen is the image of 'humanness' — which is not a single image in any recognizable sense. On the contrary, it is best likened to a wonderland of multitudinous mutually reflecting mirrors, which may, for all we know, set up an infinity of reflections. No person can participate in the whole, or even behold (much less understand) every single aspect of it. But if we are there in the midst of it, and can turn wherever we will, then even if we do not particularly appreciate the wonderland of the human world for its own sake, we can possibly at least more satisfyingly form our own focus of attention and direction of movement.

What groups are by definition, what they are in their own life and being, whence they arise — these questions have yielded answers that end up painting an extraordinary picture of the nature of this 'group' side of the human world. The extraordinariness is in fact a matter of the range of all manner of things that is encompassed by talk of groups. But without such a background, it would have been too easy to talk about the dynamics of groups — too easy, because the avoidance of stereotypes is difficult, and because one might have expected that a single level of analysis and general approach would be adequate.

We need, then, to ask how groups live, how they function, how they survive, how they conduct themselves. What is the nature of their energy, and of their motive power? All these questions are fair, but they are also rather odd. The best analogy to them, perhaps, is to contemplate posing the same questions of individuals. What is the nature of individual dynamism and energy and drive — and of individual restraint, direction, and decision-making? In the case of the individual, one is convinced from the outset that adequate answers can hardly be expected to come from an analysis of human bodily structure and capacity, even though these matters are not irrelevant. The point seems rather to be that everything is relevant or likely to be so. It seems difficult, putting the point differently, to distinguish the dynamics of groups from the minutiae of all their operations, their characteristics and their history. The fundamental question of the source of their energy will simply always recede, and reappear one stage further back no matter how far back one actually goes. But to analyse their structure, and imagine that it (in some rather static form) will reveal the answer to the questions posed is illusory. In a sense, the structures of groups are themselves liable to be endowed with a certain dynamism of their own: they are seldom completely, and often enough not just subject to the vagaries of an evolutionary natural selectivity.

It is clearly necessary to say that groups (with energy and motive power) are adaptable, that they can adjust what they do and how, that they can hang on and endure (and sometimes even let go and cut loose). Whether they can intend, decide, resolve, or have consciousness are really questions which hardly matter — in the sense that if one answers them negatively, then one is immediately committed to devising an analogous concept for groups, to correspond with each of them. Furthermore, there seems to be a quite distorting kind of reductionism involved in attempts to resolve group 'intentions', and the like, into the intentions of their members. In short, the group's dynamics are its own: which is not to say they are completely other than those of its component individual members, for these are part of its dynamics. It is rather to say that there is more to the group's dynamics than these.

One vitally important aspect in the functioning of groups is that they draw energy to themselves, and in a way channel it. The being of a group — its existence, its standing where it does and for what it is, its being involved in whatever it is involved in — can draw people to it and engage them and their energies. This capacity to draw and engage is magnet-like — and it can become limpet-like. The existence in this sense of groups has a power to focus minds and concentrate activities — and insofar as it is combined with adaptiveness (insofar as adaptiveness is part of it and a product of it) it may be seen as doubly dynamic. And insofar as groups can offer rewards and facilities to people who come to them and do their thing — and insofar as this process itself has a kind of inbuilt multiplier contained within it — such groups can become self-sustaining to a remarkable degree. They are not exactly autonomous, because their own dynamic becomes sufficient for their development without any norms. They will not keep going forever in the one direction, but their changes of direction will usually be gradual curves rather than abrupt angles — although there is no guaranteeing that new points of departure will not sometimes erupt.

It should also be said that the most dynamic groups tend not to be clingy. Not only do they draw people and energies to themselves, and proceed or work in harness with them. Such groups also function, often and often, as springboards for their members to go on to other things. They do not push people out, but help them to rise. And herein lies a purifying mystery — so long as the works do not become clogged up with dullards and nincompoops. Insofar as a group does become a springboard, it is itself given the dynamic of being drawn by those other groups to which its members have become accustomed to cling.

The fish that swims with the tide because it is going there (especially if where it wanted anyway, but hardly less if it trims its wants accordingly) not only is helped on its way, but strengthens the tide itself — and as the tide contributes to the increase of that towards which it is drawn, so it will more strongly be drawn towards it.

It has not been my intention to say that mystery is at the heart of the dynamics of groups. Indeed, the point has in a way been the opposite, that it is simply a question of endlessly prosaic particularities. Such generalities as can be substantiated about the workings and dynamics of groups give little indication or insight into the dynamics of any particular group. At best, they might provide some kind of framework with which one might start to interpret the minutiae.

Yet there does remain a measure of mystery about the dynamics of groups. For part of their dynamic — especially that of some of the more profoundly deep-seated and influential groups — seems to be inseparable from if not actually identifiable with their own life. Their being, their life, their dynamic — like a kind of trinity, we have these three; of which none is greatest, but each is itself and all go together. And when as much as can be detailed has been said, there remains a cosmic gap which somehow seems more profoundly significant than all that has been said.

It is interesting that one is apt to be less dissatisfied when the tale of an individual has been told. Thus no history of the Jews or of the Church or of the State ever does its subject justice. One never puts down such a history while giving it a pat and saying contentedly to oneself 'so that is how it was'. Yet one sometimes does this with a great biography of a great person. I suspect, however, that the difference between the two does not really exist. For with the biography, we know we are dealing with an individual, and an extraordinary one at that. And the gap which we perceive in the case of the group is filled in the case of the individual with his or her greatness — which is never precisely explained. It may be monumental, but it is ineffable.

Why do the dynamics matter anyway? Why does it matter how groups function? In short, the answer is that we are enabled thereby to grasp more fully the human world. In penetrating the question of how groups work, we expose this aspect of the human world more openly and amply to view. Furthermore, insofar that the dynamics, the origins, the nature and the characteristics of groups are all intertwined and interfused; and insofar also that a discussion of dynamics reveals that groups work through and with individuals as well as individuals through and with groups: the whole discussion serves to make plainer and clearer the inherent dynamism of the human world. It is not accidental that human affairs move: on the contrary, the extraordinary thing would be for them to stop moving.

It might also be expected that by looking into the dynamics of groups, (especially as this has been done) some clue as to their authority might be revealed. The question of authority ranges very widely, of course, as becomes plain in the references to it in the next section. But the ways in which things are come to and the ways in which activities arise and are generated are surely pertinent to questions in the sphere of authority — and also to those in the sphere of effectiveness. The real notion by which to make the transition from dynamics to effectiveness and authority is that of <u>articulateness</u>. What is the <u>voice</u> of the people? And with what voice or voices do groups of all descriptions speak?

A group voice need not just be some consensual expression of view or belief. It can express pain or pleasure, determination or disinterest, single-mindedness or diversity, and much else as well. Articulation is itself an elusive not to say devious notion. For it has to do not only with verbalization, but more generally with giving expression. To verbalize is to employ one method of <u>giving expression</u> — one that is peculiarly exact and at the same time peculiarly universal and transmissible. And words can do some justice to an amazingly wide range of responses. Not merely do justice to many of them indeed, but actually be the response: belief is the example par excellence: there is paradigmatically no distance whatever between a belief and the words in which it is expressed.

It is not uncommon for people to express their beliefs in the wrong words. But they will then not only confess their error, but will say that the expression was either not really of their beliefs at all (unless it is just a question of misunderstanding or ambiguity) or alternatively that they had failed to identify to themselves what their belief was. In the latter case they were confused in their minds, which means not that they were clear about the belief but not the words — rather that they were actually confused about the belief, though without realizing the fact. Words can be treacherous as well as expressive and wrong.

But there are other modes of expression besides words, many of them not transposable into words. Words have a remarkable status at the level of universality as we may call it. For words are always translatable into other languages — and translatable with a fair measure of accuracy, competence and comprehensibility. Other modes of expression — music, art, and the like, have no need of being translated, cannot possibly be translated indeed. Yet they may be intelligible, even immediately and without explanation beyond their own circle — which words can never be. On the other hand, these other modes sometimes cannot be explained at all.

When the subject is groups (or individuals) giving expression, and the focus is on non-verbal modes, the urge to ask what is being said must be resisted — tempting though it always is, and often almost irresistible. For it is a reductive question that not only begs the question but that also seems plainly to reflect an unwillingness to take account of any modes of expression but one. And to do this to people is to do them a great disservice. The difference of language may indeed be a Babel[28], but differences in mode of expression are enriching. (Anticipating somewhat, some modes of expression are horrendously difficult to heed or take account of in political terms. How, for example, might a government possibly respond to a situation in which the nation's writers produce better books when they are in exile? The mind boggles, and a Ministry of the Arts is surely concerned really to deal with something quite else.)

The term 'expression' is perhaps wider than the real quarry here – the 'voice' of groups or of the people. For not only might everything that a group does be regarded as expressive in some sense, but some expressions are sufficient in themselves and make no call for repercussions or anything consequential. At the cost of a certain triteness, consider the 'voice' of a choir at its annual concert: the 'expression' is its own consummation, and the listeners can go away with no further demands made upon them. But the 'voice of the people', or of other groups — the expressions which they make — with reference to what is to be done, or with reference to what should be, or who should do what, or what should be available — this is an entirely different matter.

There is, above all else, an enormous problem of interpretation. If we cannot always ask what certain expressions in various modes are precisely saying – a soundless demonstration, massive attempts to avoid taxation, a huge swing at the polls – we certainly can ask what they mean. And even when an expression is verbal and absolutely precise – a petition – we may still need to ask what it really means. For the meaning is often not apparent. Indeed, there may be a sense in which the meaning does not exist in advance of being correctly interpreted: the case of an inchoate sense, a feeling within a group, which can be crystallized only by some penetrating interpretation from outside. The process or act of interpretation is itself a part of human life — it is not that the people or groups or individuals express themselves, and that something external then interprets. The people may well insist on there being faithful, creative interpreters to do the interpretative job that it realizes all too well (even if dimly, inchoately or inarticulately) that it is unable to do for itself.

3. The Effectiveness Of Groups

The issue arises because not everything can be done. Not every way of life that humans have a mind to make can in fact be made. For there are conflicts and incompatibilities, shortages of resources, and opposed views about how various groups and individuals may be called to the aid of particular projects. Further, not all the options that are desired can be provided, nor all potentialities realized, nor all possibilities born. In the generation of ways of life in the human world, there is much thwarting of conception, much abortion, much struggling at birth, much infanticide, and much squabbling among the survivors. All of this is plain enough. Disputes about why it is so seem academic in the sense that they have no impact upon its prevalence or conduct. And it seems likely to outlive theorising about whether it is inevitable.

But the fact that the issue of effectiveness does arise — and that it can be treated along the lines that follow even if this treatment be thought inept — does imply that questions about 'what will be' are not just questions about power. The factor of power is of course enormously important — power in the sense of imposition of an outcome, by any means which simply overbear any other factors. Of course, power is a most potent factor, particularly at the point where conflicts arise, where people really do want to do things that are incompatible. For power is at its best, its most conspicuous, when the chips are really down.

It is contended later that power is the fly in the ointment in connection with many problems that arise in connection with effectiveness — that a free market in the resolution of disputes would lead to resolutions tremendously often were it not for the incursion of power. Yet power is not the only factor with which it is necessary to deal, not the only concept in terms of which to consider questions of effectiveness, or the related question of authority.

An ancillary to this which has wide ramifications is that there are no guarantees in the human world. Even when talking about the strongest power, and even when one has it in one's hand, one cannot depend upon it absolutely. These are tremendously general observations. The central point to be drawn out of them is that when one has said and done the most and best about effectiveness that can be done, when one has set up structures or arrangements or whatever which seem quite certain to be effective and to do the job one has in mind for them, some new factor may enter, some different and relevant perspective may surface and give everything a kind of turn or twist, so that one must build afresh.

The real point here is neither that everything is uncertain in human affairs, nor that one never has enough knowledge of what is going on to be able to forecast the outcome or provide for it. These factors are relevant. But there is something further and something better, to do with dynamism and development. Perhaps the best way to see this is in terms of the idea that nothing in the ongoing human world is ever cut and dried. It can be deeply irritating and distressing that this is so, particularly if a given uncertainty, which is liable to cause anxiety, appears as if it should be able to be settled. But the very fact that an uncertainty is liable to cause anxiety reveals that the matter in question is of some moment; and whatever is really of moment is likely to attract attention, new ideas and new thinking — and thus is quite likely to become the subject of further action.

<u>Stability,</u> greatly to be desired for comfort, has to be bought. In the bottom of our hearts, we should hardly be prepared to pay the price. For the price is not just dullness, but stultification. Insofar as the business of making ways of life is a continually ongoing process, with something new being continually initiated, there can be no guarantee that some unsettling, cross-cutting input will not come onto the scene.

This does not mean that everything is strife. Rather should we think of everything as an adventure. We may wish that a particular adventure would go on, undisturbed, for ever. But since we cannot guarantee this, it is surely foolish to try to fight off absolutely every incursion. By not doing so we may lose something of value — but by always doing so we are not only likely to over value some things, and to lose their real value and our enjoyment of them under the stress of having continually to be defending them. We are also likely to lose out on other things that may equally be of value.

To stop making a way of life ever afresh and anew — not completely so of course — is in a way to bring a way of life to an end. More than this, since it may be taken away anyway, we may lose it and not only it, but in addition the capacity to control what we want and will have next. Where not everything can be, not everything that is can be expected to continue. So neither the established nor the expected, neither the promised nor even the allegedly guaranteed, can truly be guaranteed. Indeed, the effectiveness of various groups is normally itself a variable quantity. All this provides the foundation, and a suitable point of departure, for turning to the question of the effectiveness of groups.

It certainly gives a certain twist to the opening question, namely what it is that makes groups effective. In a comparative sense, vis-à-vis individuals, relatively homogeneous groups have certain advantages in achieving their aims. For support and mutuality are available to their members, and their 'negotiators' cannot be shamed into anything because they are always able to say that they have their instructions. Personal considerations do not enter the case, and the firmness of intransigence is on the side of the group. But of course, this is not always an advantage — the group may have tied its negotiator's hands, and in general those advantages of groups are advantages in a buyer's rather than a seller's market, at least when there is a market situation.

It needs noting that this general discussion of effectiveness and its conditions is artificial inasmuch that considerations of power are not included in it. The bases of power are varied indeed, but the absolutely deterministic character of exercises of power places them outside the range of the central concern here. Of course where there is power there is effectiveness, but this is the point: the effectiveness of power is being taken for granted, and the real issue is, 'what else gives effectiveness, and what other sources of it are there?'

Groups have other advantages or strengths in terms of effectiveness in addition to mutuality, intransigence and impersonality. They can generate their own enthusiasm, and consensuality can be a driving force with its own inbuilt effectiveness. They can create atmospheres and climates more easily than can individuals. They can assume self-righteousness to themselves, and can manufacture an air of dispassionateness. In certain matters they can get themselves to be thought expert — and thus authoritative — particularly in the eyes of those who hold the strings of power. If their word is regarded as sufficient justification for doing something, then what they say will often be done in a world where justification and 'proof' are deemed to be good 'reasons' for doing things — also in a world in which the deciders do not know what to do.

Nothing fills a vacuum in decision-making like a reason, especially one that is thought to be good. There is a curious process of mutual reinforcement often at work, whereby not only does expertise breed authority and thus effectiveness, but effectiveness itself is often transposed — via self-righteousness and self-importance in many cases — into authority, and thereby into a presumption of expertise. This phenomenon is not unknown with individuals, although there it is always attended with some fragility and must be sustained by a good deal of push. But with groups, the process can be very strong, can be long-lived, and can also become self-sustaining insofar as the group's effectiveness results in real experts being drawn into its ambit. There is also a corresponding danger of fools making a takeover, and destroying the reputation that was there, and the effectiveness that went with it.

If we turn to 'the people', we seem to be confronted with a group (if indeed it really is a group) which does not possess the attitudes or qualities upon which groups largely depend for their effectiveness. There is seldom if ever that consensuality, seldom that homogeneity, seldom that closeness which breeds mutuality and self-support, seldom expertise (except in utter dilution, and mixed even then with ignorance and error), and seldom authority. Indeed, it is difficult to make any sense of the notion of 'the voice of the people' at all. Yet there must be something else to be said. For inchoate, divided, and unenlightened as 'the people' always seems to be, we mean something real when we talk of 'it' in a serious sense.

The starting point for this discussion is twofold. First, it seems that 'the people' as such is or can be genuinely effective only in a situation where some system has been set up for it to be so. Among other things, this involves the existence of some expression or other, some means of obtaining and formulating declarations that are deemed to be 'the voice of the people'. Secondly, we must consider how far the sheer weight of numbers can actually be effective; and related to this, what is meant and involved in what is commonly called a 'groundswell of opinion'. If the upshot of the ensuing investigation is that the idea of 'the people being effective' has weight provided that the term 'the people' has an unexpected meaning, that itself will not be unilluminating. It certainly has implications for the idea of the authority of the people.

It may be assumed for the present that 'the people' is a group, i.e., that there is something that unifies it. And it may also be assumed that once in a very long while, ever so rarely, there may be a genuine, incontrovertible and pretty well unmistakeable 'voice of the people': the persuasive case (or example) would be where the society as a whole really and unmistakeably is subject to aggression and invasion. Such eventualities may properly be allowed for, but they do not really go beyond themselves, and they certainly cannot be made the basis of a general argument about the voice of the people.

For in all other respects, the people is profoundly amorphous, discontinuous and fragmented. Size and numbers undermine homogeneity almost by definition. All kinds of unifying devices, all kinds of symbols and communications, all kinds of uniforms are powerless against the diffusive influence of size and numbers. This is not to say that 'the people' is divided, for that is different from amorphousness and fragmentation. Neither is it to say that in certain circumstances 'the people' may not be welded together for certain ends or in the presence of something comparatively rare. The assertion about 'the people' being amorphous is limited to the meaning and implications of the terms used – 'the people' while perhaps in one sense a group, is in most respects more like grains of sand on a beach, blades of grass in a lawn, fallen leaves in a heap. It is, as such, a <u>many</u>. And it remains a <u>many</u>, (like all the separate plants in a forest) even though each of its individual members may have many group links with others of its members. 'The people as such' therefore, is a term to refer to everyone, in every context except that of the rare cases already mentioned. It is a group, but only in the most extended, the most tenuous, the most inconsequential sense of the term — except, once again, for the exception mentioned.

It follows from this that in the ordinary course of things 'the people' cannot be effective because it possesses insufficient identity for it to make sense to say that it has done this rather than that. To attribute some outcome to 'the people' presupposes that we can identify <u>something</u>, when in fact the people is a <u>many</u>. And if this problem did not present itself, there would be the equally pressing problem that the agency of 'the people' — its *hand* at work — could not conceivably be isolated or detected: any 'hand' that was found would *ipso facto* be more determinate, fewer and smaller than 'the people'. Similar kinds of problems arise whenever the numbers of an allegedly effective group are large. But nowhere do they arise so utterly decisively as in the case of 'the people'.

But may 'the people' not be enabled to act and be effective? May it not somehow come about, or be brought about, that the people do something, achieve something, effect something? These questions may be pursued in two directions. Suppose an anti-litter campaign is launched because it is thought that 'the people' are sick and tired of mess — and suppose it catches on so that no-one dreams of littering nor litters. In a sense, perhaps, this is a case of 'the people' being effective. But there are two comments to be made. First, the example is one of an extremely small number that can be conceived — and almost all the others, one senses, would have a qualitative similarity insofar that they would all be concerned with something that might loosely be called 'public health'. Secondly there is a sense in which the example is not of 'the people' being effective — granted that this would necessarily involve their impact becoming externalized — but rather of the people doing something to themselves.

The second direction for pursuing the question of enabling the people to be effective is clearly voting, either for representatives, or in referenda. This has become the most widely accepted method for enabling the people to act and be effective. If there is anything the modern world believes in, this is surely it. And certainly, elections do have an impact — they make and break governments, and hardly anything is more decisive than this. Believers in elections would agree, no doubt, that the people can be effective by this means only if an electoral system has indeed been set up, and in this sense the people is effective only because it has been enabled to be so. Yet these supporters would be inclined to say that an electoral system is so obviously the proper means for enabling the people (where they are more than a handful) to be effective that it is really part of the nature of things – and thus in no sense an artificial or arbitrary human construction.

But this approach does not bear scrutiny. The alleged naturalness of elections and voting is immediately exploded when one considers not only that there are dozens of electoral systems and methods of voting (which produce inconsistent results), but also that no single system or method commands universal or even unqualified support. All are agreed to have shortcomings and flaws. The reason for this is that they are all sectional, all partial: that is, none elicits 'the voice of the people'.

Nor can it be said that they are satisfactory insofar as they are the closest practicable approximations to the theoretically perfect method. For nobody has ever been able to make intelligible an idea of what this theory is. It would surely have to be something more than everyone just saying yes to some proposition that was put to them, devised by someone else or even one of them. Lest this be misunderstood, let me make it clear that I am not saying that elections are bad. I am merely saying that they are always sectional — that they elicit or reflect the view not of the people as such but of the people in part. For practical purposes, it may be legitimate to regard this voice as that of the people. But this is a case, no matter how legitimate, of deeming something to be what it is not. So even a well-working electoral system, (accepted as such and as legitimate even by the whole society), would not really enable 'the people' to be effective. Yet no other system seems to present itself.

Turning from systems to the other aspect of the starting point in trying to elicit what 'the voice of the people' means, there is the factor of weight of numbers. To reach the most weighty interpretation of this, we must think not of mobs or demonstrations, and certainly not of petitions, but of what is commonly called a 'groundswell of opinion'. Probably only those who have been threatened by this phenomenon are able to comprehend its full weight — and they are almost invariably politicians.

A groundswell of opinion is a most potent and extraordinary thing. It is more like a tide than like waves blown up. For with the latter, only the top of the water moves, even though it may move violently. But with tides, all the water moves. Much of it moves only slightly, but the small movements of every part make for a massive impact at the point where the flow expresses itself. By the same token, if supporters drift 5% in the strength of their support for a politician, that politician comes under intense pressure. The fact that even his or her staunchest supporters are still 95% 'for' suddenly manifests itself as far less important than that they are now 5% 'against'. Those who were always 'against' will be more strongly so, reinforced by some perceived backing from everyone else. And there will be a spill over from among those who were formerly on balance 'for', into the ranks of those who have always been on balance 'against'.

Such is the nature of groundswells of opinion. It seems likely that such phenomena exist. And yet it is not the voice of the people, because it is not the people saying this rather than that. It is rather a case of some who say 'this' saying it more strongly, some who said 'that' now saying 'this', and the remainder still saying 'that' but less strongly.

All in all, the voice of the people is not there to be heard. When we talk of it, we actually mean something that is not 'it' at all. The most we can mean is that it is the voice of some section of the people (e.g. a majority) which everyone agrees to go by, and which everyone consents to deeming to be the voice of the people. It is hardly more likely that everyone would agree on what proportion should be deemed to express the voice of all than that they would agree on anything else. This makes it likely that in the course of seeking some section that may speak for all, an infinitely regressive 'third man' will enter the picture; that consensus on how many are needed to speak for all will require a further consensus on how many are needed to comprise that consensus, and so on. It would certainly only be a majority that could ever be brought to agree about the terms on which the majority view could be regarded as expressing the people's voice — and only a majority that would agree to a majority determining the terms of majority rule. Even if humans knew nothing, they would hardly trust their fellows in this regard. Apart from anything else, they would in this situation either not know enough to trust the rest, or know enough to distrust them.

In this connection, it is worth commenting generally on rnajoritarianism, which is totally antithetical to the general theme of the human world. For the fact that under majoritarianism everyone counts (in the sense of having a vote and possibly even being able to push their own views and interests) does not mean at all that the life and claims of each person are actually taken into account. On the contrary, it tends to mean that those of the minority are disregarded. Further, if a system of a more or less permanent majority becomes established, then the minority not merely will not have its aspirations catered for, but may even come to find itself deprived of the resources, facilities and expectations to which it has been accustomed.

Of course, few believe in unqualified majoritarianism. The cant phrase – cant almost invariably in fact, and cant in theory from this work's perspective — is 'majority rule and minority rights'. The main problems about this approach relate to who defines and protects the minority rights, and who can keep the majority within bounds. In a society which respected and conserved its traditions, the traditional and prescriptive rights of minorities may be admitted and looked after, and minorities may also have the benefit of the traditional rights of the whole society. But in the division of new spoils and in the creation of new facilities and options, the needs of minorities would be disregarded — unless perhaps their members went around the majoritarian principle and took direct action using whatever resources they could muster.

The greater problem relates to the definition of minority rights — granted particularly that humans are on their own and are the measure of all things. If human rights existed in the nature of things, and merely awaited discovery, then the problem would hardly arise. But they have no such natural existence. 'Majority rule with minority rights' is a cant phrase theoretically, because, within its own terms, minority rights can be defined and decided upon only by the majority. There is nowhere else they can come from. Of course, from the pure perspective of humans as on their own and as themselves the measure — and in this context, 'humans' is both the individual and the group — we are going to have to face up to a very complex series of perspectives on what rights are, and then to say something about how the whole complex can authentically be built up. If the rights of the minority are defined by the majority, then 'majority rule with minority rights' boils down to the same thing as 'majority rule unqualified'.

It would be better, of course, if everyone could determine the minimum rights which no-one (*a fortiori* minorities) should be without. But 'everyone' has no voice, as has been said already. Overall then, 'the people' is not a broken reed, but an unconstructable reed. When we get onto talking of the people, we are talking less of the life of humans than of the organisation of that life. And this is quite proper. But the real upshot of what has been argued thus far is that when we get to the question of the organization of life, 'the people' — considered corporately — is not a corporation but a fiction. Alternatively, it might be thought of as a machine, something constructed (although by whom would not be easy to say) to do a particular job. Its name is its disguise — a name that may disguise many different realities, many indeed and indeed.[29]

The issue of authority has been progressively lost in the course of the foregoing discussion, and we must return to it. Attempting to define it is the wrong approach. Better to ask, 'on what matters or types of question do groups possess authority', try to deal with the matter direct, and possibly come at the concept subsequently. The answer that suggests itself is that groups have authority on matters which are their business — matters in which they have an authentic interest, matters on which they have knowledge or expertise.

In terms of this treatise, the formal explication of 'their business' is absolutely clear: groups have authority insofar as the matters in question pertain to their ways of life. In matters which are pertinent to their ways of life, groups (and individuals equally) have a right to speak and be heard, a right to act, to do something, a right not just to wait but to initiate and take a lead. The word 'right' is incongruous here, the more one considers it: for it is too passive and too static in the context, as indeed it usually is. For on matters pertaining to other ways of life, it is really the business of groups and individuals to be speaking, to be speaking out if necessary, to be speaking in such a way that they will be heard. They must not be hanging back to catch the speaker's eye, for the conversation is one in which there can be many voices speaking at once — each making itself heard and hearing the others at the same time – and consequently each speaking not a set piece but rather reaching and adapting to what it hears as well as to what it has itself just said. It must be expected that groups and individuals will be speaking, acting, doing, initiating. Not just doing their own thing, for that presupposes an isolationism which is really quite foreign to the reality of the human world, to the interfusing of people and persons that has been discussed previously in this chapter.

This, of course, is a theory. It implies that the Trades Unions are the institutions whose job it is – and who thus <u>should</u> – protect the workers, that the Church should protect the religious, that artists are the guardians of art, and so on. But this implication takes the theory beyond itself — in a way that must be explored. Trades Unions can only protect their workers either if they have the power to overbear counteractive power, or alternatively only if 'protection' can be given without the involvement of power. But of course 'protection' would be a misnomer if there were no power. For resolutions and compromises — 'decisions' is the most general term — would flow much more positively if power was not on the scene: if ways of life were made and arrived at — if not consensually or cooperatively or even through tolerant adjustment — then (doubtless *per impossibile*) by every person and group having a fair go at cutting their coats from the cloth that they and others make.

The theory goes beyond itself in a quite different respect as well, namely that it is anti-organizational — or a-organizational. For as soon as Trades Unions become organizations, they are immediately seized with structure and hierarchy and oligarchy. So in a sense they themselves then enter inevitably into the world of power — and may, though not necessarily, thus lose sight of the interests of their members. For representative functions can easily be disregarded when considerations of power enter the scene. The case of artists is in one sense at the farthest remove from that of institutions such as Trades Unions. For artists are art's guardians in a quite different sense — the sense in which galleries and museums are mortuaries (and artists, individually or collectively make poor museum keepers) whereas art itself is served by artists at work on their own terms, not really subsidized as such at all. Tremendous efforts are always necessary for artists' organizations not to become altogether dissociated from art itself, as a dynamic element of the human world.

Granted that protection is needed, that considerations of power do come on the scene, that self-regulation as between groups is not really a viable possibility, some sort of power broker is called for, overriding all and not representing any person or group in particular. The government has no business of its own, by virtue of its overriding and comprehensive character. But in a society in which the human world is widely diverse, in which individuals and groups really do make their own ways of life, the arbitral and regulatory role of government seems calculated to become hardly less widespread (if less pervasive and penetrating) than that of totalitarian government. A free society will call for an exceedingly <u>powerful</u> and <u>extensive</u> government. And yet one that remains modest and unassuming, i.e. one which does not assume too much or too greatly: one which must never go beyond asking, as its first question when it comes upon something, 'what's going on here?'

It is often said that the government should be or express the voice of the people. In a sense this gives the right perspective — inaccurate or incoherent as it is if taken strictly — on the role of government. The right perspective should be seen negatively rather than positively. It is incoherent to suppose that a government can, in a positive sense, represent the whole people. But there is a negative sense, that it must not represent anything less than the whole, i.e. that it must not be sectional. It should surely be dispassionate rather than anything else, and then it will be the best that it can be. As soon as it begins to take sides, and more particularly as soon as it begins to do things off its own bat, then from a broadly theoretical point of view it has a disproportionate amount of power which can hardly but result in its coming to overbear some other — groups or individuals — who are doing their thing as they (legitimately) see it.

Yet there is a further problem, which vitiates this theory in practice, a problem which arises because there is always power. For individuals and groups, going about their business (and even being willing to work in with others) are likely to be overridden and overborne anyway by unashamedly sectional groups and interests which possess power and will use it. Whether it is better, in these circumstances, for the government to have (and thus use) a degree of power which is really more than it should have (other things being perfect!) so that it can say 'what's going on here?', with effect, to the powerful as well as to those who run into others in the legitimate conduct of their own lives, is a fundamental dilemma. It is a dilemma which in real terms seems to admit of no theoretical solution... Unless, that is, one says that it is a theoretical solution to take the line that such governmental power is permissible provided it is in the hands of a government which is not too ideological, not too keen on its own schemes at the expense of those of others, but nevertheless willing and able to go ahead with its own schemes if that proves necessary to counter the overbearing schemes of others who are mightily powerful, or else as a means of effectively breaking constructively through a conflict between other persons or groups, a conflict which could otherwise only be fought to the death of one or both parties.

There is perhaps a further point to be made in connection with the government as the voice of the people, a point which links with the statement in the first chapter about the people as authoritative on general matters and issues. Only a government could think of itself as representing the whole people, as bearing the responsibility for securing the interests of everyone, for having no favourites while favouring everyone. Every other group — especially every group with power — must confess to a degree of partiality — or at least that any impartiality it possesses is essentially accidental. Now while it has been argued that the people is too incoherent to be a group proper (with the exception of defence), and while it thus cannot strictly be represented, we can see something worth saying if we think of a power group (or centre) which seriously makes it its business to try its best by the people as a whole. Such a group is in one sense fighting a hopeless battle, for it will never really please anyone and will consequently be odious to all — and it can only do what it is trying to do in a partial and imperfect way in any case. But it would at the least be trying something grandly worthwhile. Its views and capabilities would not be so devoted as we might wish the most elevated views to be – yet they would be far more elevated than any others that might be envisioned. And of this breadth and generality, (granted of course that the government is making a genuine attempt to discharge what it sees as its function, and granted further that it manages to attract people of ability to its ranks) what could challenge its authority? And what superior or higher authority could there conceivably be at the level of generality that is here in question? In the human world, it must never be forgotten that authority is itself a human quality and a human construction.

This leads back to the final point for consideration, concerning control and regulation. In a human world in which power figures, such control must be exercised by the powerful, or some powerful people — even though the control itself would be far less necessary if power did not figure in the human world. The people, however, collectively or individually, are not capable of controlling themselves at all fully. And perhaps it is better so, for there would be little zip in the world if everyone was sufficiently reined in of their own devices that no discipline was needed from any other source. Zest, adventurousness and enthusiasm, the keenness to run on as the course opens up before one, are hardly less the source of disorder than zealotry, or ignorance or ruffianism.[30] That a person needs to be disciplined is not of itself a defect in him or her. But by whom is the discipline to be exercised, and how far may it go? All of this will be explored further in the ensuing chapters. But for starters, who or what could have a better claim to do the job than the kind of government referred to above — provided it does not become too entrenched, or too self-righteous: provided it keeps an open mind on the world, and provided it is not unaware of what is really going on.

How far may the regulation go? The governing principle here is clear. People can take a very great deal without being ridden into the ground — how much is impossible to say, granted the uniqueness of all disciplinary measures. But the principle is that no-one — no group or individual in the business of making a way of life off their own bat — must be overridden, overborne or utterly subdued. There is no basis for that, there can be no basis for it. Neither may group override individuals (or other groups), nor individual override groups (or other individuals). For the basis (the measure) of everything is humans, and 'human' is all humans and all groups of humans — all on their own, all making their ways of life.

6

THE POLITICIANS

These final chapters treat the overall organization of the life and lives of humans. In effect, therefore, the subjects dealt with are governance, which is primarily a national affair, together with national and international politics.

Human beings in fact live in societies, typically national societies. The more general levels of interaction within these societies call for a different approach and mode of arrangement from the less general ones. At some levels, interactions can be arranged cooperatively, and if not with ease or good feeling, then at least some sort of *modus vivendi* can be worked out as between the parties. At these levels, people basically handle their own affairs: transactions are characteristically individual, even though small groups may be involved. The 'deals' are typically person to person, face to face affairs – not for that reason necessarily good or beautiful or honest, but there is something direct about them. The issues involved are not likely to be obscured or obfuscated to any great degree. Furthermore, interactions at this level can be arranged within a framework, such as a legal system: and if it comes to a dispute, there are mechanisms for resolution and enforcement.

The position is totally different at the overall, general level.

Something has already been said about this, and it is plain that the features and factors referred to in the previous paragraph are altogether absent. There are too many people, too many issues mixed up with each other, too much confusion, too many cross currents, too much meddling, and often too intransigent an approach for these matters to be handled by those directly involved. In any event, there is a great sense in which nobody and everybody is directly involved. And in addition, many of the parties involved are not acting on their own behalf, but in some kind of representative role – although some who should be representing will always be found to be working on their own behalf. It is a world which is profoundly treacherous, in which things and people are often far different from what they seem, and in which distinct skills seem necessary to find one's way if one ventures into it.

None of this is because humans happen to be organized into national societies. If these societies were divided into the smallest conceivable fragments, it is difficult to imagine that the fragments would not still be so large that the same problems would remain. Further, if that were to be done, interaction between these mini-societies would surely assume a curious intensity.

On the other hand, if national divisions were removed and humankind made into a single so-called 'community', these problems would be vastly increased, at least for a longer period of adjustment than one cares to contemplate, due to the higher stakes, the communication problems, and the endless incompatibilities of existing practices, approaches and expectations. This is not to say that the distribution of humans into national societies is either ideal or sacrosanct. It is rather to say that the same issues, problems and factors would come into play regardless of the type of distribution which existed and was in operation.

This chapter deals first with the nature of politics, and then with its impact. In considering the nature of politics, two matters that are thoroughly intermingled are (i) what is done and (ii) who does it. Politics is a distinct kind of activity, which exists on its own level within the human world. It also seems on every side to draw to itself a somewhat characteristic type of person. Whether connections can be made between the kind of activity and the kind of person is a baffling issue which is considered later. But there are certainly connections between what is done and who does it in the sphere of politics.

This is not to say that politics is the exclusive preserve of a particular kind of person — although it may be true that people who are not of this kind but who do get involved are unlikely to emerge unmarked or unscarred. This is part of the reason for heading this chapter 'The Politicians' rather than 'Politics'. The larger reason is that 'The Politicians' focuses attention on the pre-eminent reality that politics is not some abstract activity divorced from human beings, but that it is what politicians do. Politics has no inherent nature of its own, and it is not something that humans discover and imitate or conform to. What politics '*is*' is what it is made to be by those who engage in it — acting on their own, and making their own ways of life. Of course they are also living and acting in the human world at large, where they become subject to pressures (and perhaps enabled to go in desired directions) by virtue of the fact that humans at large (including in various conformations) are on their own and making ways of life.

'Politics' is not a straightforwardly identifiable phenomenon. It is not the kind of reality which can be unambiguously and unquestionably identified, and as such measured up for a defining set of words. What needs to be done is rather to build up a picture of a set of activities and practices which can be seen to have an identity — and then to characterize that identity.

It will not be difficult to accept that politics itself is different from the study or science or theorisation of politics — although there are some points (particularly in connection with ideology in its various forms) at which there is a close joining of hands.

Politics is also to be distinguished from government. In brief, politics is broking, whereas governing is deciding. That there are close and formidable linkages is unquestionable. But it surely is odd (at the least) to say that governing is nothing more than politics (or a part thereof). My purpose here, however, is not to develop or sustain the distinction fully, but rather to foreshadow it.

It is useful to start with a comment on how and why politics comes to be, and to note that why politics comes to be is inextricably mixed up with why government comes to be. It would be too much to say that politics arises because government arises. But it is not inappropriate to say that to a considerable degree politics comes along by the coat-tails of the need for government. In brief, a congeries of things go together in this connection.

Groups form that result in many people living and living well; people multiply through living and living well; there is multiplication not only in numbers but in aspirations and in the impulse to achieve more. To a considerable degree, people must act in concert to achieve more, but because people are people there tend to be conflicts or incompatibilities about what should go on the programme of the concert. People interact, and from their enthusiasm not to mention their selfishness and intractability there arises a need for control and regulation. These are the factors out of which arise politics — out of which, due to which, in the context of which, along with which... All these phrases are equally appropriate, for the key point to keep in view and not lose sight of is that there are many factors which go together. They tend to be mutually reinforcing, and to become mutually explicable and intelligible. They go so much together, and so strongly, and so deeply into the human world that it is unlikely they could ever go away either singly or collectively, either wholly or in part. This is not to say they go on unchanged, although it probably does mean that changes are nourished to a considerable extent by what they have been.

Thus we may say that in the most fundamental sense, politics exists because humans are on their own and because they make ways of life. There is no-one designated in the nature of things to direct human affairs overall, nothing in people to confine them to such cooperation and interaction with other people as would make government unnecessary. It is people themselves who make politics necessary, and people themselves (especially people who engage in politics) who make politics what it is.

1. The Nature Of Politics

To understand politics as a type of broking goes to the heart of the matter. If we would understand what politics is by distinguishing it from what it is not, and how it relates to those parts of the human world with which it is most closely and integrally related, this is where we must start. Politics is broking, arranging, finding acceptable ways, getting acceptance from those who are involved. It is a kind of intermediate and at the same time intermediary activity.

In order to get this clear, it is necessary to ask at once a far reaching question: 'between whom does politics broke?' This question ultimately leads the way to the three major questions that need to be posed in order to grasp comprehensively the nature of politics, namely what manner of people engage in this particular type of broking, what means do they use in their activity, and in what matters do they broke.

The first of these questions admits of an apparently straightforward and simple answer. Politics brokes between governors and governed, between governors and would-be governors. More derivatively, it brokes also between groups, particularly largish-scale groups. Politics is thus a broker of control and regulation: we may even say it is a broker of government (or governance) *per se*. This is not to say that a person who has a part in governing is not a politician, any more than that a mere politician may not aspire to govern. Nor is it to say that persons with a capacity for devising and formulating ideas, ideals or policy are in that respect without anything of the politician in their being, or that politicians are precluded from having ideas of their own about policy or ideals. In fact, there is liable to be intermingling in relation to all these matters and qualities that are in themselves distinct. It is certainly not without interest that politics itself seems to be the hub of this intermingling. Politicians take a bit of the other trades unto themselves, perhaps, but even more do the other trades take a bit (often indeed as much as they can get) of politics to themselves.

To illustrate this, it is useful to talk around a phrase that is very commonly on the lips of governors and would-be-governors, policy-makers and would-be policy makers, administrators and visionaries, theorists and sometimes even ideologues: 'the politics of the matter'. In nine such cases out of ten, failure in dealing with a matter will follow on from a failure to attend to 'the politics of the matter'.

To elucidate the phrase 'the politics of the matter', it is necessary to proceed gently, step by step. Take a nation's budget for example. Normally, 'the politics of the budget' would be real enough, and would need to be taken into account. But to begin with, it is conceivable that in some nations and under some conditions, there would not be any politics associated with the budget. Certainly, in societies where politics is rife and where money counts and is valued, it is not easy to conceive of budgets unaccompanied by politics: and I shall say something in the next section pertinent to the way things would be in a society from which politics was absent.

Going on from here, 'the politics of the budget' may be vastly different in different societies or situations. There are many different procedures for drawing up budgets, and many different steps that different practices and institutions require budgets to get through before they come into operation. To put the point shortly, while all politics is broking, political broking is a rather different activity in a multi-party system from what it is in a two-party system, or again in a one-party system, or again in a system where budgets go to referendum, or again in an hereditary oligarchy. Where the relevant arranging, or 'fixing', must be done between different groups, or between people in different positions, or between people who rank the importance of the matter (i.e. monetary considerations and their consequences) in different ways, then the particular features of the political broking process may be radically different from each other.

In a sense, there is something unique about politics in every society. To a large extent this is because of a congeries of differences between any two societies, differences of traditions and power structures and institutions and many additional *minutiae* as well. In another sense, however, one is inclined to feel that there is something the same about politics everywhere. More is said about this in discussing politicians specifically. But by way of anticipation, one has an ineradicable sense, first that the differences are a matter of different applications of essentially the same thing; second that political broking is fundamentally the same thing everywhere even though it takes somewhat different forms in different circumstances and situations; third that those who are drawn to politics in one society would still be drawn to it if they were translated into quite different societies; and fourth that they would employ in their new politics the same capacities and energies as in their old politics even though the ways of applying them might be different.

Accordingly, in order to talk about 'the politics of a budget' with any semblance of concreteness, it is necessary to relate the talk broadly to some kind of political/governmental/administrative system – and a democratic parliamentary system with a more or less permanent public service serves well for the illustrative purposes that are here in view. What, in such a system, is the 'politics' of the budget? And what else is there to the budget, that is, what are the non-political components or aspects of it? For convenience and simplicity, only the short-term political aspects are touched on, partly because the long-term aspects are seldom easy to elicit or agree upon.

The politics of such a budget pre-eminently arise out of the fact that the attitudes and reactions of the parliament, the electorate, and opinion formers matter: in particular they matter to the government (i.e. the executive) which is (and is held to be) <u>responsible</u> for the budget: which must stand by it, and may fall by it.

It is worth playing this out a little. Let us suppose that the government wants to go along as far as possible with what is often called the Treasury line: this 'line' means the view of what the budget should be which is held by the public servants, the economists in the government service. Their view of what the budget should be will be dictated by their economic judgement about the best economic measures for achieving the optimal kind of economic outcomes that are consistent with the government's broad aims and conducive to the realization of these aims. There is no need to consider further the character of these aims. It is plain that drawing up and carrying through, i.e. administering, such a budget are central governmental activities. And in this sense, we may say that public servants – *qua* public servants — are typically good at governing. But they are not, typically, so good at politics — although they are likely to be good at spotting the points at which political issues will arise. If they put in some options on those points, they may save a good deal of messing about. But in some way or at some stage it must be expected that they will themselves step aside from the politics.

The politics of the matter arises at several points – first, the Treasurer (member of the government acting politically) must get the Cabinet (and probably the Prime Minister) to accept the budget, if it is to begin its journey. Then the Party Room may have to be persuaded to accept it. Then the Parliament must be brought to vote for it. In the course of this, the electorate (partly directly and partly via opinion-makers) must be brought to see the budget in such a way that it will not on that account throw the government out of office at the next election. This is all, of course, perfectly obvious, uncontroversial and incontrovertible.

What is equally true, and hardly less obvious, is that the purely economic arguments and considerations that are pertinent to the budget's appropriateness may have little part to play in getting acceptance at the various levels. What is likely to be more important is how proposals are presented, which points are highlighted and which glossed over, how prejudices are evaded and hostilities smoothed over, and how the opposition guns are spiked. Those are the matters that make up the politics of a budget. Influential people must be got on side, power blocs must be appeased, fanatics must be circumvented or isolated. Sometimes those who could matter may be blustered into acceptance, sometimes red herrings may be drawn across the path, sometimes boredom may be created, sometimes a furore in another direction may serve to take off the heat, sometimes deception or even sheer determination and fighting spirit may serve their turn. All this is what is involved in the politics of budgets.

In addition, it is likely that politics will at some stage cut across the economic considerations by demanding changes and adjustments. If a particular proposal, no matter how justified, is anathema to a group whose support is essential, then the proposal will have to be dropped – and schemes, no matter how damaging, may have to be adopted if the support of those whose pets they are is essential. Again, there are quite different kinds of factors – e.g. of justice, egalitarianism, or anything else – that may cut completely across the economic considerations. The politician *per se* cannot say which kinds of considerations should be overriding in such circumstances – that is a task for government, though for the statesman rather than the specialized expert. Neither the Treasury nor the Treasurer is competent to decide that, and often enough, sadly, there will be nobody in the whole of a government with such competence. This of course raises issues about different levels of decision-making, which are picked up in chapter seven.

To a degree, this account oversimplifies by talking just of backing off and adjusting, and of one type of consideration overriding another or not. The usual process is more complicated – some kind of compromise, some kind of deception, some kind of gesture, some kind of deal. In connection with deals, the key point is that the terms of deals in this type of human interaction are probably more flexible, various and negotiable in the broadest sense than anywhere else.

In all of this, the broking role of the politician is immensely important and prominent. Politicians do not themselves decide whose support is essential to the government: they rather know, perceive, elicit and make evident such realities. As pure broker, the politician would not be acting for one side rather than the other, but rather trying to bring the two together. In order to do this (ideally) the politician must be acting for both.

A vital part of this is that he or she must almost be better at grasping the vital interests and concerns of each than they are themselves. Politics is not the art of the possible, it is the art of the acceptable. In this the politicians are not wholly passive – they can be totally tough in negotiating deals — although purely as politicians, the threats are not their own — nor are the cajoleries or the persuasions. They are, as brokers, in the business of drawing attention to the realities of situations.

When they say to a government 'You cannot do that', they do not themselves command the strings that make the doing of it impossible for the government — although they may be in a position to give them something of a twitch. It is worth adding that this explains in part why a government can often get away with more than would have been thought possible. Impossibility in this sphere is less physical impossibility than impossibility within some system of expectations, habits, established practices, and widely accepted or shared views (almost conventions) about where various balances of power lie. And if a government wields its muscle, and crashes on regardless, its action may well prove sufficient to upset the established expectations and the balance of power that was a balance only because and insofar as it was accepted as such.

Politicians themselves need to be alive to the underlying as well as the superficial realities of all these kinds of situations, although they are at the same time themselves to some degree vulnerable to their own situation as brokers. This is amplified below, but it may be noted here that politicians are as prone as anyone else to falling prey to the illusion that the 'market' kind of situation to which they have been accustomed has a greater permanence and capacity to be self-sustaining than it really has.

In essence, then, we may say that politicians, as brokers, play a quite extraordinary role. They cannot make anything possible that was not inherently possible: but the inherently possible may not be actually possible without their intervention, without their skills and good offices. They do not actually decide anything. And yet in a sense they do: for if they are the ones who find a formula which is acceptable to those whose decisions do matter, they surely are deciding. And this is not a case of the piper calling the tune, but something genuinely unique to brokers.

While politicians do not actually limit governments, they do in a sense. For by formulating the limits beyond which anything the government does will be unacceptable — and they do this by negotiating with those whose acceptance is essential — they have not merely defined and discovered but also determined the limits, provided they were truly negotiating. And while they are not the final arbiter of governments, they are real arbiters to the extent that they are the effective agents — subordinate and yet the real deciders — in discovering or determining what the government can do or does. They may not put 'this lot' into government or 'that lot' out, but they often determine what is done by those who are in. A second, more far-reaching sense is that politicians who are untrustworthy may prevail upon the lot who are in to try something impossible, resulting in them going out and the other lot coming in.

None of this should surprise anyone who has dealt with brokers. Not merely do agents or brokers have vested interests of their own. Not merely do some agents desire to be arbiters rather than arbitrators. In addition, those who employ agents are commonly willing to rely on them to act constructively. Agents or brokers need instructions, but they also need room for manoeuvre. They often have input into their instructions, and easily become involved in negotiations which lead to adaptation of their instructions, especially if they know what they are dealing with.

Politics is an unusually self-sufficient and unusually autonomous form of broking. In many respects, and at most times, politics is conducted within some identifiable framework. There are understandings and established practices as to how things are done, the boundaries are reasonably defined and understood, and change within the 'industry' takes place at a pace and in a manner that is widely intelligible to all. Thus nobody, whether broker or client, should be entirely resistant to adapting. But such frameworks, despite their considerable strength in certain respects, are subject to an underlying fragility, and to disquieting shifts with little notice.

A government – or more generally the powers that be – may lay down certain rules for the conduct of politics, in much the same way as with stockbrokers. The government may then be strong enough, at least for a time, to enforce compliance with these rules. But in the nature of the case it cannot guarantee to itself, of itself, sufficient power to do so. For its capacity to do things is always in a basic way dependent on factors outside itself, and its capacity to be on top in this relationship is in large part dependent on its handling of the relevant politics. If its own rules for politics fail, then it will likely be forced to let them go. Any rules imposed on politics are calculated to inhibit it and isolate governments. This is always more dangerous for governments than anyone else in the long run, even though free politics may also be dangerous for a government. It seems in the nature of the case impossible to formulate a recipe to kill off politics permanently, especially by a process of supposed containment.

In the end, governments could control politics only if they could control all the forces at work within the societies they govern — emergent as well as existent forces. And not only the existence or non-existence, not even only the effectiveness or non-effectiveness of all these forces, but also the ways in which they function or operate. This is hard to envisage, at least in modern times, as possible in the long run. For as new forces, new ideas, new interests emerge and take shape, they will need to be taken into account — which clearly calls for broking as good as broking can be.

This in turn calls for openness, and potential adaptiveness. For nothing is surer than that if new forces do not find brokers in the ranks of established politicians, then would be politicians will fill the gap, and play the role in their own way as dictated by the clientele they have arisen to serve.

Politics is always the same, yet equally it is always being revamped and freshly adapted to new situations and conditions. The reason why new parties find it hard to break into well-established two party systems is not that the new parties are disallowed, but that they can seldom get a foothold without it being taken immediately from them. As soon as they find or create a bit of ground that will take some weight, the established parties move in, claim it as their own, and squeeze out the newcomer.

In the end, then, there is no framework within which politics operates, and there are no binding rules upon it. It is *sui generis*, a maverick and uncontrollable kind of broking activity because it brokes between forces, impulses, and ideas which are themselves *sui generis*, i.e. between those kinds of forces which are the makers and sources of the only rules and frameworks that there are or can be for humans and for human life.

Those who try to understand politics have a good subject insofar as politics is always the same. In this respect they are not unlike those who try to understand art, or literature. For while the subject of politics may be less elevated and may penetrate less profoundly to the real life of the deepest of human beings, it is none the less fascinating because of the pre-eminence within it of new techniques for applying its own fundamental character. Nor is politics itself perhaps any less influential on the life and world of humans overall. But students of politics are perhaps less to be expected to be critics of current practices in politics, for they are unlikely to have the eye (unless they are also something else as well) to get insight into what is developing on the scene where politics is engaged upon broking in the present. Ideologists — or even ideologues in moments of detachment — may have a better chance of grasping the nuances of current political practice than do political analysts. For biased though they may be, they can at least have some sense of whether politics is catching hold of current and developing forces and pressures.

Politics then, is an activity or function which is identifiable, basically definable and in a curious way limited. It is definable insofar as it can be likened to a well-known type of human activity, insofar as the difference between it and other varieties of broking can be pointed out, and insofar as the characteristic and unique features of politics itself can be formulated. But the kind of definability in question here would not of itself allow the novice or the politically illiterate to pick out political transactions straight off, without some training in them — and much less would it allow anyone to enter competently into the practice of politics.

The sense in which politics is a limited activity is both interesting and fundamental to an adequate understanding of what it is. Thus, while politics essentially has no boss, and while it makes its own rules and works out its own ways of operating as it goes along, it is not the arbiter *per se* of 'life and death' in the broadest senses. It is, however, often in effect the arbitrator. If the broker cannot arrange something, some deal, then things will be left to take their course, and the course that follows if political mediation is absent is likely to be tyrannical if not bloody, and certainly sectional and divisive to a uniquely damaging and destructive degree. In this sense, the importance of politics must not be underrated. In a very vital sense, it really can call the shots. And flowing from these shots, it is likely to have impact on the kinds of artillery and missiles that are devised for future contests.

But politics does not have the say as to where the power lies, where things are going, which beliefs and practices have had their day and which new ideas are coming to the fore. In the face of all this, the impact of politics is comparatively slight – the strength of traditions, the determination of protagonists, the adaptiveness and resilience and sheer strength of people at large are far more important. This is the truth of the saying that politics will go with anyone — who can pay in some coin or other.

To say this, however, is not to say that politics is a derivative activity. For it has its place, its very own place, no matter what the forces for and against each other may be, no matter what impulses may be arising or what practices dying. It is limited but not derivative, and its power within its limits should neither be underestimated by those who think they may be able to take the bit between their teeth and defy everything else, nor overestimated by those who think they can do nothing without their own political machine.

The thrust of these observations is that politics is not simply the handmaiden of government, much as governments might wish that it was. Governments may try to buy politicians off, but they do well to resist if they would not be supplanted — and indeed governments bring all the odium of politics upon themselves when they do succeed in monopolising politics. Nevertheless, politics is the arena to which those who would engage formally in the business of control, i.e. those who would govern, in fact and inevitably gravitate.

But others also gravitate there. Not surprisingly, professional opposers go there, i.e. people whose disposition is to be critical and try to do something about the imperfections of things. Opportunists of all kinds go there — people with a sense that they will in some way be able to find a niche and/or make their mark in this particular arena which seems to many who hardly know it to offer virtually unlimited opportunities to do things. A great variety of people come thus to politics – and they are apt either to go through a wringer that dispels their illusions, or to slump into hard-working makeweights.

Among the least successful of those who enter politics in the normal run of things are many of those with 'original' ideas to sell. This is partly because their ideas are too unoriginal, but their thinking is often broken by the arena they have entered. In seeking a *modus vivendi* for their ideas as well as themselves, they are apt to lose the idea itself. On the other hand, under this rubric come some of the most spectacular political successes and world figures. They may be few, but they are inestimable.

In addition, there are those who come willy-nilly to politics: they come because fixing and dealing is their nature: and once come, they grow into the mould, and bear their burden of fixing modestly and cheerfully. They are not so much the hacks of politics as the draughthorses. They bear a great deal of the brunt, without much thanks or reward and without wanting much.

The preceding paragraph has been less concerned with why people enter politics than with pursuing the nature of politics by exploring who engages in it. The first point here is that the life of politics is not so much no great thing as an incredibly varied and diverse thing. It may have a sameness in a hidebound society. But — thinking again of a parliamentary system — there is simply no comparison between life on the front bench and life on the back bench; between the life of the successful and the unsuccessful candidate; between the life (if such it can be called) of the government party *per se* and of the opposition party *per se*; between the life of those who do and those who do not have the ear of the big players. There are many lives of politics — not only because there are many levels of politics, but also because there are many levels of politician.

There is a great tendency for politics to live off politicians. It always makes a bid for a monopoly of their time and energy, and it often is successful. When this happens, the situation is dangerous for the human world. For insofar as politicians become personally remote by being cut off and detached from the main business of this world (i.e. making ways of life) they are the more liable to lose perspective on the inner function of their broking business. And insofar as politicians are monopolized by politics, they surely are detached from making ways of life and thus remote in the most fundamental way (that of non-involvement) from this world. For the life of politics, in general, is a life dominated by panics, a life which involves reaction rather than action, and making (i.e. arranging) somewhat at second hand. It is not the role of the politician to generate matters for broking, but to broke when pressures have already built up. So most of what comes the politician's way is something of an emergency, needing immediate resolution.

It is perhaps the salvation of the human world from the worst excesses of politics that there are so many varieties and levels of politics. If politicians always sold simply to the highest bidder, and more if all politicians meant the same thing by 'the highest truth', then it is hard to imagine the inroads of modernity, change and development ever gaining any sort of grip at all. In this respect, one senses that politicians who would be governors, and politicians who are oppositionists, have a common interest in letting in the new, giving it a chance to break into the charmed circle so that it may 'have a go'. Potential 'governors' will want to see whether it can be any use to them, oppositionists whether it will help at all. The oppositionist pure and simple is the person who will almost tend to favour change for change's sake.

Granted that some politicians are, as whole people, 'on about' something more than simply assaying deals — i.e. granted that they are broking neither simply for the sake of broking, nor simply for reward — it inevitably happens that the whole character of political broking is raised somewhat above pure broking. Politicians can become encouragers, helpers, facilitators, suggesters. They can give advice, not only about the best means to certain ends, but also about possible ends. In particular their skills should enable them to say something about the ways in which ideas had best be developed and given form if they are to have any chance of becoming anything real. Those politicians whose aspiration is principally to be big brokers are in a way dangerous, because of their involvement and commitment to broking for its own sake. But by the same token, if they take a long view — especially if they are in a *milieu* where others are doing something more than brute broking — they will see that they need to develop something more to offer.

In a way, politicians become concerned with everyone's life but their own. Insofar as they are sticky beaks they probably develop a more acute feel for their marketplace than would otherwise be the case. And the more dispassionate they are about this, the more to the point will be their feel — except in the rare case of the political statesman who lives to the full and whose own moods and mores run in harmony with those of society at large. Insofar as politicians becomes busybodies, they already begin to soften up their market, to prepare their people for the fact that there will be deals which they will be arranging.

The politician is plainly not a retiring kind of character. Politicians' concern with the lives of others — at the expense of their own — is not an act of selflessness. Their loss of a sense of their own identity, their detachment from the activity of making themselves something in and for themselves, is not of their own choosing. It results from their involvement in political activity. It is the character of the activity which takes its toll, unless the politician takes the greatest pains (using considerable strength of will and calling upon considerable reserves of 'wanting something else as well') to keep politics in a place which leaves room for the rest of life, and for the making of something that is more than reacting to others and mediating between them.

For in politics pure and simple, it is not oneself that makes one's way of life, but politics that does so. It can make practitioners — rough, tough and perhaps above all ready to grasp anything available to use as a lever or probe or ram or whatever else may serve their turn. To understand this is to understand one of the first rules of politics, that one must never be unwary if one is bringing something into the political arena or wanting to take something out of it. Politicians arrange, but so incompatible may be the materials they must arrange that the process is apt to involve distortion and even metamorphosis of ideas and proposals between inception and outcome.

This leads to the matter of the means which politicians use, the methods by which they go about their business. In general — or perhaps *in extremis* — anything that will serve may be used, and anything may serve, depending on the time, the circumstances, the situation and the issue. Broadly, the means needed in politics are both commonplace and unique. Their uniqueness consists in the ways they blend together, and they are commonplace in that there are no political techniques or tricks which are distinctively political, which are not to be found in everyday life whether high and low.

It is because there is no framework in any ultimate sense that any means may serve and/or be used in politics. Nowhere, indeed, are there more likely to be greater difficulties than in political broking — for there are the highest issues at stake, the strongest powers at mutual odds, the newest and most untried as well as the most established and entrenched ideas and practices needing to be brought together. All of this helps explain why there is no framework, and makes plain the need for the politician to grasp at anything that will serve a turn.

Of course, some matters that need broking are new, and some simply do not fit with others. Political broking is not just a case of oiling wheels. More than in any other sphere of broking, the arranging process may necessitate breaking new ground and making fresh departures. It may require the people making the input and coming across each other and into conflict needing to be constructive, needing to go backwards, forwards and sideways in the search to make real what they are on about, while others also make real what <u>they</u> are on about. On the other hand, what is new for dealing with by politics is always comparatively slight, quantitatively, by comparison with the factors and forces that are long-standing and well-recognized, though not necessarily easily manageable, adaptive to the new, or absorbent of it on that account.

In a sense, the means by which politics operates is always talk. Most of the following discussion amplifies this. 'Talk' of course takes many forms, and comes in many guises in political arenas.[31] It must be broadly understood, and its many dimensions appreciated. To begin with, the reality that politics is mostly talk reveals the comparative powerlessness of politicians, the fact that they can do little off their own bat. They cannot take their burdens upon their own shoulders and carry them through regardless of what others may do or think. This is the sense in which they are not doers but brokers, who must arrange things and get acceptance. They may bite and threaten – and force and violence do come into play in the course of politics. But in a quite basic sense, the threats politicians make are not their own. They control great forces insofar as they are able to still them, to satisfy them, to bring them to rest. They do not themselves force the weak to give way, except indirectly: they rather get them to see the way things are, to realize what will happen unless ..., and to understand what they may best hope to achieve.

Irresponsible politicians may practise deception and foster disaster, or simply allow things to take their course with similar results. This illustrates the unwisdom of delegating total responsibility in anything to brokers. Humans can never abdicate the final responsibility for their own lives. In line with this they must do their best to ensure that the brokers they turn to will do the right thing – otherwise their situation is grim, and they must make the best of what may turn out to be the worst. There is nowhere else to turn if one cannot get a suitable broker and great powers are arrayed against one.

Where does this lead? The significance of politics and politicians varies according to situations and the traditions that obtain. At one level politicians may be regarded as the facilitators of communication. Their task is then to bring together parties who do not understand each other and translate the words of each to the other. But mere mutual understanding solves few problems, although there may be some basis for a meeting of minds or even a synthesis or compromise. But the opposite situation may equally ensue, that understanding may breed a greater mutual revulsion, a more intransigent attitude and approach to the other party. If this happens — as it does — then from a purely political point of view the engendering of understanding has been damaging.

This brings out the point that there are some disputes, some conflicts, which *should* not be settled politically — or some aspects of some disputes. For if there is some demand or pressure which is unconscionable, which makes bold to destroy one or other aspect of the human world, then it should surely be put down. Perhaps one should first try to make it go away by talking it out of existence: that is probably the least unpleasant way, even though it is seldom likely to be effective. But such talk is not in itself political, there is no broking in it; such talk is pure polemic, pure destruction, stamping something down. Insofar as it becomes political, it becomes something else, for it is already starting to go around the thing, perhaps to divide it, but not to wipe it clean off the face of the earth. And if such a thing, such a demand, cannot be put down by (non-political) talk then it should be put down by other means or at least kept clear of everything else. For if it can get itself into the sphere of politics, and be treated in that way, it has already succeeded in drawing to itself a certain legitimacy; it has got itself to the point where it is not just to be discounted and ignored and blotted out. Putting the point differently, by being allowed into the political arena it has acquired a respectability, a claim to be taken into account in no matter how small a way. Of course this can and does happen, and the decision that it should not be allowed to is always tremendously difficult to take and justify. But that it may sometimes be necessary is really nothing more than the other side of the coin that politics will go with anyone and anything.

Granted that talk which enables communication is sometimes counter productive – e.g by making an arrangement impossible – it is plain that political talk may sometimes need to be designed to deceive, to conceal, to distort, or to obscure. This is going from one extreme to another. But the politician may need to see that certain prejudices must be kept at bay, that misunderstandings will sometimes follow on too much revelation, that wild ideas may start flying unless those concerned are addressed in a particular way. Again, politicians may need to promise more than can be given, knowing that initial acceptance will sustain continued if reluctant acceptance of less; or promise less to begin with, and then secure acceptance by adding more. They need, when dealing thus with clients, to have foreknowledge of where the deal will end up, and they probably need to know this better than the clients. Insofar as they have room to manoeuvre, they are in a position to do more than merely politics: they may then, if they choose, wield some power, or buy some favour with someone else by doing what they would want, or do what they think right, or possibly something else again.

When politicians do thus arrange by deceiving and distorting — by misrepresenting a situation as it really is so that those involved may not misrepresent it despite their misconceptions about it — they are plainly engaged in the kind of talk that will do little for their own reputations for straight dealing. When what they have done is found out, as it often is, there will be annoyance — and there is no way around this, they cannot avoid it, they must in a sense suffer it and go on to rise above it, or more, they must keep on and leave it behind. And probably, unless they really are terribly nasty, it will be half-realized that their deviousness is not simply to be deplored but is rather an unavoidable element of their trade and the tools in their bag. If it leaves a nasty taste, they must say 'so much the worse for that'; but those with the taste should not go into withdrawal, for they should know themselves enough to be able to realize, at least retrospectively, what really did happen to them.

When politicians act in this way, they are in a sense engaged in manipulation — and yet in a more important sense not. For while they are bringing people to a certain position and in a way beguiling them, they are bringing them to it more in the sense of getting them to realize that it is their position than actually changing their position against their will. It must nevertheless be conceded that it is a delicate distinction, one that is probably seldom found in practice except in a more or less flawed condition.

This leads on to the situation in which politicians, trying to arrange and broke, come up against real conflict, genuine incompatibility, and not infrequently a fair measure of intransigence and intractability as well. In this situation they may be called upon by their role to manipulate. They must talk in order to move people's positions. They must somehow induce them to change, by bluster, deception, threat, or indeed whatever will come to hand.

One thing that is undoubted is that in such situations politicians seldom find that any truly rational persuasion or argument serves their purpose on its merits alone. At the end of the argument, minds and wills and positions are seldom changed; and even more seldom is the argument actually ended. It could go on for more time than is available, or than practical people would be prepared to listen. And the conclusiveness of the arguments that are advanced bears little relationship to the degree of conviction that is produced. It is in general necessary to speak to the person, rather than to the mind, to strike chords in order to convince, to appeal to interests rather than to rationality. Political argument is perhaps the great paradigm of the *ad hoc* – it is not characteristically leisurely, and the broking spirit of its practitioners is apt to make it lively. The point about it is that any consideration, any thought, any word that will serve must be adopted and put to use. Its restlessness — and that of the issues at stake — keep it on the move in such a way that it will take every kind of distortion and rational aberration in its stride. The point is always to get a result, and the very flow of the thing can itself be used to forward that end.

In this perspective, it becomes apparent that means which are talk only in the most extended or attenuated sense can come into play. To let things speak for themselves by doing nothing but simply letting them run on is one classic method. Situations of unmistakeable drift, or situations when silence is palpably leading either to unacceptable stationariness or unacceptable spates, can move people or make them willing to move. The appearance of precipitancy can sometimes do the same. There are many variations on these themes, as well as additional themes which are not greatly dissimilar. To list them all would be tedious, interminable and impossible; and the foregoing gives the general picture of these techniques.

It is worth considering some questions of professional ethics in relation to politics. For the impression will certainly have been given thus far that anything, any means which will serve, may be regarded as having at least a certain appropriateness if not positive legitimacy. But the same or similar results may sometimes be obtained by using different means. There can be no doubt that a genuine issue does arise in connection with the ethical question. But neither can there be much doubt that this issue is exceedingly easily confounded by something like sentimentality. The realm of politics is not sweetness and light, and tough assignments often call for hard measures which often enough have unpleasant aromas.

A pragmatic point – which is both long and short term — is that politicians cannot hope to flourish for ever if they use, even with success, means which are unacceptable in the society in which they function. The chances of their not being found out are too slender, and unless they reckon to carry the society with them they will at the least need to adopt this much of a professional ethic.

So to the question whether we get the politicians we deserve. Much of the answer to this is contained in two propositions: first that no society ever quite deserves the politicians it gets; and second, that no politicians ever quite deserve the societies they get.

To say that standards of acceptable behaviour are wholly the product of political practices is quite implausible, and in this respect societies do get the politicians they deserve. This does not mean that they deserve every particular politician (especially not those who flourish only briefly), or indeed every action of those politicians who do and should flourish: for societies will sometimes act in ways that are unworthy of themselves and certainly of their better parts. Sometimes, indeed, the only thing for politicians to do is to give their societies a jolt.

Politicians as such — possibly as distinct from government - are clearly not in a position simply to impose upon their societies the kinds of practices they may themselves fancy. Insofar as this is so, there is a certain truth in saying that we get the politics and politicians we deserve. And yet this is unwarrantedly general, even with its inbuilt qualification. For the 'we' in the question treats people as if they were nothing but the largest group — as if there were not other groups not to mention individuals who might very well each deserve — and be best handled by — a politician somewhat after their own image. Perhaps the best overall conclusion is that we get the politicians that the worst of us — and the best in our worst moments — deserve.

On the question of a professional political ethic, it is implicit in the preceding analysis of politics that no set of principles, deductively applicable to whatever case may arise, could possibly be arrived at or be workable. For there is of necessity a continuing need to devise ways of making arrangements that are in a sense new, and which may well therefore fail to fall straightforwardly under any discoverable principle of this kind. Therefore a manual of legitimate and permissible means would seem an inappropriate aspiration: there can be no code.

Nevertheless, in the light of the whole analysis of this work, it is possible to formulate a very general guiding ethical principle for the conduct of politics – one which bears not only on the means by which politicians bring arrangements to fruition, but also on the kinds of arrangements which it is appropriate for them to promote. This principle is that of sustaining to the highest degree humans as the makers of their own ways of life. This is a principle of general attitude, of orientation, of approach — one which would be extraordinarily difficult to teach, but which somehow may be absorbed.

This principle means that all people and all groups of people must be revitalised and enabled to the maximum degree possible, none cramped, none cornered, none dominated, none snuffed out. The aim must be to make possible anything that is possible. The snowball syndrome — some fad on the move gathering everything to itself — must above all be resisted. But so must fragmentation. In short, the politician should promote the human world in all its diversity and mutuality, in all its individuality and corporateness, in all its separateness and interaction.

To apply this principle, and equally to decide whether it truly has been applied, is quite extraordinarily difficult. There is probably no saying whether it has been, and perhaps no absolutely certain saying it has not been. When there seems to be an excess either of fragmentation or of unification, or when there seems to be stultification or monopolisation or destructive strife, the impulse must be to say that the politicians have failed. The same is true on a smaller scale when an individual or group is continually thwarted, or unable to get a hearing, or pushed aside.

There are even deeper problems when individuals seem not to have ideas or desires to bring forward, or when everyone seems to want the same thing, or when groups do not form, or when dullness and a kind of sullenness seem to blanket a society. Politicians can probably do nothing about that, and it is hard to say what could possibly bring vitality or revitalization in such circumstances. But while the impulse to blame the politicians must unquestionably be strong in such circumstances, it is hard or impossible to be sure. For it is never certain how much manoeuverability they have, never clear that they could have made arrangements which are in the relevant respects better, never demonstrable that they were not dealing with degrees of power, intransigence, complicity or general lifelessness which rendered them incapable of anything better.

Yet to say this is not to say the principle is worthless. Politicians may have trouble applying it, and may sometimes be too weak or lazy or unimaginative even to try. Nevertheless, the principle, if they bear it in mind — and more if they aspire to follow it — surely gives them some greater sense of the full dimensions of their activity, and some very general push in directions that are desirable. By the same token, it provides the rest of society with something by which to judge what is going on.

Granted that the human world is dynamic, it is not unreasonable for people to expect better of their politicians even if they cannot rightly be blamed. For that expectation, if really pursued and followed through in its ramifications, would itself become an impulse to improvement and betterment, to a shift in the direction of more satisfactory arrangements.

Having considered the kinds of persons who engage in politics, the means they employ, and the standards by which they should act, it is time to turn to their distinctive skill. What is it that enables a politician to broke successfully, and to broke well? The clue to the answer lies in the point of which so much has been made, that there is no limit to the possible means by which political arrangements may be concluded. Accordingly, the real political skill, basic and supreme, is to be able to decide which means will be appropriate to each case as it comes along. Bluster, no matter how good it may be as bluster, simply will not serve if cajolery is required. To know, or be able to judge, the right kind of approach is the beginning and main part of political wisdom.

To be able to do well in actually employing the approach once chosen is almost secondary, at least in the sense that without the right approach the task is effectively impossible no matter how well the shots are played. But this distinction obscures the vital points that the approach is only partly chosen in advance of actually engaging in the broking, and that the amalgam of approach (which may itself often be a compound) and application is in a great many cases unique. Choosing an approach is less like dentists choosing a drill than it is like artists making their own colours and placing them on their palettes as they go to work. There is interfusing between the choice and the application of the approach, and the best of politicians must plainly be good at both. Those who have come through the fire to the top may be in a position on some occasions to delegate to others (whom they would need to choose well) the actual application, following along the approach pointed out to them.

Political skill must thus be seen as rare, and precious in itself. It appears rare even in politics, which helps explain why so many political arrangements are less than satisfactory. Indeed, insofar as it is rare, and insofar as there is no way of ensuring that it is well distributed among politicians, there is bound to be much that is unsatisfactory in political arrangements.

This really matters to the human world. For political arrangements tend to have far-reaching ramifications and echoes for our world. Those badly affected are not just directly involved individuals, and seldom the politicians themselves, but frequently the people in large groups, and indirectly those who interact with such groups.

The supply shortage of able politicians may thus be seen as a reason for the human world being organized in such a way as to minimize the need for politics and the prevalence of politics. A society that is self-regulating to the greatest degree possible, where people and groups look after their own affairs, and manage their own arrangements and interactions with other groups — where neither party is either inclined or driven to go to the politicians except as a last resort — is better calculated to produce a flourishing human world.

Are there satisfactory methods for training politicians? The task should surely be more mechanical and manageable than training statesmen — and the idea of it less controversial if politics is understood in the sense suggested above. It would probably never be possible to require that politicians be trained, for ultimately they operate at levels where they can thumb their nose at any such insistence. Nevertheless, if a course could be devised, and in an environment in which qualifications are required in most occupations, it might be expected that trained people would at least predominate.

But there are great difficulties. To begin with, the skill to be taught is not wholly mechanical — in that a professional ethic is implicit in it. One doubts whether the skill involved could ever be characterized without embodying some moral presuppositions, and to this extent there could hardly but be controversy about exactly what the skill is that should be taught. A greater difficulty is that no matter what the ethical content may be, the skill in question is bound to involve handling people and groups, and bringing them together in relation to matters about which they cannot get together by themselves, or of their own efforts and initiative. This is bound to face profound difficulties as something to be taught. That a good deal can be discovered, written, and read with understanding about the handling of human beings is unquestionable. Whether the skill can be taught — and taught by formal instruction — is a different matter.

To understand on the one hand, and on the other to be able to apply, appear very different with this particular skill. This is not to say they are mutually exclusive, or that the one may not sometimes lead to the other. But it is to say that proper training would need to include a programme for bridging the obvious gap between having the understanding and having the skill. There clearly exists no standardised method for filling this gap. While this should not in itself cause dismay — for supposed standardised methods in education are never such in reality — the difficulties of bridging this particular gap look ominous.

It is inconceivable that the skill of politics could be taught except in some kind of apprenticeship system. Such systems take time, and they need to be selective. These are precisely the conditions that would be unacceptable in a training course for politicians. A further difficulty would be finding people who could and would be willing to teach. A short — crash — course for budding politicians could have value – although it could hardly be made either selective or compulsory. Real training in politics must come less formally — and can only come well where politics is comparatively well and widely practised. It can only come where many are called and few are chosen; where there are lots of pseudo-political opportunities, which only slowly become minor political opportunities and which in turn only slowly become major ones; where there is a kind of dominant consensus (the domination wielded by strong politicians at the top together with discerning people fully engaged in living) about who should and shall keep moving along and get places higher up the ladder. Such selection methods are dangerously open to abuse — yet if they are abused the condition of society would surely be such that any other method would be even more dangerous, whereas if they are not abused then they probably work better than any other methods could possibly do.

To a thriving human world shall be given challenges; to an embattled human world, tribulation. That is the way things are. Granted that humans are on their own and inadequate to the task, there is no other recourse.

The remaining question about the nature of politics is what it deals with. This has been touched on at every point of the foregoing discussion, but the threads need gathering together. What does politics broke? The answer in general terms is plain. In the ultimate — the extreme — politics brokes between ways of life. Humans make ways of life. But the human world is a world of many people and groups — and they interact. They interact in — or because of — their ways of life. As one person is making one way of life, another will be making another which cuts across it. As one person comes to want some resource or opportunity, another person will be wanting the same resource — or perhaps an incompatible opportunity. As a space is perceived and proposed to be filled in one way by one person, it will equally be perceived and proposed to be filled in another way by another person. The ways of life that people would make they cannot necessarily have. What they can make must be understood in two senses, one being abstract potentiality, the other practical possibility. The two do not go together in a vast number of cases.

In many parts of the world, human beings — at least within established societies — dwell together in sufficient harmony, are sufficiently restrained, and have sufficiently compatible interests for the major role of politics to be one of dealing with aspects rather than whole ways of life. Partly because each person and group exists in an historical and regulated framework, and partly because people think along similar lines far more than along radically opposed ones, it is comparatively rare for any two proposed ways of life to be diametrically opposed at every point — much less for either of them to be so integrated that any part is impossible without all the rest. And where it is a question of competition for space or opportunity, it often turns out that there is more to play with than was realized.

Further, in an established society — and the great majority of people live in societies that are more or less established in this respect — there always exists a framework of regulation, and some sort of government which implements and enforces these regulations at least from time to time. Such frameworks, at the same time that they create expectations, also limit, direct and focus aspirations. Few people find themselves really wanting to play a shot that is totally alien to the game as they know it.

This all serves to make life easier, and the making of ways of life more productive and fulfilling.

The nature and functions of government are dealt with in the next chapter. But seldom if ever is the government totally remote from the society. Its voice does not come to the society like that of God to Moses on Sinai.[32] Indeed, the government is part of society no matter how remote and self-sufficient it may become, no matter how much it may try to set itself apart.

Politics brokes, therefore, not only between people and groups directly involved in making ways of life — and running into problems they cannot themselves handle in the course of doing so. It also brokes between the government — the deciders, the controllers, the regulators — and the society — groups of all kinds as well as individuals. This at least, is the function of politics. The alternatives if it is absent are considered in the next section. Thus wherever governments go and whatever they want to do; and whenever individuals or groups run into difficulties with each other, or want what they cannot get but which may be collectively provided: all such matters call for political broking.

Whenever machinery becomes more than a cottage affair and begins to have a wider impact, questions arise about controlling it and defining its place. Whenever facilities, such as the provision of television services, become available – especially when they tend to become irresistible and inescapable — for one's children if not for oneself — questions arise about controlling them and defining their place. Whenever ideas become ideologies or to any degree imperialistic, questions will arise about what sway they should have. Whenever anyone gets any sort of stranglehold or monopoly on anything, questions should arise about whether it should not be broken and limited.

Politics brokes in the sphere of regulation and control, of dominance and influence. Governance, in the broadest sense, cannot but be tremendously widespread. And there is a sense in which governments which do little ensure the presence of other forms of control which must be looked at (and arranged and controlled) with no less care and scepticism and suspicion than governments themselves.

To leave everything but criminal and civil law to some supposed free market is certainly to give to a narrow instrument the role of settling some very delicate balances. How far or effectively can the market settle, for example, the question of whether it is good for children to grow up in an atmosphere where they must watch television for 10 hours weekly or be socially unacceptable among their peers? In all of this, we are treating of a very basic and supreme kind of broking indeed, and one that is bound to have an impact on the human world not only because of what it does but also because of what it is.

2. The Impact Of Politics

To begin with, it must be realized that the nature and characteristics of politics give it a truly central and permanent place in human affairs. Politics, if not precisely the hub, is something like the spokes of the wheel, and always has its being in a kind of intermediate position. Politics is called into being by other facets and factors of life, and to that extent is not a primary element.

But this does not mean that it is dispensable, or that there is any effective substitute for it. On the contrary, without it the human world seems certain to lapse or at least to languish. Politics is not perhaps wholly inescapable, as some later references make clear. But without it — when it has not come into being or when it is significantly done away with — there are not only deficiencies, shortcomings and inconveniences, but quite fundamental threats to the human world and assaults upon it.

For politics seems to abound not only when there is an interplay of power (and I mean interplay rather than actual warfare). Politics also abounds when the making of ways of life is in a flourishing condition. Insofar as this is true, we may say that politics should be inevitable and in a sense inescapable. In such circumstances it may possibly pass some people by at least in its more direct and overt manifestations: those who live unto themselves, who make few demands on others, and who are content to make do with facilities that are there. But even here, the ramifications of politics are evident. There may be some negative ramifications if the people in question live quietly because they have been put off by politics; and there are certainly indirect ramifications insofar as the facilities with which they make do have come there by way of political arrangements made between other people. Certainly those who want more — who are less content to make do with what is available, and more desirous of abundant interactions, involvements and commitments with commensurate opportunities and facilities — these are people who come almost systematically within the ambit in which politics is influential.

Were it not for politics — and more particularly were it not for the particular political arrangements that are made and that have been made — the situation of humans would be different in an almost limitless number of respects: their situation in the sense of their expectations, their opportunities, their standing, even their capacities insofar as these depend on factors outside themselves.

THE POLITICIANS

It seems that in the absence of politics, the human world and situation is bound to be either primitive, or subject to domination. There is a sense in which politics may not arise at all, and this is surely a kind of primitiveness. In such situations possibilities are basically taken for granted, and it is *de facto* presumed that facilities, opportunities and the like are part of the nature of things, and that the same is true even about the disposition thereof. Such a society is non-questioning, and without restlessness or adventurousness in its parts. Humans have their being much more at the collective than the individual level, and individuals make their lives in entering into the life of the group — in coming to terms with what that life is. The life of the individual is one of conformity and identification, and the life of the group is static.

If problems do arise — and not many can without the fabric being endangered — then there are likely established authority structures which hand down decisions as to what should be done. The system relies upon there being no questions asked about how such decisions should be made or whether a better decision might not have been made. The survival of the system probably depends (especially when the authorities need to act) upon those in authority having a good measure of the political broker in them. They must not lead people to contemplate complaining or to feel they have been hardly done by. In short, the authorities essentially need to do what would have been arranged if political broking between the relevant parties had actually been going on. One conclusion to be drawn from this is that politics is implicit in primitive societies if it is not explicit.

The other human condition in which it may be said that politics is absent is when all branches of a society are subject to the domination of an overriding power. This is the situation where 'arrangements' (decisions) need not be acceptable to be made to be effective or to be enforced. It is not that no-one thinks of raising questions about whether different decisions might not better have been made, nor that the legitimacy of those who do make the decisions is accepted on all hands, but that those who would question are subdued and put down. There is no effective distribution of power, but rather a concentration of power — a concentration that decides without consulting, and imposes without securing acceptance. The logic of such a system is that acceptance is not necessary for there to be compliance, and that the desires and aspirations of those who lack effective power, or whose power can be nullified or overcome, have no effective claim to be taken into account.

In modern times, there would always, even in situations of the greatest tyranny and domination, be politicking and power broking as between the members of the inner sanctum. And it is probably a fantasy to imagine that domination would ever be so strong as to obliterate politics completely from within society. It is even more fantastic to imagine that the most dominant of rulers, having obliterated politics, could then take the further step of ceasing to be his or her own politician. This would mean they could do what they liked no matter how disagreeable to their subjects, and deal with reactions by force or any other means that come to hand. This would mean thumbing their noses at their subjects completely. The word fantasy needs to be taken seriously. The potentialities of force and fraud would appear to have been explored pretty thoroughly, but those of psychological and physiological and pharmacological manipulation not. And we simply cannot say that the means may not be discoverable whereby rulers might be able to dominate their people with absolutely no regard for any wishes or ideas but their own.

The impulse to do this would surely need to be ideological. Domination for its own sake could be relied on to turn sour, and so careless, and therefore to collapse. But an ideological impulse could be far more thorough-going and self-sustaining. For an ideology is apt to contain within it some pattern of life to which all should conform. From an ideological point of view (whatever the content of the ideology may be) while all people should have a way of life, they should all have the same one rather than all of them making their own.

Ideological rulers, having got rid of politics and risen to supremacy, are in a position themselves to make the ways of life of others. Or that is where they would like to be. It will be no satisfaction for them to be dominating robots or morons or addicts; and in this respect it seems unlikely that the potentialities of manipulation are unconfined. But only less likely: for it remains conceivable that the essential elements of being human (from the perspective of the ideology certainly, and possibly from other perspectives as well) might conceivably be preserved at the same time that those retaining them could be irresistibly manipulated into the way of life in which the ideologue believes. The ideologue believes in humans living ways of life, but also in only some people making ways of life. This is because the ideologue does not believe that humans are the measure, but only some humans — or alternatively, perhaps, as the ideologue would put it, in some humans perceiving the measure.

The approach just scrutinized does seem anachronistic — and it probably flourishes in the world as we know it partly because a great many people lack the energy to bother about making their own lives, partly because it has become possible for hitherto unimaginable amounts of power to be amassed, and partly because influence over others seems to be penetrating into more and more segments of life. This in turn, no doubt, is partly due to the interdependence of people. Governments in modern times have certainly become increasingly powerful, in the sense that they have come and are still coming to be involved with more and more parts and aspects of life. But at the same time — probably for different reasons — government itself has tended to become both more open and more accessible.

This has led to a boom in politics. When the business of government is minimal and when governments themselves are comparatively impregnable — and when most arrangements follow fairly traditional lines and are made without great difficulty – politicians are apt to be left out on something of a limb. The best they were often able to do (not that it was not infrequently highly significant) was to mill around among themselves on the floors of their own 'changes, and try to stir up flurries from time to time. But when there is openness and accessibility, when there is no knowing which areas of life governments may lay their hands on next, and when virtually all areas already feel that hand in some respects and to some degree: in that situation the politicians are in constant demand, and their efforts have far reaching significance in human affairs.

It is not just that politics is underneath everything, or that it is threatening. It is rather that much of what we experience, much of the control and regulation to which we are subject as well as the facilities and opportunities which are available to us are so because of the way in which politicians have broked. The very openness of government, its very accessibility, the fact that what governments do could have been done differently or not at all, and the fact that some of what they have not done might have been done – all of this is in very large measure due to politics.

The more there is room for manoeuvre about who governs, and the more there is room for manoeuvre about what is done, the more politics must be seen as playing a central role in the human world. Doubtless it is not the largest force, not the key, not the decider. It has little capacity, for example, to determine its own parameters or to decide which matters it will get involved in broking, whether to pull down tall strong trees or raise small ones higher. Its function is very specialized, its limits are tolerably clear, and what it can do off its own bat is probably in one respect about as little as moving the interest rate a point or two may seem to be. But tiny things can rise like mushrooms and sometimes grow like snowballs.

Nowhere more than in an interdependent world (which is precisely where politics flourishes) are marginal considerations absolutely crucial. Nowhere more than in a milieu in which one is encouraged to think one can have everything is it an incident to be deprived of or to be just unable to secure one small thing that one wants. So insofar as the impact of politics is capable of affecting those marginal considerations, it has profound significance. The brokers will be quite properly wooed to use their influence this way rather than that; and people may even turn broker themselves or try to get their own brokers to work on their behalf — to stop others, and help them get what they want.

The importance of politics is particularly conspicuous if one considers the costs of political failure. If arrangements cannot be made between those in conflict or at odds with each other, there is a far greater likelihood of bad blood, of real bitterness, of conflict that is increasingly difficult to contain. The next round of negotiation is likely to be marred by greater intransigence and less cooperation, divisions become clearer and more strongly battled for, and lines of battle are drawn:

all of which is unlikely to help anyone in the end. For insofar as the world is interdependent, it is better overall that no-one is put down. And no way of life is really enhanced to any extent by the need for extended battles.

The importance and impact of politics is substantial for all the reasons given, but politics is at the same time ambiguous in its significance and value. Politics, in the broadest sense, brokes between ways of life and the makers and shapers thereof. As concerned in such an intimate and immediate manner with ways of life, politics may be seen as almost sacred. But as broking them, how can it not be seen as sinister, as a potential threat to that which matters above all to humans, that is, themselves and that which they above all make. To broke in shares or stock or land may be all very well, but to broke in people and their ways of life may seem barely different from broking in human lives themselves.

Indeed there is no greater truth in this sphere than that politics is sinister and dangerous when it becomes insensitive, when concluding the deal becomes the end in itself, when the concerns and claims of both parties are not taken into decent account, when issues are oversimplified, when some relevant considerations are not given their due weight. Politics is the more dangerous in this connection to the extent that those who suffer at its hands are thereby rendered increasingly incapable of doing anything about their plight.

Whether politics goes this way or the better way — or how far in which direction — depends nevertheless not only on its own traditions as well as on the particular practitioners at any given time, but also on how much those affected will tolerate. It depends particularly on those who are likely to fare badly taking a stand from the start. Unless they do this, their position can be permanently weakened, and they may be continually yielding as much because they put themselves on the defensive from the start as because they are being pushed around.

The higher class of political brokers obviously have a quite different impact. These are the politicians with a capacity to grasp, in detail as well as outline, what really matters to those with whom they are dealing. They will discourage those who would take advantage or press claims too hard or seek what they regard as trifles at the expense of what others regard as central. Their passions are to find a way rather than merely to do a deal; to look on all sides of issues; to make balanced and even complex (though not overcomplicated) arrangements. They will be absorbed without being swamped by their task, dedicated and yet detached, dispassionate and yet sympathetic. In a way, in order to perform in such a way, the politician almost needs to become something of a busybody, although they no sooner go down that road than they become interferers rather than genuine brokers.

The apparently negative, oppositionist streak that seems always to be present or lurking in politics is no doubt calculated to give politics a bad reputation. No sooner does one get a bright idea, which would surely be to everyone's benefit (even though especially attractive or advantageous to oneself) than the politicians start to make difficulties. Sometimes, it must be conceded, sheer negativity is at the bottom of this: the need to be cautious can breed a negative approach.

Furthermore, the institutionalization of political processes is usually calculated to bring in its train some unduly sticky red tape. And yet to make difficulties, of the right sort; to damp down excess and enthusiasm even; to be sceptical about whether the most apparently brilliant of ideas really will be universally advantageous — much less acceptable: all this, in proper proportion and measure, is surely the right response from the politician.[33] Schemes of universal happiness almost never turn out to be so good, and even the most constructive politician needs to be wary.

To be a broker in ways of life, in that by which humans set the greatest store and even have their inner being, is clearly to undertake an enormous responsibility — provided, of course, that the task is undertaken for what it really is. To rate the importance of this responsibility against that of actually deciding or governing is obviously most difficult. The putting on of controls, the final decision about which controls should be put on, and the arranging that needs to be at the back of the whole process: these all go together in importance, and it would be pointless to try to say which is the more important. But it is certainly wrong to say that politics is any sort of evil because it brokes ways of life: its inescapability means that the greatness of what it brokes invests the broking itself with profound importance.

There is some temptation to say that because politics is so important, politicians should be given every facility in doing their job, that they must be endowed with a very great deal of power. This is a misconception and a dangerous one. Certainly to be a broker in ways of life, and between people and their governors, is a supremely difficult as well as responsible undertaking. And obviously, politicians should not be deprived of what they really do require in order to do their job well. But to give them power is to deify them, to give them that whose use is quite inconsistent with their doing their job well. To impose arrangements is the opposite of political broking, for the task of politics is to make acceptable arrangements. No doubt politicians often imagine, with the highest motives and intensity, that they can see what is best, and that they could make everyone happy if they but had the means, the power to do what needs to be done. But even if they were right, they would surely be more fundamentally wrong, for an imposed way of life is the antithesis of one which people make for themselves.

To talk of giving politicians every facility is hardly less dangerous. For they are likely to become slick operators anyway (especially the more disreputable of them), and if they have every facility they are the more likely to be able to 'put one over' those with whom they are dealing. Human beings very often think, at the moment when they are listening to the honeyed words of the privileged, that something would be acceptable to them — and deceive themselves thereby. Obviously, it is never going to be possible to prevent people from deceiving themselves in such matters. But equally, it is inappropriate to set up systems which are calculated to lead to a situation in which such deception is likely to arise.

In general, one suspects that politicians probably do their job much better when they do not have too many aids or set methods to distract them from the job in hand. Certainly to give facilities or power to politicians who have proved inefficient without them will not improve their performance. Power is calculated to snuff out the political skill. Facilities are likely to dampen the realization that the task of finding a way rests with the politician. Nevertheless, it is very difficult to imagine that politicians, like everyone else, will not grasp at what they fancy would ease their roles and their job if they are given the chance.

Often there is an accretion of power to politicians. This is apt to become mixed up with a blurring of the lines between politics and government. As this happens, politics becomes important in a different way, simply as one of those powers or forces of which it is appropriate to beware. A proper wariness is the more difficult to achieve because unless one would go too wild or too quiet, one must still use politicians as brokers. Indeed, it is always necessary to be wary of politicians: for they are always subject to the greatest of pressures from within society, and are therefore tremendously vulnerable. The temptation must be great and often irresistible, even for the best of them, to give way to pressures from one direction unless they are pressured (or sustained and supported as we might say) by pressures from the other. If politicians cannot be trusted but must always be watched, this is perhaps less because they are untrustworthy than because they are inherently open to being manipulated. In the flow of events and pressures, their role makes it virtually impossible for them not to take silence for consent: which means that those people who fail to keep their ball up to the politicians are apt to lose out.

This cannot be otherwise. But at least, as the overall position has been presented here, humans do not simply have to sit back while politics disposes. Politics does have a certain autonomy of its own, but it is autonomy in the midst of heteronomy. If we do nothing, we certainly cannot rely upon things to go our way — indeed we can, unless we are passive parts of a larger active group, probably rely upon them to go against us. If we do something, we may still get less than we deserve — and almost certainly less than we think we deserve unless we are disproportionately powerful. But if we do something, we are at least putting ourselves on a par with others in the stakes of getting some sort of acceptable accommodation. There is, however, a *caveat* to this: providing that other things are equal. And they never are, and cannot be when the human world comprises groups as well as individuals.

If a politician is caught between a powerful and established group, and a lively but solitary individual, it is not hard to predict the outcome — no matter how sympathetic the politician may be to the individual, and no matter what efforts the politician may make on the individual's behalf. To go it alone is to tread the most uncertain of paths: for if others cut across the way one is going (and they can hardly be blamed for doing that), then one is going to have to turn aside and possibly make a fresh start. Things cannot be otherwise, no matter how sympathetic one may be to the person who would go it alone. Those who go it alone usually in fact go along one of a very limited number of paths taken by others who go alone: so inasmuch as there is something of a movement, it is easier for these paths to be kept open. The way is much harder for the person whose original and solitary way is unique: but we seldom become aware of such cases.

To lament the need to organize is unquestionably as futile as to lament the existence of power in the human world. Both are in a sense the product of the fact that the human world comprises groups as well as individuals, and there is certainly no basis for lamenting this.

What must if at all possible be avoided if the human world is to flourish is the development of situations in which the need to organize and to be political becomes all-consuming. This can happen if some groups become so powerful that they have the resources and capability to set aside energies and agents who will, on their behalf, keep on and on about whatever concerns them. There are organizations which will never give up, which regard every compromise less as a setback than as a spur to renewed activity. Sadly, such organizations make the business of making arrangements a matter to which everyone must devote more effort, to the detriment of getting on with making ways of life on the basis of accepted arrangements.

This is really an argument against any group having more power or resources than it knows what to do with. Much the same thing can happen if the pressures on available resources become too great — if society as a whole and in its parts is unwilling to cut its coat according to its cloth. If the disease takes this form, it is calculated to be particularly virulent. For the more all-consuming the infighting becomes, the more the cloth available tends to shrink.

To compound the problem, the disease itself seems to be the outcome of something that is healthy in itself, namely diversity of desires. For insofar as diversity really abounds, there will be a demand for such a spread of resources as may become too thin to be satisfactory for anyone. When put this way, the problem is not even so much unwillingness to cut the coat to the cloth; for since the coat and the wearer (the way of life and the person making it) are bound up with each other inseparably, it becomes difficult to make the distinction between the people themselves and their unduly high expectations. This problem is pursued further later.

An excess of organization leads inevitably to politics to an undesirable degree, and one which is indeed detrimental to human life. For politics in this situation, so far from being the delicate activity of broking as between ways of life, becomes the indelicate activity of broking around ways of life. Ways of life become goods to be handled, for the politicians will be unable to resist going with the strongest pushes if the organization of life has deteriorated to the point where it is a matter of pushing and shoving above all else.

The typical politician is probably prone to that anyway, and the whole class of politicians can easily be pushed over the edge. If politics does indeed come to that, it has reached a point where it is profoundly, even fundamentally harmful to humans. For it demeans that which humans are really on about. Humans can thus demean themselves, allow themselves to be demeaned, even insist upon that which demeans them.

This highlights the importance of the earlier points about politics being a strictly limited activity, occupying an in-between kind of position. When it is impelled, or goaded, or even allowed to become more than this, politics can play a crucial role in the devaluation of that which it is meant to serve, and can serve to distort disastrously a role that is of basic importance and profound value.

What politics can do _for_ humans — as distinct from what it can do _to_ humans — is of measureless value. Interactions between people — between group and group on the one hand, and individual and group on the other — are both a bane and a glory of the human world. There is no escaping rough passages in these interactions — and bad politics can make such passages worse. The outcome of bad politics — divisive or even abrasive, and certainly insensitive politics — can be as destructive of the human world as is destruction of human life itself. But good politics, in the sense outlined above, can streamline human interaction, can make it productive, constructive, and dynamic. Even controls and regulations can come — within limits — to be seen not as what governments do _to_ human beings, but _for_ them.

7

THE DETERMINATORS

As human beings, we are subject to influences on all sides. Some come from within and some from without. Of those from without, some come from individuals and some from the world at large. Some we can master, some we can take advantage of, some we must adapt to, some we must give way to. To classify or categorize all of them would be tedious. To compare their relative importance is to attempt to generalise cases that are unique.

A study of the human world must absolutely take serious account of these external influences. This is no less true because we make our own ways of life or because we are on our own. Indeed we are what we are both because of and in spite of the influences to which we are subject. To grasp what 'making our own ways of life' and 'being on our own' truly amount to, we must understand what influences us generally — and we need a broad perspective.

The type of influence this chapter is about is not easy to categorize, though it is less difficult to recognise in practice. It would be easy to say that the matter under consideration is a specific source of influence (e.g. government) or a specific type of influence (e.g. domination). But terms like these focus on a range of straightforwardly identifiable factors, while diverting attention from less overt or less well recognised factors. The chapter is headed 'The Determinators' partly to avoid preconceptions about the character, the scope, or the sources of the influences that require consideration — and partly because the word 'determinator' breathes strength without evoking preconceptions.[34]

There are two expressions which turn our minds in the right direction: calling the tune, and cracking the whip. Our subject is not so much influence upon particular individuals, but rather social determination or social causation at the general level. Concepts such as ruling, controlling, dominating and regulating come to mind. Government is certainly a core notion – perhaps the fundamental tune-caller and whipcracker — as evidenced by its prominence in the chapter's second section, which deals explicitly with government and its role.

But in the world as it has come to be in the Twenty First Century, government goes nowhere near encompassing all the 'players' that need to be factored in. There is the media, including social media and other communicators. There are political parties, trade unions, employer organisations, statutory bodies. There are the arts, including great writers and musicians. There are international bodies such as the United Nations, the World Trade Organization, NATO. There are education and research institutions, including pre-school, primary and secondary schools, trade schools, universities and research institutions. There are religions, with their creeds and faiths and structures and practices. There are global corporations. There are communications platforms. There are robots, and there is artificial intelligence. The list goes on, and will continue to expand.

Some of the big 'tune-callers' have no power but that of vision and imagination. Some are essentially facilitators. Some are essentially forces. Some play their part as arbiters of the future rather than of the present. There is usually another breed of functionaries as well, who may have a proper place and function, yet who may sometimes be regarded as usurpers of the function of government.

There is a place for ruling – directing rather than governing — a society, using the term broadly. It often happens that a good deal of such ruling is done, not by governments or anyone else with due authority, but by other centres of power. In brief, it is because government is often not so much at the centre of ruling as it should be, and equally because where it is at the centre it is so in the wrong way, that this chapter is titled 'The Determinators'.

It is a major aim of the chapter to avoid studying government in isolation from other forces, influences and determinants which in practice are in some relevant ways on a level with it. The word 'determinators' should not be interpreted too strictly — any term which could be taken strictly would indeed thereby disqualify itself from being an apt term for the job required. Furthermore, some of those referred to above as determinators are probably less a breed than politicians, and so to some extent the determinators are probably less important relative to their decisions than are politicians to politics.

It is important to be aware that the determinators are not necessarily in harmony, that they need not form a homogeneous group. On the contrary, they are frequently opposed to each other, and it is sometimes the role of government to 'take on' some or all of the others. The chapter has three sections, the first dealing with determinating in general, the second with the role of government, and the third with the overall impact on people.

1. Calling The Tune

People are on their own, but are seldom isolated individuals. Indeed, the real point is not so much that individuals are on their own as that humans, in the totality of that expression, are on their own. People do live to themselves, but they also live in groups and in societies. Without attempting to get at the heart of what it means to say 'society', the aim of this chapter is to explicate the reality that societies do not exist without controls, nor without rules, nor without widespread if not precisely universal practices.

To a degree, societies may hang together: but they are also kept together. Some activities are not allowed; some activities are made impossible; some are frowned upon, or made difficult or costly. By the same token, some activities or attendances are made compulsory; some demands and practices become virtually irresistible; some practices and attitudes become — or are made — in effect all-pervasive. Individuals seldom have choice about the currencies in which they can deal in relation to various matters.

Putting this general point pessimistically and negatively, we may say that the parts which make up societies (individuals and most groups) are substantially 'imposed upon' both at the societal level, and from the societal level. The effects of this are far from uniform. Many rules apply to all, but few affect everyone equally or in the same way. Much that is imposed only catches those who fall into a relevant net — whether we think of conscription for those under forty, or income tax for those with incomes. In some societies many people can stand out against widespread social pressures, whereas few manage or wish to do so in other societies.

Talk of 'tune-calling-decisions' thus encompasses a variety

of different requirements and pressures and inducements and impediments to which people are subject in any given society. We are dealing with a broad, a loose, a variable, and to some extent an arguable category. Its looseness must not be allowed to obscure its importance as a category. That there is a difference between governments banning the use of steam-powered automobiles and the patent-holders of steam-powered automobiles refusing to allow those automobiles to be manufactured is unquestionable: but the difference matters little to ordinary people. That there is a difference between the social pressure on children to watch screens and the legal compulsion to attend school is unquestionable: but the difference means little to children who do not like screens, but want to have friends. It is unquestionable that for certain purposes, distinctions ought to be drawn. But it is no less unquestionable that there are some contexts in which adverting to such distinctions can only be deceitful.

Plainly, there is some need for some tune-calling and for some whip-cracking. Human life needs a framework, and 'societies' function as frames only because some tunes are called, and some whips cracked. Perhaps, if humans were not on their own, none of this would be necessary. But humans on their own must make arrangements for themselves. Without control and regulation, nobody seriously believes that humans could get along. Further, it seems almost equally clear that more is needed than the mere restraint of ruffianism.[35] — especially if every generation is not to be starting off from scratch.

If human life is to possess any dynamism, then society must provide some direction — must not only point the way in an amiable sort of fashion, must not only merely give people a push. In many respects, the great bulk of people surely need to be carried along to an enormous extent if they are to find their own way and make their own life at all. But the question is always there — how much control and direction are needed: how much, and what is really conducive. As we shall see, the question admits of little generality by way of answer.

Putting the same point from a different perspective, we may say that a free market is a very sophisticated idea. It presumes not only that people know what they want, but that they know a fair price. It also presumes that people will be able to get what they want — or possibly what they need — at a price that they are willing and able to pay. It presumes not only a congruence between people's purchasing capacity and their needs and wants, but also presumably between both these and their productive and selling capacities. Or if it does not make these presumptions, it certainly presumes that there can be no better mechanism.

It further presumes that markets can be free, which is at best dubious. For unregulated markets always become phoney or fraudulent: they get rigged and cornered. On the other hand, regulated free markets are inescapably illusory because the regulations can never really be adapted to the dynamism inherent in the pure idea of a free market — apart from the difficulty of keeping those operators who need to be regulated away from influence on the regulations that are adopted.

These are all potent considerations, though none of them shows that the freest possible market should not have the maximum sway. But the point about people knowing what they want does mean that a free market can get going only when people have come — been brought — a significant distance. It must also be pointed out that a free market means not only buying and selling, but also persuading and manipulating. At the same time, to contemplate regulating manipulation in a free market savours of setting a maze to catch a maze.

The idea of a free market has been noted because it is sometimes regarded as a mechanism by which humans *per se* can become the deciders. But the reality is that this idea seems subject to severe limitations — that it makes people the deciders to the extent that they become traders. If it does or did this, it would certainly have called a most potent tune, resulting in a most unenlightening uniformity.

How far, however, and in what ways, does the tune need to be called? In detail, the only answer is: 'it depends'. We may say, pessimistically, that insofar as humans develop to the point where they can with tolerable readiness get a sense of what they want, of what they like, of what way of life they will make, the machinery of society is likely to have developed to a point where it cannot easily let well alone. Aside from that, it is possible to make the abstract remark that the tune presumably needs to be called up to the point where people – groups and individuals — are in a position to make their own ways of life.

This must surely mean, among other things: first that people know what they are after, or are sufficiently on the way to work that out for themselves; second that they have the means and capabilities to go ahead with their making; and third that they will neither be stopped in making their lives, nor stop others in making theirs. This is both an ideal and an abstraction. Even as all three, it suffers the shortcoming of not allowing for the coming generation, which will always be there, always in the condition of needing to be brought to the point of knowing for itself what it wants.

Beyond that shortcoming, what could the ideal mean concretely? In general, it must mean that somebody or something must take or have taken some enormously difficult and inescapably imperfect decisions both about the ways in which tune-calling should have been leading, and about where it should taper off — or even leave off entirely. Apart from everything else — and there is much else — this involves the impossible task of catering for every individual case with general procedures. Even apart from the problem of the coming generations, there is always also the reality that some people never grow up and never reach maturity, while others are champing at the bit from their earliest ages.[36] Nevertheless, it is something — which is taken further subsequently — to have an abstract statement of what is needed.

The more immediate point here concerns the differences between needs and actualities in tune-calling. There can be too much or too little tune-calling; there can also be wrong-headed, misguided, perverse, or irrelevantly motivated tune-calling. Very little tune-calling is designed, or deliberately adapted, to fulfilling or measuring up to the needs just referred to. Even in the case of governmental tune-calling, it is rare for there to be a clear focus along these lines, or adequate scrutiny of the appropriateness of what is being done — or of what is not undone.

It is not possible to generalize about the value of much governmental tune-calling. But it is possible to convey an overall impression about the ways in which things go awry. One great tendency of governmental tune-calling is to become unduly absorbed and involved with detail. Rather than indicating generalities, particular ways of conforming come to be mandated. Policies about public buildings, for example, tend to result in the specification of corridor widths. This becomes extremely degenerate, partly because those conforming are themselves easily led into an undue concern with details.

Again, the impulse to be systematic or symmetrical can

lead to the imposition of needless controls in matters that seem analogous even though they are not. The practice of regulating and registering everything can become a passion, so that the immediate recourse, when some difficulty appears in any sphere which is unregulated, is to legislate or regulate. Governments find it hard to remove controls which have passed their used-by date, or to adapt controls to changing and developing situations. This all tends to create excessive tune-calling. The reverse can happen when governments lack the resolve or strength to do anything about seriously problematic situations; when they will not take bulls by horns; when they proceed *ad hoc* and decline to treat problems systematically; when they are blind to developing situations until too late.

Agencies of social causation other than government can equally bring about enormous disparities between needs and actualities in this sphere. Shortages, for example, can occur and be perpetuated; it can be made difficult for people who are not well-regarded to embark on various activities; particular observances, attitudes and ways of looking at things can almost be imposed upon people. Various kinds of conformity, which bear no relationship whatever to human needs can come over a people. Expectations about how people should react to various situations, almost by rote, can be set up and then can prove hard to resist. People can be stereotyped — with the result that some can hardly escape being drawn into certain pursuits, while others, no matter how suitable, are shut out. It can be made unnecessary or needlessly hard for people to think for themselves. Prepacked, pre-digested ways of life can – without too much exaggeration — be dangled out for purchase at the cost of one's soul: a cost which can even be made to seem a bargain!

There is also another side. Over-organization, rush and crush, can lead to anonymity, to depersonalisation, to the loss (or incapacity to attain) a sense of identity. People can be engaged to a degree that leaves them with unspent resources but also results in their being isolated so that they cannot do much. The rationalization of facilities can eliminate opportunities. On the other hand the rush to satisfy markets can lead to a paralysed bewilderment where there is too much on offer for people to be able to make choices.

It cannot be expected that non-governmental tune-callers would take account of the needs of people at large in any general way. At worst, it may be expected that such decidings would be perverse from a human point of view, i.e. that they would be seeking an advantage or power over others, or some power over them, or simply to make some use of them. At best, not greatly concerned about people or thinking about them, such tune-callers might point the way to the future, although that would certainly happen indirectly.

Between those extremes there are two other categories of tune-callers, the do-gooders and the disinterested. The do-gooders are the more likely to be wrong-headed or misguided, for they see no need to look beyond their own ideas about what others need. But they can sometimes perform useful if modest services. The disinterested, going about their own business, sometimes drag others in their wake. This is potentially very dangerous, for its accidentality might lead anywhere — in directions which the tune-callers themselves would be horrified about did they but realize. But equally, its impact may be benign.

It must be borne in mind in these discussions that what is really involved is humans bringing various forces to bear upon themselves. It is always by <u>humans</u>, whether as individuals (including as office-holders), or as groups or organizations that the tune is called. There are other determining forces at work on human beings, of course — especially facts and mysteries as previously considered. People also work upon themselves, in mysterious and complicated ways — often, indeed in ways of which they are unaware.

Perhaps nowhere more than in this sphere is the complexity, interdependence and interrelatedness of humanity to be seen. In considering tune-calling in broad, it must never be forgotten that it is by people as well as to people that tunes are called. Tunes called by some may be completely alien or repugnant to others — either other tune-callers, or those to whom they call — and who may lack either the option or the wit or the strength to resist. But it is still very different that they are called and bidden by fellow humans rather than by forces that are not in any way of their kin or kind.

What enables some to call the tune? To generalize is dangerous, for there are almost always unique features and factors. Furthermore, there are cases in which a person will be unable to be effective in spite of possessing what would seem the right resources. Again, what will work in one milieu may count for nothing, or very little in another. And yet again, different resources are often required for different kinds of tunes.

There is a basic level at which something like power — often underpinned by material wealth — provides a base for deciding to call a tune. In the first instance, this is more likely to induce compliance to the letter of given instructions than anything far-reaching. It goes further only insofar as compliance becomes a habit, and even so the habit is unlikely to outlast the power that was responsible for its inception. Another source of ability in tune-calling is being recognized as authoritative — though again, this with nothing else is fragile, and needs constant shoring up. It is probably in general over specific pieces of behaviour rather than ways of life more broadly that tune-calling which derives from such sources has sway.

To have at one's command those resources which afford control over people's options would seem a far more profound source of tune-calling capacity. Money, or financial resources generally, can be a source of such a capacity, though only if they are well-employed. 'Well-employed', in this context, means that it is necessary to be doing something which has impact on others. Control over options is a very broad idea, for it includes more than making some things physically possible and others not.

In many spheres, and to a greater extent than is often realized, people's options depend both on their own perceptions about them, and also on what others are doing or find attractive and acceptable. While it is true that all individuals make their own ways of life, few individuals do so with any great independence. A great many people allow the tune to be called to them.

But it must be a tune that is called. Nobody can call the tune if they have no tune to call. Nor can a tune be anything but minimally effective if nobody wants to hear it. Nor can a tune really hold sway unless it somehow manages to get itself into the bones, the heart or the heads of those who go by it. For when it does that, provided it does so on a broad scale, then it may imperceptibly yet irresistibly, if also reluctantly, draw into its ambit some who would rather be free of it.

Plainly, there are great differences between more or less forcing people to comply with a 'tune' which they may find unattractive (paying taxes, obeying speed limits), offering something which people readily grasp hold of and make their own, and drawing people into some ambit whether happily, resignedly, or even against their better judgement. This reveals the importance of presentation in connection with tune-calling. Good tunes may catch on no matter how badly presented, and the strongest uses of power may exact compliance no matter how nastily presented. But in between, where fall most of the tunes by which humans go, the presentation is hardly less important than either the calibre of the tune itself or the backing by which it is supported. There is need for drive, for bringing the tune to the forefront, for ensuring appropriate impact.

How far all of this can be calculated and contrived is a difficult, moot point. It is doubtful whether presentation can be separated completely from the character of the tune itself — although some advertisers have at least short-term success with completely false or inappropriate pretences. Furthermore, advertisers as such can find a role only in a milieu of mass-media. But in such a milieu, tune-callers must either be their own advertisers or else employ one: and if they are employing one, they need the judgment to pick the right one.

What then are the characteristics of tune-callers? And is there a quality that is common to them? Both these questions call for a negative answer if tune-calling itself is comprehended sufficiently broadly. For its variety is too great for stereotypes about 'rulers' to be appropriate. Of course, if one is thinking exclusively of those who operate by power, those who impose their tunes, then it would perhaps be possible to isolate characteristics such as strength and determination, intransigence and an unwillingness to be distracted, decisiveness and the habit of using others, as characteristic of the tune-caller. We may almost say that a certain kind of ruthless determination is a necessity in all tune-callers apart from those of genius — ruthlessness, determination, and a wholly businesslike approach. All this is required because of the competitive nature of tune-calling, i.e. because there are always more people making a bid to call their tune than there is space for tunes to be heard. But that said, it must be added that these characteristics are all exceedingly general and may take a variety of forms. Furthermore, that which enables people to become tune-callers may bear little relationship to the kinds of tunes they call. Again, some people seem to become elevated, by virtue of a type of prominence which they possess or attain, into professional tune-callers — and they are then respected as such even when they have nothing more to offer. They typically become a type of 'front-person' at that stage. And as such they tend to be peculiarly irresponsible kinds of brokers of tunes unless they happen to fall into someone else's grip.

Tunes are called not only by individuals. Indeed, in the increasing complexity of society it is perhaps more likely that they will emanate from organizations and institutions. This is particularly true of those tunes which really have to be called, as distinct from those with their own power to catch on. There is probably no way of snuffing out completely the impact of greatness or genius in the occasional individual: no way in which the seminal idea, the profound perception of the direction things are taking, can be completely absorbed into the toils of some machinery. And yet the human world is increasingly an organized world, one in which there really is far too much to cope with, too much on the go, too much to absorb and accommodate.

This explains why tunes are so apt to be called by institutions rather than by individuals, by organizations (or by individuals with an organization behind them), by groups that are organized rather than those that are loose and unstructured — and then, in turn, by organizations that know what they are about, which not only have something to push, and which not only wish to push, but which are organized to push. The generality of people may be imbued with a kind of conservative lethargy or resistance, but they also grow weary. Individual tune-callers may be sufficiently underlaid with sensitivity to decline to go all out in pushing their tune when it does not make its way easily or suffers setbacks. And people being called by an individual may react adversely, and resist simply because the caller is no more than an individual such as they are themselves. But the picture can change quite drastically when there is an organization which will not grow weary unless it is carefully sabotaged or weakened (an activity which itself calls for a considerable degree of organization), when the push does not let up, when every step is but an encouragement to a further step rather than something on which one may pause, when there are images of the superhuman and of infallibility being purveyed.

Organization *per se* in fact puts a different face on human relationships. Face-to-face, person-to-person contact is distinctly sobering. And the perspective, the proportion of such a relationship may almost be said to be written plainly upon its face, to be virtually unmistakeable. Certainly it is apparent in such transactions – the more so as the going becomes tougher — that the matters at stake are human beings and their lives, not mere blueprints or ideas or gains. But organization removes all sympathy, all feeling, all sense that people as distinct from mere matter are involved — all sense that the game is not just a game, but is for real. Part of the strength of organization lies in this very quality of being detached, although much also lies in the fact that organization means that nothing is left to chance, that nothing is overlooked, that matters receive the attention they require rather than simply what one might feel like giving them. Organization defines the labour to be undertaken, and divides up the functions to be performed.

All this enables organizations to be extremely effective in tune-calling. Organization may be said to mechanize the ordering of human life, to go solely by its own lights, to be able to disregard everything it regards as extraneous. And when organization is brought to the provision of services that humans need — or when it is brought to the aid of selling services that can seem attractive — it can place itself in something very like an impregnable position. Few if any of the natural constraints that limit individuals in imposing themselves on others apply to organizations. So the very effectiveness of organization may be regarded as one of its most dangerous features — even though it is a feature which can also make for enormous advancement in human affairs.

Most organizations are in a sense artificial — which means not merely that they are made by humans, but that they essentially continue in being as a result of being propped up. They depend less, in a way, on their own structure (although that can be made strong) than upon the functions which they perform or which are given to them. Further, they are dependent upon, and for the most part derivative from, the work done by their agents — even though the totality of such work may add up to something considerably more coherent than anyone directly involved might realize.

It is arguable, however, that some institutions are to a substantial extent natural, that they can hardly be avoided, if at all, in the human world. Among these, perhaps pre-eminent among them, stand the family and the state, and possibly some ecclesiastical establishments. These institutions can assume an enormous number of forms, some of them radically inconsistent with others.

The family presumably admits of the fewest variations, and each family presumably has direct impact on fewer people than any other institution — and yet the impact of families (and thus of the family, presuming that some degree of generalization is possible) is profound. This is tune-calling at its gentlest yet most insistent, at its strongest yet most unpredictable.

The state calls stridently, by contrast — and while something more is said about it later, its calls must needs be very substantially adapted to the tunes the society is already hearing, and those it wants to hear. By contrast, the call of ecclesiastics can become plaintive when their tune is not much liked: they are perhaps less adaptable than any other tune-callers, and must either be capable of surviving spells in the wilderness, or else fade away completely. In that eventuality, others may rise in their place, unlikely contenders often enough.

While many tunes may seem to be called by 'forces' of one kind or another rather than by individuals, and while individual tune-callers vary, we may nevertheless ask the question of the qualities that deciders or tune-callers should possess. In doing this, we would likely find ourselves viewing institutions and organizations anthropomorphically. To a degree, the qualities we would seek must depend largely on the sphere in which the tune calls. Nevertheless, the presiding desirable quality is surely quite unmistakeable, no matter how unlikely it is to be present. And this is that tune-callers should never cease to be alive to their high office in human affairs — that they are, even if at the same time making their own ways of life, having a quite profound impact upon the way in which others make their lives. This factor need not be unduly at the forefront of their minds, especially if they are creative deciders, for then it could turn them into do-gooders and even destroy them. But when those who are doing their own thing and making their own way are also calling a tune, one wants them to take into account that they have an impact upon others. The name for this is 'acting responsibly'.

Apart from this, it is easier to articulate the undesirable than the desirable qualities. The greatest danger is when tune-callers gather some influence and become too big for their boots: when they extend their influence because they like dominance, or because they attain a position of being able to do what they like with their subjects. Those who will brook no opposition are dangerous, as are those who think they know what is good for others.

The worst thing is tune-calling for its own sake. For necessary as it is in itself, tune-calling always has a compelling aspect that is antithetical to the very idea of the human world. There is always an element of making common moulds and putting people into them — and thus tending to make those who are put into the moulds something less than they might be.

Tune-calling exists across the whole range of human life. One of the great difficulties in writing this chapter is to treat together and keep in proper proportion the extraordinary diversity of human influences. For not merely do governments or technologists or industrialists call the tune: so do artists, so do teachers and parents, so do inventors, so do trend-setters, so do thinkers and musicians.

This is not to say that everyone calls the tune in some limited respect, although there would be some truth in that. But it clearly is to say that the breadth and extent of tune-calling is far more extensive, far more diverse, far more many-sided than can easily be comprehended. The interplay of social causation and social determination is fantastically elaborate, and fantastically complex.

So complex indeed, that there is something decidedly odd about trying to isolate the relative importance of various tune-callers and deciders. Do the artists or the statesman have the greater impact, the thinkers or the advertisers, the machine-makers or the opinion-leaders? To pose these questions is to reveal their inadequacy. For apart from the fact that their relative importance would vary with time and circumstance, there is the vastly more telling point that what is worth knowing is the impact that each of them has. In this respect, the proper approach is not to start with the tune-callers and see what they do to people, but to start with people. And this is the reason why this chapter comes before the next one — why, even though this chapter says something about the impact of tune-calling on human beings, the broadest and most comprehensive perspective on tune-calling and social causation is seen in the discussion of people in the next chapter.

There are other aspects of tune-calling to be considered. This is the point at which to consider how far it should be private and how far public — how far publicly or privately controlled, how far in public or private hands. The distinction between private and public tends to collapse — or be transformed — as the so-called public realm is expanded. For it then invariably becomes a clique, which increasingly determines its own membership, admits whom it will from outside, and swiftly becomes accountable to no-one. But the distinction can serve its turn even though it is not systematic. There are some kinds of tune-calling, such as that of artists and musicians, which cannot be collectively or collegially practised, even though it may be possible for public entrepreneurs and financiers to have some impact on the marketing of the tunes.

The point on which there is room for controversy concerns private control of those material resources (and to some extent of access to position and status) which can provide a base for tune-calling. It can hardly be doubted, for example, that there would be something unsatisfactory about a system in which a private person had a monopoly on some particular resource (such as steel) and prevented anyone but their own manufacturing companies from using steel. But it can be seen at once that it would be equally unsatisfactory for the state to have the same monopoly and to use it in the same way.

Public control does not of itself imply that tune-calling will do more to advance or enhance the human world, more to enable people to make their own ways of life without undue impediment or difficulty. On the contrary, indeed, it is often far more difficult to gain access to what one might want, to buck the system, to evade the tune, when one comes up against public rather than private tune-calling. And indeed, a private law-making and law-enforcing system — even this — would, if fair, surely be superior to a public one which was corrupt and unfair. It is just that private ones never are fair, whereas public ones often try to be and have some success.[37]

In this sphere, then, it is hardly appropriate to consider what is best or right in the abstract. What should really be considered is what control of which resources is most likely to result in the calling of tunes which people will want to hear. Which are best adapted to — and will take further — practices which have already begun to grow but require development? Which are most conducive to the calling of tunes which are not too domineering or too exclusive or ill-adapted to the ways of life of the society, of the groups within it, or of its individual members?

It is also important to consider what can be done if things

turn sour: the question of having some recourse. For it is tune-callers above all who may need to be controlled. This matter is considered further in the discussion of government. But before moving on, it is right to note that the need for control is a different notion from that of being accountable: tune-callers who really are accountable are so vulnerable that any creative spirit in them must be seen as greatly at risk.

A good deal of tune-calling is covert rather than overt - and in general, tune-calling goes unnoticed to an enormous extent. 'Covert' need not mean deliberately shrouded in secrecy, but simply that it happens without fanfare. Of course there are always backroom operators, and those who like to pull strings simply to be in control. But the more general point here is that the tendencies of things, the fashions that take on, the attitudes and feelings that people find themselves assuming, often seep into the system, and often have no single source. There certainly are tune-callers who have no sense that this is what they are. There are tunes called which assume a different pitch from anything that would have been envisaged for them. And some mere melodies unexpectedly turn out to have a most potent call.

All of this is both dangerous and re-assuring. The danger is its unpredictability, which in turn makes for uncontrollability. Humans cannot know, in a sense, from what quarter they may next be seized and dragged along. Something deleterious that might seem to have been controlled may break out again from a fresh quarter.

By the same token, a set of controls that might have seemed perfectly satisfactory might collapse or prove impotent in the face of some new type of tune-calling. This is reassuring in that it guarantees that tune-callers cannot rest on their laurels, in that it provides some hope for those who wish for but cannot discover or construct any new points of departure in tune-calling, and in that it means that those who control the controls on tune-calling do not have that aspect of society by the throat in perpetuity. In short, it is the guarantee of the only kind of development or renewal that is worth the name, i.e. something which is not deliberately and consciously contrived from within the existing framework.

Deciders are not wholly their own bosses, especially those who are consciously calling tunes. They are dependent on other tune-callers, on people with power, and in a way supremely on the people whom they have the power to call. For the fact is that unless the people called in fact follow, the deciders' power is nought. In some measure, those called may have a power or capability to resist, to find alternative ways, or to rebel. Accidental tune callers — especially in the arts – who are not actually in the business are the most independent.

These independent ones are their own bosses, and go their own way. There is no guarantee their tunes will catch on. It is not that they call the tune, but that they make a tune which others turn out to follow — even decide to follow, with no pressure to do so. Those thinkers and artists who are in the business of making their reputations, of consciously trying to lead or mould attitudes and beliefs and practices, are of course much less independent. For they must have an eye to trends, to what will appeal and make a hit. But they have no power, especially in the long term, to ensure they will lead the way into the future. To the extent they consciously try to lead, they may actually undermine whatever creativity they possess.

The most independent tune-callers are those with the power to enforce conformity with their decisions, and those with a monopoly on necessities. Limits remain with both. The danger really comes when monopolists call advertising, public relations and manipulation to their aid. The combination of monopoly and manipulation is among the most sinister of exploitations: which has a great capacity to wear down resistance, and which is resistible only by fervour or real coolness. Humanity's best hope in such situations may be that monopolists will fall into error and overplay their hands — and thus bring down some reaction on themselves.

In many societies there is an almost unconscious conspiracy between tune-callers and the generality of people at the expense of minorities. It is perhaps unexceptionable that unprofitable lines get cut out — but people in general suffer when it is troublesome lines that are cut out. The ease and comfort of tune-callers is the worst excuse. Minorities can often do little or nothing to protect their interests — unless they develop a fervency which matters at issue rarely warrant.

Tune-callers have curious relationships to each other. In some respects, they are in competition and arrayed against each other. But they also have much in common, to the extent that they conspire together at the expense of people in general. Collective interests are certainly in many cases opposed to the public interest.

This leads to the question of the extent to which politics enters into non-governmental tune-calling. In general, whenever tune-calling does not involve a genius pointing the way, one wants politics of the best kind to be involved. This ensures that the interests and wishes of those affected are at least consulted. This is something, even if not much, because the preponderant influence likely remains with the tune-callers, especially if their position is monopolistic. The tune-callers are likely to be able to make the politicians their agents rather than independent brokers. Further, when tune-callers turn politician, they are likely to play rough, or turn manipulative.

It is nonetheless valuable for there to be lines of communication, and desirable that those whose fate or desire it is to call the tune should be placed in a situation which requires them to be responsive. The danger of their becoming unduly political — whether for their own good or that of those for whom they call the tune — is probably best coped with as and when it arises. Non-governmental tune-callers seem in general to be excessively free of politics and its constraints.

The fact that tune-callers may be political does not of itself mean they are subject to control. It is plain that enormous problems arise in connection with controlling tune-callers, both governmental and not. The idea that governments should do something to control non-governmental tune-callers is elaborated in the next section, and controls on governments themselves are also considered there.

A general point about balance needs to be noted here. Taking again the supreme case of the arts – of creative genius pointing the way — we must keep in mind that control can be truly monstrous. It has certainly been monstrous historically, as exemplified by the case of Galileo. Those who set themselves to control are so often inept, so blind and ready to pervert the greatest potentialities which human genius has developed.

There is some carry over from this even to the monopolistic tune-caller. There is clearly a good case, granted the way monopolists operate, for breaking monopolies. Yet how should this be done, and who should pay the price for losses in efficiency that may occur? Those who call tunes often do better than they know, better even than they would wish: better for humanity. And those of them who wish to do well are sometimes able to do very well indeed for people at large: better than anyone with eyes set on 'controlling' them would be able to do.

Control for its own sake is in fact more likely to result in gratuitous interference in the affairs of those who are calling good tunes than in effective restraint of those who call limiting or pernicious tunes. Furthermore, insofar as controls are imposed on those who call tunes, it becomes the more likely that they will cease to feel any obligation to be their own guardians, or to act responsibly because of their prominence and position. This is not an argument against controlling controllers. But it is an argument against pettiness and small-mindedness in the devising of controls. The controls themselves must obviously be strong. But they must be viewed as dealing with the strong rather than the weak; there must be bigness about them and the approach behind them if they are to work well.

While there is a place for responsibility in all decision-making that involves tune-calling, the question 'which kinds of considerations should be brought into play in reaching such decisions' obtains little grip with non-governmental decisions. The point here is that such tune-callers are essentially acting on their own behalf. They should, perhaps, take account of certain negative considerations — that this or that would be peculiarly damaging to others. But as soon as they become involved in consulting the best interests of others, they are likely to become interfering nuisances. Their power and position, if they use them in what they regard as the interests of others, will allow them to intrude intolerably. For then the situation of those upon whom they impose themselves becomes less one of making their own way in their own situation, and more something like feudal dependence.

Non-governmental tune-callers are in no sense representative.

Their role is to go their own way, and follow their own lights – not the lights which would seem appropriate from a more general perspective. Here again we see both the dangers and the value of tune-calling. In this non-governmental sphere, tune-calling is not accountable — it cannot be and should not be. It is part of the human world, it has a dynamic impact even though from one perspective it may be or seem stultifying. Without the possibility of it - and thus without it - the greatest stimuli to humans are eliminated. And yet much of it takes little account of people's interests or lives or development. Its benefits can be expected to accrue only contingently — so to gain these, some risk of damage must be accepted.

It is fair to ask whether societies get the tune-callers they deserve. There is certainly a sense in which they get those they want, especially in the non-governmental sphere. For there is the sense, already noted, that the tune can be called in relation to a matter only because or to the extent that the matter is one which people care about or value.

There are needs, of course: people cannot do without food or shelter; but in many respects, when we talk about what people cannot do without we are really dealing with what they want. In this respect, humans allow, and themselves decide upon and determine, those spheres of influence in which tune-calling can become a possibility. We should not be unaware that certain spheres of influence are calculated to draw to themselves certain kinds of tune-callers, who will then proceed to call the tunes that may be expected. But this point does not go very far. There is no basis for saying that societies get what they deserve in tune-calling beyond where it goes.

So what is the scope of tune-calling? What spheres of effectiveness are there? Are there any types of tune to which people are impervious, no matter how insistent the call might be? In the light of a central theme in the foregoing presentation, one major issue that presents itself is whether values can be imposed. A second is whether it is possible to tie matters of indifference to values which are held. The governing point in relation to this whole subject seems to be that there is nothing inherent about humans which sets any limits to the extent to which they may be dominated. People's being on their own, and the indeterminateness which enables them to make their own ways of life, may be seen in this context as a kind of defencelessness.

Humans are not, of their own nature, armed against their fellows. They may be able to arm themselves, and make themselves impervious in certain respects. But then again they may not be able to do this, or not successfully. One is inclined to say in the abstract that the limits of resistance cannot but be coterminous with the limits of domination: which will mean that in practice, everything will depend upon the wit, the resources, the determination, the strength — together with all the other qualities that are relevant — or that may be made relevant — of the protagonists. Furthermore, there seems to be no reason of principle why tune-callers who go for something like total domination need fear that they will reduce their subjects to the mentality of slaves: there may remain, in fact, a very considerable capacity for a kind of genuine if embattled human doing and making. Of course, the total domination of a person does not mean that there is someone with a monopoly on the domination. There may be, although where there is it is perhaps the more likely to come from a source which, while single in one sense, is also multifarious within itself. But perhaps the more fearful kind of domination is that which comes from many quarters, and ends up not only leaving a person with no room for manoeuvre, but also means that in attempting to evade domination from one quarter the subject falls more decidedly into some other kind of domination. While such people may retain some capacity for human doing and making, they can hardly be said to be making or doing for themselves — they are precluded from making their own ways of life and their condition of being on their own is deprived of all nobility.

2. The Role Of Government

The place of government is one of supremacy and superiority among tune-callers. This should not be taken to mean, however, that governments always are in fact supreme, or always superior. One great indicator that supremacy and superiority is their place is the universal admission that it is the lot of the government to lead. What leadership amounts to is something we shall come to, although it certainly does not mean sovereignty, i.e. does not mean total control. No other tune-caller ever has the role of leadership normally attributed to government, even though a great many tune-callers may be regarded as legitimate, and even though it may be thought proper that some of them should be prominent and have major impact. Even such tune-callers themselves would not say it is their function to <u>lead</u>, even though they might maintain that they should take a leading role. Further, those who wish to minimize the functions of government do not thereby say that it should not lead, much less that something else should: they are rather commenting on the way in which governments should lead. These points — begging for the moment some questions about what a government is, and also about what governing and governance are and involve – are taken up later in dealing with what governments can and should do, and considering forms of government.

In exploring the notion of leadership, it is appropriate to take account of the fact that 'the people' will always be divided, and etched with conflicting interests. Does this mean it is incoherent to want government to be non-sectional and dispassionate? The answer is that it is the role of government to take account of all (or at least not to overlook any) of the elements of the society over which it presides. This does not mean that a government can be all things to every group or individual within the society. For that is impossible, and to attempt to make it seem possible sets up a kind of trade in delusions. Nor does it mean that no government is ever entitled to decide against some person or group. In fact, it means nothing very precise because it is more a matter of the perspective from which governments should act, of the comprehending approach which they should adopt, of the attitude of mind which should be engendered in them.

The contrast between governments and other tune-callers helps make this clear. Other tune-callers need give no consideration to minorities - or majorities even: they need simply go their ways, acting in the light of those considerations that are pertinent to their own concerns. Governments, however, must in some way consult and take account of considerations which are pertinent to all concerns. Further, governments cannot go about the business of calling those tunes which they think appropriate, while regarding themselves as one tune-caller among others. They must also adopt a kind of supervisory role in the whole tune-calling business. They must call tunes for other tune-callers as well as for societal groups and individuals.

To say that leaders must be dispassionate and non-sectional, and that they should take account of considerations relevant to all concerns, gives little guidance in relation to the question of what leadership amounts to concretely. The problem posed by this consideration appears the more acute because there is some tension between tune-calling leadership and it being up to people — individuals and groups — to make their own ways of life. There is a sense in which it is not possible to give much positive guidance on this question of what governmental leadership means concretely. There seem, for example, to be no useful general principles which could tell a government, faced by a conflict between economic and egalitarian considerations, which it should follow.

In this question may be seen the profound limitations which beset public servants as governors. The treasury, for example, may be presumed good at deciding what should be done in the light of the economic considerations: but at least from a professional point of view, it is completely incompetent to decide whether it is appropriate to go by the economic considerations. The statesman is the person who is needed to make such decisions. But how are we to say what qualifies statesmen to do so, or what is to lead them to their decisions? Some of those in government believe in and possibly use overarching principles — concrete ideals or ideologies from which they deduce in some fashion what to do. But any such principles are certainly antithetical to the central theme of this work that it is for people to make their own ways of life.

The clue to the problem lies in this very theme. It is a hope rather than a principle. And it cannot be made a principle, certainly not one from which governments could deduce what to do, or even how to proceed. But as a theme, it suggests an analogy — which is time-honoured if often perverted — with the activity of being a parent. This has nothing to do with paternalism as generally understood, nothing to do with being patronizing, or squeezing into moulds, or imposing values, or taking the decisions of others out of their own hands, but a great deal to do with some very different ideas. In fact, it has as little to do with paternalism in this sense as do modern ideas about parenthood. Parents know best, no doubt, in certain matters. But to think they know best in relation to their children's way of life, for example, is for them to impute to themselves a knowledge of a future which they will never even experience. The role of the parent does involve the provision of protection against dangers of which the child may be totally unaware — as does that of government: although even here the parent needs to beware of being overprotective. Again, the parents must provide for the child — food of course, but teaching and training as well — yet only up to a point; and certainly not beyond the point where what they may have to offer turns into a kind of bandage. The role of the parent — the leading role — is surely to lead the child (no matter how old the child may be) to become himself or herself. To assist, to provide resources and opportunities, to point out — and possibly ferret out — possibilities and potentialities. In certain respects, it may be seen as the responsibility of the parent to detect what the child is really on about even though the child may not himself or herself be aware — and while this pursuit is fraught with extraordinary difficulties, and while it should probably be undertaken in a very low key and with the minimum disturbance to the other potentialities that may be present and may possibly turn out to be the 'right' ones, it cannot properly be evaded. Parenthood — thinking of the situation where there is more than one child — also involves the kind of dispassionateness that seems appropriate to governments — although it is again impossible to generalize about what it should amount to concretely.

This analogy is useful, not only because of its direct relevance (which may be contested), but also because it places government in the camp of those kinds of activities which can hardly be regarded as reducible to exact sciences — and which it is possible to dispute about — dispute in the sense that there is room for substantial disagreement and difference of opinion about the way in which the activity should be undertaken.

If the notion of the leadership of government is viewed from the perspective afforded by this analogy, several stereotypes get cut across. For example, government may be seen as in some sense leading from both in front and behind, although neither of these notions hits the nail perfectly on the head. Again, good government leadership is quite unlike good military leadership — more subdued, though not wholly cooperative, not collegial either – in short, not this, not that, but itself, a very distinct and at the same time exceedingly variable phenomenon.

It is a leadership that need not be too pressing, that need not always involve tune-calling (and certainly not always that of the enforceable kind). Particularly in times of difficulty, it is likely to call for a kind of inspirational or visionary approach which could seldom be appropriate in parenthood — and because of its scale, it is not unlikely that it will become overlaid with irrelevant vanity and pretension in the persons of those who provide it. All of which reinforces the point that while the analogy with parenthood gives some vital clues to the proper perception of governmental leadership, it is still necessary to view and conceive of it in its own terms, i.e. as unique. It is certainly clear that other tune-callers are in no sense engaged in a kind of leadership that comes anywhere near it.

Leadership conceived along such lines is highly compatible with the idea of humans as makers of their own ways of life. It also moderates an extreme conception of what is involved in allowing that humans are on their own. In particular, it reveals a number of the ways in which this condition is not one of isolation, or solitude, or aloneness. None of this is especially surprising, for it is partly because of the ideas of humans as on their own and as makers of ways of life that this conception of governmental leadership is appropriate.

This conception of the role of government, while not extending to the functions of government, does lead easily into a discussion of the kinds of qualities to be sought in governments. This concern is with desirable qualities, although it is difficult to generalize because of the variety of circumstances and needs — and in the light of the foregoing discussion it is difficult to evade the idea that perceptiveness is the fundamental quality. Much else needs to go with it. But insofar as governments do call tunes, they must surely above all be alive to what their peoples are on about.

Perceptiveness calls for much more than good communications — it requires something more like prevision. This is always a dangerous quality in practice, for in its mere appearance it can become unduly self-confident; and individuals may easily mistake their own visions for those of others. But unless a government can take account of what is becoming, then the society is bound either to get at odds with itself or else to bog itself down. One key thing about this quality is that it can pretend to genuineness only where it is rather unassuming.

The impulse to play God becomes almost irresistible, but must above all be resisted. For nobody can read the future of others (even of groups of which they are themselves members) solely out of themselves. It is a matter of ear to the ground, feel for the winds, and eye on the horizon. The greatness of spirit that it requires is quite distinct from the delusions of vision which we may in fact have to put up with in our governments.

Along with perceptiveness — and often uneasily allied with it — there are the obvious qualities of strength and determination, efficiency, good management and the like. A government obviously needs the capacity to choose the right functionaries, to strike the right note, to be persuasive. It must be able to look after the administrative side of its job. In crises, as already noted, it may need inspirational qualities, just as in all situations (no matter how perceptive it may be) it needs to be flexible and adaptive. It must be profoundly realistic. It must not make unattainable demands, nor push policies because of their purity and rightness if they will in fact result in any extremes that are less than the best attainable.

Governments must be profoundly alive to the realities, the possibilities and the potentialities of real situations. They must be able to balance carrot and stick and all other inducements. They must have an eye that can never be shifted from the main point (and which invariably picks the main point) while at the same time being aware of and alive to prejudices and minutiae that matter to people. All this is very demanding indeed: yet it also calls almost for a kind of 'common sense' ordinariness - certainly not for high-flying genius or brilliance in their usual senses.

If the role of government is viewed as analogous to that of parents, it is difficult to resist asking whether we get the governments we deserve. The question is itself perhaps hardly less paradoxical than whether governments get the people they deserve. Yet there is an element of mutuality, of interaction - particularly at the level of quality of life. It sometimes happens that pig-headed governments somehow come to power, and that they cannot be dislodged - whether because of their own cunning, or because they really do make a society bow down or even give up for a time. The inertia of governments in office should certainly not be underestimated, nor their capacity for ensuring their own survival.

But there is an important truth in saying that a people can bring out the best - or the worst - in its government, just as a government can do in its people. Tune-calling does not, as has been discussed, go all one way. A people that simply submits itself gives no help, no encouragement, no stimulus to its government. Nor does it do itself any good, for such submission involves letting a great deal of potentiality slip. Of course the means by which societies can keep their governments on their toes and up to the mark are difficult to pin down — the thing itself probably happens more as a by-product of a general aliveness in the society at large than because of any deliberate moves. In this general connection there is a most interesting issue about minorities and ginger groups. For it is unlikely that society as a whole will ever be sufficiently alive and vibrant to keep its government up to the mark. There is a need for those who are the salt of the earth to be at work. But distinctly sectional minorities, particularly where they have been mobilised for some particular purposes, can easily come to play a disproportionate role in moving government in particular directions which may run contrary to what would seem appropriate from a truly dispassionate perspective.

Thus we are led to the question of what governments need to do, and what they should do. To an enormous extent, any tolerably cohesive answer depends on what else — everything else, almost! — is going on in the society at large, and particularly on what other tune-callers are up to.

There is plainly a protective role for government, and also an enabling role. In the sphere of enabling, the crucial point of departure is the presumption that neither groups nor individuals nor other tune-callers will provide all the opportunities, the options, the possibilities, or the perspectives which are to be desired. There is no agency apart from government which has the comprehensive and comprehending sense, or grasp, or capability to undertake this role.

This is not to say that governments should attempt to monopolise the field. Indeed, it is arguable that it would be preferable for governments to encourage others to provide what needs providing rather than attempt to do it themselves. But governments, granted their <u>leading</u> role, should surely make it their business to perceive shortcomings and look ahead, and thus to open and keep open those doors through which people may wish to pass in making their ways of life. At the same time there must be restraint; for the provision of opportunities is always a costly business, and it is no less vital that opportunities be provided than that people are not stripped of the capacity to take them. This is why foresight is so crucial in government: the task of government is not to open doors which people <u>might</u> wish to go through, or even which they may <u>contemplate</u> going through, but more importantly those which they actually <u>will</u> choose go through (although governments may also have some role in inducing them to want to go through these doors, while not manipulating them this way). The balance in all this is plainly very delicate indeed, calling for great perceptiveness and sensibility.

The protective role of government is in a sense more fundamental. People must be protected against other people, and within limits against themselves; against machinery, against institutions, against organizations, against other tune-callers, and certainly against government itself.

The key point of departure for making progress with the ancient and intractable problem of 'how much protection' lies in the two big ideas — first that humans must not be removed from the condition of being on their own, and secondly that they must not be prevented from making their own ways of life. There is no reason to think that there is any better guide to the point at which interaction between people changes into interference with them (and thus calls for government protection) than is afforded by these ideas.

The question of interference and thus of the possible appropriateness of protection arises initially at the point where persons are impeded in the making of their ways of life, or where their being on their own is subverted. Thus can be seen how a kind of relativity arises: for what would be interaction between some people (granted the ways of life they were making) would become interferences if it was a different way of life that was being made. But it is one thing to say there is interference, such that one party in a conflict must be restrained that the other may be protected. It is often quite another thing to say which party should be restrained and which needs protection. There is probably a presumption that the offended party, the one run across rather than the one running, should be protected: but this distinction is often not easy to draw, when both parties are involved in the making of ways of life. So governments are sometimes required to balance judgements about how integral conflicting aspects are to different ways of life.

For governments to set about protecting individuals against themselves certainly smells paternalistic. For most people, some licence must surely be granted. It is not just a question of the law helping individuals to keep a check on destructive impulses which may arise from time to time and which they could probably keep in check on their own account anyway. Nor is it just a case of playing a role in bringing the young to maturity, or caring for those who remain perpetually green. It is more tied up with the continuity, the ongoing nature of human societies and of the human world in general. What it is essentially to do with is that many people are neither good at, nor interested in taking account of the longer term. What governments need to do — granted the certainty that many people will be imprudent in this regard — is somehow to protect them. This necessitates government taking steps to ensure that such people will not end up wholly without resources and incapable of continuing to make their own ways of life when the zest and adaptability of youth will have gone, and when needs and desires have assumed different complexions and proportions.

Providing protection against other tune-callers — including all other organizations, institutions and the like — is a fundamental role for government. This role is far-reaching and fascinating, demanding and dangerous. But if one thing is absolutely clear, it is that the human world can hardly be more at risk than it is when government is in the pockets of the other power-holders and power centres in a society — when government becomes their creature and their agent. For humans (especially individuals) are then without recourse. It is because these other power-holders and power centres call tunes to people at large while being essentially concerned with themselves rather than those they call to that there is need for such restraint. The interaction between them and those they call is altogether one-sided. The balance will need redress. They may sometimes need to be called off. To some degree, government need not play God in deciding where to intervene because those called by other tune-callers may themselves appeal to government for protection. There is probably some presumption that government should side with those who are weaker when this happens. Yet this presumption is not absolute, and a government still has to make up its mind where the balance lies, and where it should step in. This is even more so in cases where no appeal is made because those who should be appealing have been seduced. A government must then consult its own judgement. And even though it may be able to act in such a way as to weakens the strength of the call rather than alter the tune — and thus enable people to make their own choices — its decisions are hardly any easier than in any other cases of stepping in to protect some against others.

In order to take on, and thus restrain or control other tune-callers, governments plainly need not only power, but also integrity and independence. Without the power, they will be unable to stand up to other tune-callers: they will not be able to stop what should be stopped. For the resourcefulness of private tune-callers, especially when attempts are made to back them into corners and weaken them, can scarcely be overestimated. And people can hardly ever be persuaded to give over their power — it must be taken against their resistance. It is especially because one form of resistance is to attempt to attack or take over the government itself that governments are in particular need of integrity and independence in this regard. They must be willing as well as able to stand apart, they must simply not entertain offers and blandishments which may be held out to them.

But neither must governments be too self-righteous or self-important. For insofar as their integrity goes in that direction, insofar as they come to think of themselves as really being the arbiters, their power makes them supremely dangerous. For if they stand above other tune-callers in power, and at the same time grow to regard their own position as authoritative because it is they who are calling the tune, then they themselves need to be restrained — and it is difficult to see where such restraint can come from.

There is no possibility of devising a structure containing some element — some institution — which provides a remedy for the difficulty that arises here. And there is no way of guaranteeing that governments will not become too big for their boots, although some systems — such as certain electoral ones — can help make it less likely. The best kind of remedy — or chance of remedy — is to have and maintain a loose and open social and governmental structure. It is in taut and rigid systems that superior agencies are able to elevate themselves irresistibly and within limits permanently. Where there is some looseness and openness, then moves are likely to lead to countermoves which may redress the balance. Balance is all in all, or almost that, in this matter. And it is not just a kind of theoretically contrived balance between the designated powers of formal institutions which is required. It is rather a balance which permeates the society as a whole, and thus one which can probably only develop over time. For it is not only a matter of power in the pure sense, but also of attitudes and ways of reacting, of capabilities and resources that are both entrenched and hidden, and also imbued with an inherent dynamism. Whether it exists, whether it can be brought into existence, and whether it can be sustained — all of this may be said to be a matter of fact, for the contributing influences to it must plainly be manifold. But at a deeper level we see that it depends on people: on what individuals do and think, on the ways in which groups function, on the behaviour of institutions, on the kinds of relationships which those groups of people we call societies construct for themselves.

All talk of what governments need to do and be is in a profound way one-sided. For it is not always open to governments to be in command of themselves, to act at their own behests, in the way that such talk presupposes. We must ask not only what governments do, what they can do, what they should do. We must also consider what governments in fact have to cope with, and what it falls to their lot to attend to. Governments cannot precisely define their own role. It is artificial to suppose that any abstract decision can be made by anyone about what it is their business to deal with. For matters arise which governments can turn their backs upon only with disastrous consequences. This is not to say that every difficult issue should be passed on to the government to deal with. But it is to say that some issues do arise which cannot but be referred to government in the end.

For example, all efforts might be made, by government and society together, to make and encourage people and groups to be self-sufficient, to be able to deal with their own business. But there can be no way of providing against some natural disaster which may occur. No matter what preparations and provisions may have been made, the magnitude of such eventualities may make it incumbent on a government to act.

But matters for governments to cope with arise not only from outside the human world, not even only from outside the particular society (prime examples of this are imperialism and war). There can be some control of what can arise from within a society, even if not much except over the pace at which large and major new eventualities loom upon the scene to take their place. One could instance among such factors industrialism and unionism, technology and communications, international production, and the assertiveness of youth. These things happen, and that is what matters. Whether one approves or disapproves is largely immaterial. And governments must respond to such happenings. For they are so momentous in their impact that for governments to do nothing is to do something, i.e. to sit by and allow transformations to take place without any consideration being given to their appropriateness or desirability.

A major aspect of such phenomena is that they are new: so governments must not only do something about them, but must cope in the sense of having to work out what to do without there being anything much to learn from previous experience. There is no necessary harm in there being a need for governments to experiment and make shift: indeed, the need to do so is a good antidote for unduly fixed routines. But granted that governments are freed to feel their way, it clearly would be foolish to expect too much of them, to imagine that they should never go wrong or make mistakes. Here we find humans as government being on their own.

In considering the kind of performance we may expect from governments, it must be kept in mind that they have to cope with intransigent attitudes, with non-cooperative stances, with entrenched forces, with pig-headed resistance, with passionate enthusiasm, with muddled determination, with doctrinaire principles, with ignorance, with unimaginativeness, and all other such shortcomings as are found amongst human beings when they are gathered together. These shortcomings exist in human societies, and they must be taken into account in practice. To cleave a way through them, or to ignore them, may be possible on paper but never in practice. When we consider that governments are always up against all this, we may be less inclined to judge their performance too harshly. Further, governments are themselves but humans, so we must expect that they will themselves be riddled with such shortcomings, whose deleterious effects may be compounded by the necessity for governments to act, to reach decisions.

In short, it is a great error to dream that the best attainable performance of governments could possibly not be open to substantial criticism.

It is also important to recognize that government is a comparatively blunt instrument. It can distinguish classes of case with considerable precision. But it cannot effectively distinguish cases. It operates at a level of generality which does not easily cater to the needs or aspirations particularly of individuals. And when it tries to cater for individuals, it falls easily into the trap of arbitrariness.

Government lacks a degree of sensitivity by its very nature. It can restrain individuals, and what it does can be beneficial to individuals. But governments cannot, of their nature, ensure either that these restraints are appropriate to individual cases, or that these benefits are real for individual cases. Furthermore, governments are limited in their impact, at least directly or immediately, to overt behaviour rather than to the attitudes or aspirations or even the policies of individuals or groups — or other tune-callers. And where governments attempt to transform attitudes and the like, they can hardly but become a profound threat to humanity – especially individual people — almost as such. Certainly the combination of their power and their bluntness suggests the likelihood of an insensitive handling of aspects of human life that surely need extremely careful handling. It is partly because this seems inescapable that it is difficult to resist the view that for government to tamper in this field is an unduly dangerous assault upon people as beings who are on their own.

This begins to say something about the proper limits of government. Thus it may be said that government should not venture into areas which call for greater sensitivity than it is capable of; that government should respect the condition of people as being on their own; that if an attempt by government to do something for people is bound to prove fruitless or be damaging to people, then the attempt should not be made; and that it is damaging to people to have their integrity assaulted, or (other things being equal) to have impediments placed in the way of their making their own ways of life.

Yet there is something artificial about attempts to elicit general principles about the proper limits of government, or to make general statements about presumptions that governments either should or should not intervene unless something or other is present. The only presumptions that seem useful or appropriate are that governments should come in when they need to, or when the indications are that they would be able to do something positively to facilitate people's attempts to make their own ways of life. And if it is asked 'who is to be the judge of when such occasions arise', the answer in the end must be the government itself — if only because the power to make such a decision, even though it may be invested in some institution which is separate from those which make and administer governmental policy, is essentially of a governmental kind.

But saying that the decision in the end lies with government does not mean that there is nothing else to the matter. For the government should obviously consult and test the water — and when it goes wrong, or intervenes when it had better have abstained, then a vibrant and vigorous citizenry should be able to make that fact plain soon enough — or at least not too late. Hard and fast rules are certain to hamstring a government, and hardly necessary where liveliness abounds. And where it does not, the rules are not only likely to be ineffective with respect to the government, but also to deaden further the absence of liveliness.

In deciding whether to act and what to do, the great consideration for government to take into account is what it can do for people — for both individuals and groups, and preferably to the detriment of no-one. This must not merely be an attitude, for it then cannot but degenerate into a form of do-goodism. The thinking within government must be developed in such a way that it takes account of and becomes related to the influences that are at work in society; to developments that can be capitalized upon; to potentialities that may be grasped, and to desires that can be brought within reach. The underlying attitude that is crucial is that level of dispassionateness and that commitment to non-sectionalism that has been stressed throughout this discussion. In considering what they can do for people, governments must always have their eye on people as makers of ways of life. It is not to bolster the weak if they will not go on to anything that governments should intervene, nor to restrain the energetic because they are diverging too far from the mainstream. The consideration which governments must take account of, then, is not one which itself says what should be done, but one which forms the foundation and guides the construction of policies of action.

In reaching their decisions, in going by relevant considerations, and in practising dispassionateness, governments need to be independent of other tune-callers. For these others are not dispassionate in anything like that sense, nor should they be. It is virtually unimaginable that they will not, given the chance, attempt to foist their own sectional perspectives and problems upon government.

But it is much easier to say that governments should be independent than to ensure that they can be or that they are. The difficulty that arises here is not due only to the pressures that other tune-callers may be able to exert on governments, great though these may be. The further difficulty is that insofar as government is not the only tune-caller, it must to some extent be in harmony with those other tunes that are being called. Unless it takes account of them, it is ignoring some major factors which will bedevil its own aims. But as soon as it does take account of them — adapt to them, and to a degree harmonize — it becomes unavoidably caught up with a kind of sectionalism. There is no way of getting completely around the problems and dilemmas posed in this connection — except for the worst solution, namely that government monopolizes tune-calling. All that can be done for the best is that the government should give the fullest possible attention to maintaining dispassionateness, and that groups and individuals themselves apply a countervailing pressure to governments in order to help neutralize the sectional impact which may come upon them from other tune-callers.

It can be expected — or hoped — that governments should be assisted in this problematic area by politics, and by the political training that government personnel will often themselves have had. There are dangers in this: insofar as there are temptations to do deals with those who are strong or insistent. A political background might unquestionably enable the members of a government to find plausible alternatives to dispassionateness. But equally can it assist them to be as dispassionate as possible, both by calling upon their own political experience and by making use of political brokerage to the most extensive and comprehensive extent.

Governments themselves can play a major role in ensuring that politics is well done — especially insofar as government members tend to be past masters of the political art. Further, insofar as their own tune-calling role requires a fair measure of political consultation, they are bound to be in a position to judge how well politics are being conducted. And insofar as they can maintain a level of detached dispassionateness, they can possibly call the tune a little to the politicians in order to ensure that their own best efforts at tune-calling are not sabotaged or derogated from either in their conception or their reception.

Governmental tune-calling — unlike other kinds — is in fact, at its best, tremendously dependent on effective politics. It is not merely that governments are not gods, but more importantly that governmental decisions need to be such that they can find acceptance as well as compliance. While governments should be held in esteem, it helps no-one if they are held in awe or regarded with fear. If the members of a society have a negative attitude to their government, much of the good of which government is capable is likely to be soured or lost. More than this, not only is the difficulty of deciding what to do nowhere greater than for governments, but the fact is that great assistance, advice and even guidance can come to them from politicians.

It is important, in considering the role of government, not to overstress its personal aspect. A government is not just any group of people with some power, but is that group of people which occupies the offices of state within a society. Government is a machine which people have made as well as a group of mere mortals doing a job. Thus it must be borne in mind that there are institutional as well as purely human dimensions to the *modus operandi* of a government. There is — or should be — interaction between the institutions and their occupiers, between offices and office-holders. One expects that the institutions, acting purely as institutions, would be impersonal, without much human sympathy or warmth, and probably a bit rule-bound and inflexible. Whereas one might expect that the office-holders as people might be understanding of difficulties, might be able to distinguish rightly between human differences, might be willing to bend a little where bending will do no harm and may do some good — might, in short, be ready to display something of what would seem from an institutional point of view to be the weakness of human warmth.

In the conception of the functions of governments which has been developed in the foregoing paragraphs, it seems that interaction between, as well as the combination of, the institutional and the human sides of government is calculated to have beneficial effects. It is essential, as a foundation, that the institutions be constructed in such a way as to lead easily to the right decisions — that they should facilitate appropriate consultation, that they should be endowed with suitable powers, that they should be attractive to the right sorts of people. But this foundation is never enough: the very rule-boundness of purely institutional functioning, by itself, inevitably allows for unsatisfactory decisions on the one hand and for evasion of the proper or right decisions on the other. To counter this, there need to be the human qualities of perceptiveness, adaptability, flexibility: office-holders need to bring their own human capacities into play to ensure that the decisions made do take proper account of the hard cases, and do limit and restrain in the proper quarters. But by the same token the office-holders themselves, as people, can be subject to such sectional pressures that it is useful for them to be kept in line, to be always drawn back towards dispassionateness, by the institutional quality and requirements of the offices they hold.

A discussion of the role of government can hardly be complete without some reference to forms of government — and so we come to that, before proceeding to the final section of this chapter which deals with the impact of tune-calling. Some negative hints about the idea of ideal forms of government were thrown out towards the end of Chapter Four. The general thrust of the ensuing discussion may be summed up in the following synthesis of two famous sayings, as follows:

> Of forms of government let fools contest,
> Whate'er best serves its proper study's best. [38]

Not only is every classical 'form of government' flawed, not only would none of them adequately serve humans and their world, but forms of government are always mixed anyway. Every actual form of government that has ever existed has inescapably contained elements of government by one, by some and by all. While the quest for the best form of government has proved futile, it seems no less pointless to seek the least bad form — because of the variety of societies. What one surely wants is to discover and develop the most satisfactory ways of making arrangements for each particular society — drawing upon the most satisfactory people, using methods which provide for appropriate restraints upon them so far as that is possible, and adapting the structure to the particular needs of the society in question. If the role of government amounted to the same thing concretely in every society, or if there were the same governmental traditions or comparable pools of governmental potential to draw upon, or if every society could be relied upon to react to its government along similar lines, then it might conceivably be possible to generalize. But none of these conditions holds good.

Further, to invest forms of government as such with any degree of sanctity seems calculated to give a false perspective on the essentially instrumental character of government. A form of government cannot be an end in itself, for the most important thing about government is that it should play its proper role and discharge its functions. And while some generalizations may be made about the functions of government, the *minutiae* of these functions seem to carry more weight in considering which governmental structure or arrangement would be the most suitable and effective. We need to know something about how effective any particular governmental structure would be in a given society; how well it would be accepted; how adequately it would take account of the level of interest in government which obtains in the society; how well it would be able to cope with the matters that will fall to its charge; how it would relate to the structure of other tune-callers in the society. For without some grasp of the answers to these questions, we cannot possibly begin to work out which governmental structure or 'form' would be best suited to enable the government to do what it should.

The very idea of a 'form of government' is in fact inadequate to the issue that really arises. What we are really talking about, surely, is a set of governmental institutions, organizations, practices, and customs. And we say a set rather than a system because the latter term itself implies a greater degree of interaction or coherence than may be appropriate. For a governmental structure may even be more satisfactory — particularly as less likely to do too much or become too strong if it contains within itself a certain amount of disunity. In this, as in so many matters, the only general response to be made to general questions is to say that 'it depends'.[39]

3. The Impact Of Tune-Calling

Tune-calling in general may be seen as both a part of the human world and an intrusion on the lives of people. It helps people but at the same time breaks in on them. It both increases and derogates from their independence. Governments should not relate themselves to their subjects in overbearing or overpowering ways. On the contrary, governments should be cooperative when acting to enable their subjects, and professional when acting to enforce laws. Other tune-callers often have little incentive to establish relationships along such lines — they may to a considerable extent simply go their own way, and call as and where they wish and are able.

A human world with no place for tune-calling is difficult to envisage — even though tune-calling itself might seem in certain respects inherently at odds with the general perspective presented in this work. But for so long as there are limited resources and competition between people, for so long as some people are more effectively ambitious than others, for so long as the bulk of people have no impulse or inclination to be self-sufficient – then not only will some people take a lead and call the tune, but it is desirable that they should do so. By the same token, insofar as the generality of people become slack and manipulable, tune-calling is likely to grow into something more extensive and demanding than it can usefully be.

For there is no question that tune-calling can be damaging to human kind. It can in effect make moulds and pour people into them if it is allowed to do so. Where this happens nobody gains, except in purely material terms — and in a sense everybody loses. Tune-callers lose all the stimulation they may have gained, and the moulded persons go even further along the track of losing the strength to make effective any ideas they might have about their own ways of life. In general it would seem that there must come a point, somewhere along the way to where everything is regulated and controlled, at which the will to make ways of life would begin to be weakened. Over-regulation, the situations in which tune-calling penetrates into too many spheres of life, or too deeply into some key spheres, tends to crush creativity, incentive and initiative. When individuals within a society are seized with a feeling of 'what's the use', then disillusionment, drabness and deadness appear at both individual and societal levels.

The point at which tune-calling becomes excessive is difficult to determine. There is no reason to suppose it is the same in all societies. Some peoples may need a level of control to be enabled to mobilize themselves which would be demoralizing in other societies. Some peoples may have their energies sapped by certain kinds of control, where others would be spurred on. Great attention must continually be paid to whether tune-calling is reaching levels at which people begin to feel either that it does not matter whether they find the tunes acceptable, or that any thought of resistance or of action to change the tunes is worthless.

For tune-calling must be such as to leave people in the condition of being on their own and in the way of making their own ways of life. Unless it does this, it begins to destroy the human world. It begins to transform people into machines, and create a condition of enslavement.

The dangers of excessive tune-calling are great, particularly when the tunes are made to be seductive, and when the calls are insistent without seeming to be compelling. It has already been pointed out that governments have thrust upon them the major responsibility for ensuring that tune-calling is not excessive. Individuals are hardly in any position to resist even for themselves, much less to do anything to enable others to resist the widespread, damaging, dominating power that major social organizations and institutions and corporations are increasingly gathering to themselves. In this situation, individuals have little recourse but to appeal to government to act on their behalf.

We may say that this is merely a new form of ruffianism for governments to cope with, and there is a certain truth in that. But it is more illuminating to view the matter as something that requires a new approach to control on the part of government. The offenders may be rogues, but it will not do to treat them like criminals.

Nowhere is this more plain than when government itself is the offender. For such a procedure in that eventuality is likely to result in society either being torn apart or even more firmly put down. The problem of keeping governments in check is clearly of horrendous proportions. The inclination to say that an electoral system must make contenders for office responsible — and that it should require them to respect minorities — is desperately lame. For it seems that the promise of more and more governmental action is a major key to electoral success. It really seems that the only recourse in the end, when governments rise up and further up, is for people as people to rise higher still.

It is perhaps not too much to expect that this might happen. For good tune-calling, strong tune-calling, extensive yet regulated tune-calling, can in fact lead people to greater heights — or can be a great contributor to that dynamic process by which people proceed more and more on their own in the making of their own ways of life.

Effective and appropriate tune-calling can in fact do an enormous amount for people. It can protect and enable —

and these are tremendous boons and bonuses. It can also, in a most useful way, direct. It can mute the less attractive aspects of people's isolation. It can enable them to discern their real capabilities. It can assist greatly in helping them to focus their own interests.

This is not simply a case of people being manipulated, although it can degenerate into that. It is rather a case of their being, in the most profound sense, <u>enabled</u>: not merely having facilities and opportunities externally provided, but becoming able to discover and determine and focus their own interests, and to grow into as well as to make the ways of life they are truly their own.

8

HUMANS

The foregoing focus on the roles of government, politicians and other deciders has been essential. For while people themselves, they all impinge greatly on 'the people'. It is impossible to understand how the human world functions without an understanding of the workings of government and politicians. It is impossible to relate people's being to their potentiality without an adequate grasp of the role of government and politicians. Government and politicians can do too much or too little, they can do what they do well or ill, they can overprotect as well as protect, they can overwhelm as well as enable.

But it is important not to concentrate unduly on government and politics. Government needs to be put in perspective in relation to decisions across the whole spectrum of human affairs. Politics and decision-making need to be considered in the context of an account of how people relate to each other. Considerations of social and political affairs need to be connected with an understanding of the groundwork of human life.

Each previous chapter has been treating an aspect, a dimension, a boundary condition of the human world. There are many roles that are played and need to be considered in connection with this world. Indeed, the foregoing chapters can stand on their own as an approach and a theory to explain human affairs in general.

But the role of people themselves still awaits consideration and treatment. In dealing with this role, it is necessary to consider in very general terms the threats to people and the conditions of human achievement on the one hand, and on the other hand to examine and explore again, in the light of all that has been said thus far, the condition of humans as on their own, and their all-in-all nature as makers of ways of life.

This condition of humans — on their own; and this nature of humans — makers of ways of life: has provided the orientation, the point of departure, the basis of resolution to each issue that has been considered in the foregoing chapters. This has been done – in the only way it can be done — without either notion being fully developed. But each has seen a good deal of development in the course of application to the issues. Particularly important matters that have come to light about these notions are that they are not hard and fast, and not absolutely clear or predetermined. What has been going on in the previous chapters has not been a case of dealing with everything in some predetermined way, or fitting everything into a predetermined straightjacket. At every stage, something has been revealed about these notions themselves in the course of applying them to the various issues.

It would seem to have been shown that it is possible to do a good deal with these notions — for it is more than nothing that they have provided some basis for an approach to the issues raised in the previous three chapters. It is also noteworthy that this approach has involved coming to terms with the issues in the broadest sense: for at the same time that it has generated understanding, it has also generated attitudes. It amounts, in fact, to a way of looking at human affairs. It has to do primarily with what human affairs are all about, rather than just with what they are. It provides a basis for explaining the way things are — a point of departure, a perspective, an orientation on the whole question and issue of the matters that need to be explained. But the approach that has been offered does not itself explain the facts, in the sense of providing the key for the immediate discovery of the 'why' of every particular eventuality or isolated happening.

The proposed way of looking at human affairs gives primacy and pre-eminence to certain aspects of people themselves. But as these aspects have been used (and explored in use) it has become increasingly apparent that they are far less simple than they may appear on the surface, or at first glance. If it appears initially that they are aspects of each individual, then it quickly becomes clear that they are at least as much aspects of combinations of people — and thus complications and complexities arise. That this is so is not a defect in this way of looking at human affairs — quite the contrary. But it does mean that there is a need, in this final chapter, for a more systematic explication than had hitherto been possible of the full dimensions of these aspects of humankind.

Another way of coming at these points is that in the foregoing chapters, most of the issues raised have been referred back to, and dealt with, in the light of the ways in which the issues may be seen to bear upon these aspects of humans, and these aspects to bear upon the issues. That these aspects are pertinent to such a range of such fundamental issues, and that these issues are in turn pertinent to them, certainly suggests that these aspects can hardly be ignored, that their significance is substantial, that to take no account of them is bound to result in an inadequate view or conception of human affairs. More than this, there is an implication, which this chapter seeks to substantiate, that these aspects are crucial, fundamental, and utterly important.

In short, this chapter must make plain the measure of the alleged primacy and pre-eminence of these aspects of humans. It must clarify further and more fully what is actually meant by saying that humans are on their own and that they make ways of life. It must substantiate more fully the claims that humans are indeed on their own and that they do indeed make ways of life. And it must draw out the reasons why these aspects of human beings do indeed provide the basis of both a comprehensive way of looking at human affairs, and a conception of that human world which is, at the most general level, what we humans must come to terms with.

One central claim which is being made is that it is far more important that people are what they are (especially mature people) than how they came to be so. This is not to say that it is impossible or worthless to explain the development of human beings, both individuals and groups, in terms of various antecedent factors. But it is to say that the true importance of such explanations is that they increase our knowledge of what the people concerned are: only thus, however, only mediated via our knowledge of the people concerned, only indirectly, do they help us to predict. But in that way they do help with prediction: indeed they almost become part of prediction in the sense of that term that is relevant to human affairs.

For what people are, how they came to be what they are, what they are on about, what they are doing, what they will do — it is hardly possible to separate these various notions from each other. This is partly because there is temporal overlap between each of them — which is another way of saying that people are always in a state of development. It is also partly because we cannot effectively get at, get a proper sense of, what persons are doing (much less of what it really is that they will be doing tomorrow) unless we have a grasp of what they are and what they are on about. And what people are on about is almost invariably much more perspicuous if we know something about their circumstances, both past and present (not to mention prospective); and about those other people, including both family and friends, with whom they have and have had much to do.

What people are seems to be hardly distinguishable from what they are on about: certainly one cannot get to the heart of the first except through some considerable grasp of the second. And what people are and are on about is surely at the heart of a genuine understanding of them; surely the basis of the possibility of genuine and constructive interaction with them; surely necessary for effective sympathy, for a sound grasp of their needs and wants and desires; for an appreciation of what they are and do. When all these notions are put together thus, they not merely seem to go together: they seem obviously to be inseparable from each other.

Yet there are many perspectives from which none of this is obvious. In particular is this true of an exclusive obsession with explaining, the passion to make sense of some action or factor by reference to causative factors. In the first place, this passion leaves one with what is at best a partial picture: it is always particulars that are singled out and that need to be focussed upon from the point of view of this approach — and so exhausting does each particular enquiry about each factor become, so incomplete the conclusions that are reached, and so absorbing the analytical approach that is appropriate to such enquiries, that the pieces are never put together. The fragmentation that has occurred would make the task difficult anyway, the conclusions that have been reached are likely to be too disparate (if not positively lame) to be put together, and the analytical habit is not conducive to a combining, synthesising effort.

But the obsession to explain has the deeper defect that it always cuts out yesterday, and leaves you behind. It is not in any sense (apart perhaps from some optimism about mechanistic prediction) forward looking. By concentrating on how people came to be what they are, it loses all effective sense of what they are on about. And insofar as they come to be viewed as the thing of real interest and the *explanandum* is merely taken as given, this obsession with explanation is apt to deprive its practitioners even of a sense of what being human really is, much less an appreciation of that.

Explanation is background; it adds depth; and it gives perspective on what a person (or a group) is. But if one is trying to come to terms with human affairs, background is insufficient, and depth without a real sense of human immediacy and potentiality and dynamism is hollow. It must matter that people are not dead, but living; that what they are now doing and getting round to doing will shortly be part of the *explanans* rather than the *explanandum*; that they are not merely made into something by the past, but that they are making the future. To have no sense of this, or to lose one's grip of it; to fail to realize or keep at the centre of one's awareness that people are agents and actors, rather than simply products: is to become divorced, remote and removed from what human affairs quintessentially are.

The stress being put on what humans are should not be taken to mean that there is some human nature which must be located — some uniform or universal set of characteristics or qualities which are either common to all or else distributed by predetermined patterns — which itself enables us, when it has been articulated, to come to terms with human affairs. It may be that the content of human nature can be discovered with sufficient determinacy to cast a general light on human affairs. Certainly, if there is such a thing as human nature, people are more than their natures. No matter how much may be made of their nature, it still remains much more important to get a grasp of what people make of their nature, what they do with it, what they do and become as beings with that nature.

For there can be no doubt that humans must find themselves, and make themselves. This, above all, is human nature — or we may say that it is humans' fate, their lot, their privilege. And in the most comprehensive and illuminating sense, people are what they make themselves; they define and measure themselves in themselves and for themselves; they measure the world in relation to themselves, and relate that world to themselves as well as themselves to it; they make ways of life, and they are defined by that. This definition of humans, this account of them, this way of looking at them is immeasurably the most illuminating, the most real, and the most true. Human beings are, in the end, their ways of life: they live what they are because they are what they live. Everything else about humans — even their nature as defined at the top of this paragraph — is subordinate to this.

How do humans find and make themselves? In a sense, this is absolutely the central issue of this chapter — and virtually everything that has been said in the other chapters has some bearing on it as well. In asking how they do it, one becomes caught up at the same time with the question of what is involved in their doing it — with what it is for humans to find themselves and make their ways of life.

One also comes up against the question of what it is for people to fail to find themselves and to make their ways of life: the question of how such failure occurs, of what such failure consists in, and of what brings such failure about. For there can be no doubt that some people do fail in this whole business. Perhaps nobody ever fails completely but some people certainly fail lamentably.

It has been emphasised, in the last three chapters particularly, that finding oneself and making one's way of life neither is nor can be a completely solitary or isolated undertaking. Humans need to be protected, and most if not all humans need to be enabled. Humans, while on their own, are tremendously dependent upon other humans. And it is no diminishment of persons being on their own, or of the originality of what they make, that they sometimes receive stimulation as well as gaining more capability from facilities which are made available to them. The originality, the condition of being human, is enhanced rather than detracted from by this — in much the same way as it is elucidated by the understanding that humans have their being in a world of facts and mysteries, and also by taking note of the fact that each generation of humans succeeds previous generations.

But while it is clear that people need help, it is not clear what they need this help for. When all appropriate help has been given, what must people do in order to find themselves and make their ways of life? How are they to proceed? What should they do, and how should they cope, if the help which they receive is inappropriate — if they are smothered with kindness, or edged in ways they do not want to go? Those are very fair questions — and yet it is hardly possible to answer them in the terms that the questions seem to imply. For in the nature of the case — and we may sum this up by re-iterating that humans are on their own — there is no method or procedure which awaits adoption by human beings.

Ways of life surround us, but none of them is in its nature a model for any individual's way of life. If people decide to model themselves on some way of life which they have observed, then in a sense they make their own ways of life in making that decision. In another sense, if they are slavish in conforming to their model, then they bid fair to fail in making their own ways of life – although it is unusual for people not to put their own very considerable glosses on their versions of their model.

It is probably more common for people to have a number of models — and here it is particularly evident that people must at every stage be making their own ways: this is the essence of it. People make ways of life by making them — by acting: by acting in such a way that they build up (or possibly evade building up) patterns of action; possibly but not necessarily by consciously adopting such patterns as their principles (although if they do this their principles will tend to keep growing to accommodate their actions, or else their actions will become cramped by their principles).

It is the nature of this business of making ways of life that each person and each group makes their own; and in the end, the only answer to the question of how each does so is to give an account of what each does, or possibly of what each sees itself as doing (particularly if such self-consciousness in fact is present). People do it by the method of doing it. What they do, of course, can be tremendously variable — which makes difficulties for giving a general account of what a way of life amounts to. But this is to be expected, for ways of life would not be so basic as they are if this was not the case.

In one way, peoples' nature, lot and privilege — this need to find themselves and make their own ways of life — is hard. It is always hard when there is no track to go along, or at least harder and more demanding when there is not than when there is. Some human beings certainly struggle, and wrestle with themselves as well as the world in the course of finding themselves and making their way. Some – who knows but that they are not the most acutely self-conscious and self-reliant of all — cannot bear to go on with it beyond a certain point. Again, there are those who, having made something which has the appearance of being a coherent and even a satisfying way of life, cannot really bear it but turn right away from it, and try to start afresh.

But while there are some who find that the challenge to make just what they want so demanding that it becomes a burden — and some who find even the prospect of trying intolerable — there are others to whom the making of a way of life comes easily, even naturally. They simply make — perhaps blithely unaware that they are doing without a care or trouble something that is agony for others, though not necessarily unaware of this. There seems little reason to suppose there is any significant correlation between taking easily the making of one's way of life and simply falling into some conformity. There is too large a variety of factors in play in the determination of whether ways of life are creative or derivative, constructive or empty — and too many apparently unrelated factors which bear upon a person's dispositions and general outlook — for such a simple connection to have any plausibility.

One other aspect of whether the nature, lot and privilege of humans is hard or easy calls for comment. This is that 'hard' or 'easy' are scarcely applicable categories in any general sense. For there are no effective comparisons to be made. The lot of those creatures who have no life of their own to make is neither easy nor hard. But it is not seriously possible for human beings to contemplate living the life of an ant: for the imagination of what it would be like includes a consciousness and an awareness which could not possibly be present in the actuality. Accordingly, humans cannot really consider whether such a life — life according to the nature of ants — would be harder or easier than life according to the nature of humans. When it has been said that it is human nature to make one's own way of life, and when a full realization of what that amounts to has been attained, then the question of whether it is hard or easy on humans that their ways of life await their own making simply cannot arise.

It is because humans are on their own, because it is humans' nature to make their own ways of life, that there is a human world, and a need to draw attention to it. From certain perspectives, this world may be viewed as hardly less drab than the world of facts, and possibly as qualitatively no different from it.

Of course, ways of life once made are facts, if sometimes shot through with some mystery. But a way of life in the making, or in prospect, is something quite other. This is not to say that we cannot regard it as an assortment of facts and emergent facts. But it is to say that we can regard it in a very different light. We can look to the sequences and collections of components, rather than only to the components in isolation; and thus detect qualities such as coherence, integrity, and worth — or possibly the absence thereof. We can see imagination at work, we can see courage and zest and creativity and determination and a whole range of qualities and characteristics that are on a par with these. They are all purely human qualities, exclusively human qualities. They have no application whatever to the world of facts and values. Whether there are noises where there are no hearers is clearly arguable, but there can be no doubt that there is no integrity, no zest, no determination where there are no human beings.[40]

The human world is not wholly divorced from facts, any more than a work of art is wholly divorced from canvas and paint. On the contrary, the human world is dependent on matter, and largely made with matter, out of matter, even into matter. But the human world is not characterised by material qualities: and the material qualities which it possesses are wholly (or almost wholly) immaterial in any account that we may give of it. Indeed, the accounts or descriptions that we give of what I call the human world are couched in a language of their own. We have concepts and categories which go together and form a system (or set of systems), and which seem to relate to each other in quite different ways and at quite different levels from those which are applicable to the world of facts.

It seems a fatal error to presume that the qualities for which we have concepts in the human world relate or may be related to each other in ways that are analogous to those in which we can relate factual qualities to each other. One cannot avoid the impression that there are the most integral connections between the types of qualities and the types of relationship that they can have to each other. For what we invariably see happening when persistent attempts are made to establish material kinds of linkages between human kinds of qualities is that the qualities are stripped right down and completely lost. For the material analogues that are built up to replace (euphemistically, to interpret) them can be viewed as related to them only by contrivance. So simply can the study of humans be lost, when the human world is not treated on its own terms through and through.

The fatal flaw theoretically about attempting to reduce the human world to the material world for purposes of analysis and comprehension becomes apparent when we call to mind that humans are the measure of all things. The terms in which we talk of the facts do not belong to the facts, but are devised for them by people. And there is no reason whatever to suppose that they will be illuminating or prove appropriate for talking about everything. They have no standing apart from what humans have given them. So it seems at best gross folly for humans to propose to take account of every aspect of themselves in terms of them.

So in what sense is the human world a world — especially granted that it does not stand wholly on its own? The answer is that in spite of people's dependence, human affairs and ways of life can be taken account of on their own terms: they can be understood and made sense of, viewed, assessed and regarded by themselves. They can be seen as systems, they can be examined for coherence, they can be evaluated for what they are. And insofar as it is qualitatively different from that other world of facts and mysteries, of sheer materiality; insofar as the concepts relevant to facts pass humans by; and insofar as there is a set of concepts pertinent to human affairs and a congeries of activities and dynamics which make up human living: what else is there to say but that there is a human <u>world</u>? Although dependent, it is a self-sustaining, self-sufficient, self-developing dimension of reality: and one which human beings cannot, must not suffer to lapse into the sphere of brute facticity.

Only people can sustain their world at its proper level. People bear a great responsibility in this regard, to themselves no less than to others. Human beings are far more dependent on each other than upon anything else. Insofar as they are interdependent, helping and encouraging others is a good investment to say the very least. For such help and encouragement are in fact a great stimulus to continuing social dynamism. Furthermore, any help and encouragement that may be offered must be enlightened. Humans can damage their world as well as enhance it, they can destroy ways of life as well as create them, they can feed foolish dreams no less than they can dampen initiative.

An issue that illustrates this general problem concerns the attainment of a balance between the stimulation of enterprise and the promotion of realistic expectations. To tell children that their lives are their own, that they may make of them what they will, and that they should not back off from making the way of life they want merely because some difficulty arises before them, seems on the face of it a not unreasonable encouragement. Furthermore, for those of the present generation to take pains and make efforts to maximize opportunities, and provide facilities for those of the next generation seems not only meritorious, but calculated to enhance the human world to the greatest possible extent. To do anything else would seem calculated to cramp and confine future generations, to make it needlessly difficult for them to attain what they aspire to, and possibly lead them to aspire too low.

But the problem is that when people have been offered the earth — even if explicitly on the condition that they must display the capacity to attain it — they may tend to think that the earth is their right, and thereby come to covet it even if they lack the capacity — or even just the energy — to attain it. In this we find a condition of things in which discontent and disillusionment are apt to become rife. For to readjust, to lower without bitterness one's expectations of what is realistic, is difficult. And disillusionment is seldom productive of determination and initiative. On the contrary, it produces a tendency to fall back on supports that have been provided as springboards rather than as resting-places and retreats.

This tendency easily assumes epidemic proportions. Humans must therefore beware of promising too much. Particularly must they avoid indiscriminate offers or provision of facilities and opportunities which will create expectations that are bound to turn sour — even though at the same time they must not promise or offer too little, especially to those who could do well with more. The problem as posed here demands a responsible attitude towards equality.

The real equality of humans, surely, is that everyone should be brought up in self-confidence, not being ashamed to be what they are, to do what they do, or to want what they want. In the human world there is room for difference, and a need for some to lead, even command in some respects, and for others to follow. But there is neither need nor place for status, for feelings of superiority or inferiority. Other notions of equality can be nothing more than practical approximations to this – unless they are based upon misconceptions of human nature. Construed along these lines, equality is an extremely powerful but at the same time virtually utopian ideal, at least on a wide scale.

There is, in the first place, a problem of achieving and maintaining harmony between what persons are, do and want — and then the problem, albeit related, about how they are to arrive at the condition of being satisfied and not ashamed of all that. The most general comment to be made about this equality as an ideal is that it is none the worse for being utopian, none the less to be sought and promoted because it can never be completely attained. And it would never, even in utopia, be a kind of permanent condition of things: not only does it need to be uniquely achieved in every single human being, but even that achievement cannot be a 'once for all' affair in persons who are continuing to develop: its development must be a part of their general development.

Further, if one considers this notion of equality from the point of view of those bringing the next generation to maturity, there is the very great practical difficulty of needing to breed that type and measure of confidence in each child which will be appropriate to wants and a way of life which is at that stage largely if not completely unknown. It would seem on the face of it easier to conduct each person towards an appropriate self-confidence and satisfaction with their place, themselves, their role, and their aspirations, if one knows something about their future. And certainly, to make the true doctrine of equality a practical object lesson — to produce self-confidence in people by teaching the doctrine to them — would seem unlikely to be effective.

All of this may be regarded, perhaps, as highlighting something that is obvious anyway, namely that bringing up the next generation is always a substantially empirical business, which calls for new judgements and new points of departure at every stage. Nevertheless, it is possible, in the light of the general perspective being offered here, to venture one particular line of observations about what 'upbringing' really consists in.

The real point of departure lies in the notion of wants. Considerable stress has been laid on the requirement that human beings should be able to do what they want: that in making their own ways of life, they should be making what they want. (Indeed, if what they make is not what they want, then they can be said to be making their own ways of life only in an extremely limited sense.) In working along these lines, it has been noted that people's wants may change and develop, may even undergo various metamorphoses. But what has not really been dwelt upon is the issue of discovering, or forming, or ascertaining one's wants initially. And there is in this connection a quite fundamental importance that there be provision for such growth. It is an affair of the greatest uncertainty, and it has a quality that seems unattractive to many people insofar that discipline seems to be an unavoidable aspect of it.

But if it is true that there are enjoyable activities, activities which people really want to engage in, which can be enjoyed only by those who can do them well. And if it is also true that there are some activities which it is impossible to learn to do well overnight, but which require time and training and experience, even perhaps a degree of initiation and induction, not to mention an appropriate background knowledge... If there is truth in these two statements, then it follows at once that human beings can probably find out what they want only as a result of being led along paths which they do not greatly wish to tread, at least in advance of treading them. There is in this, of course, a need for tremendous discernment. To drag people along a wrong path — one which they will always regret having traversed, possibly one that prevented their traversing another that would have been beneficial, possibly even one that results in their losing or being diverted from their proper direction – this is a dreadful prospect, and the fear of doing it should quite properly haunt all those who teach. But there is no formula which guarantees immunity from such mistakes, and even the most discerning can still go wrong. Nevertheless, the argument against instant wants and instant things stands as a powerful reminder about one aspect or sphere of the responsibility of both mentors and authorities.

Two further aspects about wants are worthy of comment. First, there are some things which people want, enjoy and value only if they have made or achieved them themselves. Clearly, the upshot of this is that there is need for training so that people will acquire skills. But of course such skills must be appropriate — and all the difficulties of discernment referred to above clearly arise in this connection. The second point is the converse — that there are some things which people want, enjoy and value only if they have always been accustomed to them and have not had to make or achieve them for themselves. This seems to give rise to an argument for some kind of principle of inheritance: the difficulty being to choose at birth those who can do with the inheritance.

In practical terms, it would seem that the least unsatisfactory way of arranging for the bringing up of future generations is to have some sort of system which always has its money every way, and is strictly incoherent. The aim must be to provide, not equality of opportunity, but quality and appropriateness of opportunity.

To give everyone the same chances is not only wasteful. It denies to teachers in particular the responsibility to cultivate their own discernment. There can be no more certain way of ensuring that some useful opportunities will not be available at all, and that some children will be driven into taking opportunities that are totally inappropriate to them, than to insist that everyone should have the same – i.e. so called 'equal' — opportunities. It is unquestionably deplorable that anyone be disadvantaged in respect of their opportunities by virtue of considerations or factors which are extraneous or irrelevant. But this line of argument becomes treacherous when it is asked to bear weight.

From the perspective of this work there is a basic flaw in the idea of universalizing any substantive concept of disadvantage: the flaw being that any such concept can only be postulated on the assumption that there is some universal measure. Thus, we can say that it is unfair that a child should be disadvantaged because the parents are poor: but we cannot infer from this that any child actually is disadvantaged, other things being equal, if their parents are poor. This inference would be legitimate only if there was some universal measure of disadvantage. Putting it differently, the opportunities open to a particular child as a result of parental poverty might be appropriate to that child, and any others which could be added by neutralizing the limitations which are part of that result quite inappropriate. By the same token, the opportunities open to a child as a result of parental wealth might be inappropriate. The line of argument could be amplified and refined, but its general thrust is clear.

I would add that in the course of the following sections of this chapter, several other classic concepts of political thought (e.g. freedom) are explicated in terms of the overall perspective that is developed throughout. These concepts — freedom above all — seem capable of being continually renewed with the vigour of eternal youth. These are all concepts which relate directly to humans themselves. Concepts which laud for its own sake anything other than human beings are apt to be immortalized with an overlay of senility — which is probably so because such concepts seem inescapably to belittle humans.

1. *Threats To Humans, And Conditions Of Achievement*

It is rare for there to be no difficulty about discovering and providing the conditions under which human beings can find out and achieve what they are after. By the same token, there are invariably substantial difficulties about balancing those general conditions which seem likely to optimize achievement overall against the particular conditions which specific individuals and groups require. Further, human beings have needs *vis-a-vis* other people as well as *vis-a-vis* the material world. Human as well as material conditions unquestionably need to be satisfied if humans are in fact to succeed in making their own ways of life.

In general, there is obviously a need for order, and for containment of conflict. And those with power and authority, governments and deciders both, need to provide a conducive framework, conducive conditions, if achievement is to flow easily. At the same time it should be noted that a challenge can itself be a stimulus. This means that it may be counterproductive to try to iron out every difficulty that might present itself. And while the deciders and the powerful have a major responsibility in the determination of whether the most conducive conditions are provided, there is surely no-one without responsibility in this matter. Even the most private way of life can be exemplary. Individuals must stimulate groups and groups must stimulate individuals. Centres of power become crass and dull unless they themselves receive some stimulation from outside themselves.

The supreme condition of achievement is surely achievement itself. This is not to say that human affairs can only be in good condition if everything is frenetic. It does presume, however, that the mere provision of facilities and opportunities and incentives and encouragement is not a sufficient condition of achievement. The real stimulation must come from the fact that ways of life are being made around one, that people are doing what they want: from an abundance of energy, from liveliness, from a widespread productivity in the most general sense.

There is no greater stimulus to the making of one's own way of life than to see others thriving on making their own ways of life. This is the real dynamism of the human world, the real source of the development of civilization, the only true incentive. And where people are making and achieving, producing and spending in order to make their ways of life more fully, there is bound to come into operation a kind of multiplier. People become drawn into the way of following their nature.

One reason why a milieu of achievement is the supreme condition of achievement is that more facilities, options and opportunities can themselves create in humans a condition almost of dependence. They can be relished and wallowed in, and messing about with them can become so absorbing that one never gets beyond them, never takes them up or makes use of them. When they make life too easy, they become a substitute for life itself: and 'too easy' here simply means that the facilities in question can be enjoyed without being used.

It is not exactly a case of a person going on and on without ever getting anywhere, but rather of going round and round the same sets and the same level of essentially preliminary activities. So arrangements and facilities must be good without being too good. And what is too good is relative to the level of dynamism in society generally. For what would be too good in a sluggish society may well be a genuine stimulus when combined with the greater stimulus of a generally high level of achievement and activity.

It is also vital in the provision of appropriate conditions that arrangements and facilities should not be allowed to outlive their usefulness. The past, and its achievements, can certainly provide an excellent springboard from which humans can pursue their nature: if we always had to start from scratch we would never be able to refine and civilize ourselves — never be able to develop our world.

But the past becomes a constraint when traditions and

practices become entrenched within it to the point where they will not give way to new opportunities and facilities which have become more appropriate. The inertia of established, entrenched arrangements is a perpetual threat to liveliness within society. This threat becomes more acute when combined with a situation in which facilities and opportunities become so plentiful that it becomes difficult to find one's way around them sufficiently well to be able to make proper use of them in following one's nature — and when machines and reliance upon machinery become so all-embracing that it is difficult to prevent oneself from adjusting one's wants to fall into line with what the machines can do.

We are led to ask, then, whether humans and their world are at greater risk, subject to greater threat than ever before. For there is every reason to think that the circumstances just described are characteristic of our times. Every age probably has a sense of its own peculiar dangers, problems and threats — but by the same token, every age probably also underestimates its own human resourcefulness and potentialities, its own capacity to solve the problems which it confronts and which it creates for itself. It can hardly be doubted that mechanistic contrivances are almost inevitably two-edged swords — they can be turned against humans and their world no less than they can be used in support of its development.

The same goes for organizational or institutional structures which are essentially instrumental: they may be a bit clumsy when turned against people, though still possibly none the less damaging for this. To be sure, our times are such that people need to adapt and adjust the ways and procedures by which they go about the business of making their ways of life. But this presumably is always the case, especially in situations in which there is some vibrancy and vitality in the human world at large. Accordingly, there seems no basis to think that the threats are greater now than at any other time — or rather that if they are, then there is a greater capacity at hand to cope with them. There is no reason in general to presume that this capacity does not increase proportionately with the strength of the threats. Accordingly, there seems no basis for general laments — which is not, of course, a basis for taking any threats too lightly.

The most encompassing threat, already mentioned, is that humans might be swallowed up by their own worlds, by their own creations. Organizational strength and domination is one particular facet of this, which poses particular threats to individual aspects of the human world. The accelerating decrease of elbow room — more people, more needs, higher expectations, a greater use of available resources — is another facet of the same thing. Related to both is a general increase in cost-consciousness among human beings at large. Each of these facets merits some consideration.

One reason why cost-consciousness becomes more pervasive is simply that demand in general seems to outstrip supply — and consequently everything has a price put upon it. There are other ways of coping with this problem, but restricting those who are entitled to come into the market is probably harder to justify than making everyone pay and thus excluding those who cannot pay. But one fears that there may additionally be some deeper reasons, to do with the failure of people to grasp what they are on about, what they want and are really doing. If people seek material potentiality for its own sake, without really knowing what they want or what they are doing, then their condition is disturbing, and is calculated to be worsened by their quest.

Cost-consciousness taken to any lengths also tends to produce a kind of reductionist mentality. Those who go in for it are prone to lose the capacity to consider things on their own terms. If one can reduce everything to some purely quantitative measure, especially one which seems to be a universal standard (for it is hard to remember that different people value money differently), then the tendency to laziness becomes extremely hard to resist. Individuals are certainly not helped in making their own ways of life if there is a dominating underlying attitude of mind which drives them always to ask what they can afford. This breeds passivity apart from anything else, but it also seems to make cost-consciousness into a way of life — as if only what can be bought (or sold) is worth doing, making or even being.

Cost consciousness also feeds upon itself. For it progressively reduces other bases of comparison to itself, or rather distorts them out of existence. It assaults and batters down other criteria of comparison and assessment. Even if it ultimately appears as unsatisfactory, it is likely to have done a good deal towards engendering that frame of reference which will seek some other all-embracing single criterion. And anything else of the same kind is likely to be no less limited, no less reductionist, no less unsatisfactory.

The threat of insufficient elbow room is tremendously difficult to comprehend or face up to. There can be no doubt that people need scope and space in order to flourish. But as soon as one asks what kind of space they need one is immediately made to wonder whether shortages and limitations and general closeness are genuine threats to people at all. There seems, for example, to be no reason to suppose that there are any inherent limits to moral space, or any genuine (or unavoidable) shortages of those materials which people really need in order to make their own ways of life. The answer to the question of how much space people need is different when there is perceptibly a lot of land around from when there is perceptibly not. To be sure, a shortage of physical or moral space can be a constraint (although it is to some a spur).

But there is a vast difference between a simple constraint and a real threat to people's capacity to make their own ways of life. That limitation of space and scope, that degree of crowding, would need to be unimaginably great that would seriously begin to prevent persons from following their nature altogether. Perhaps people need to consider, in times of explosive growth of numbers, whether they should commit future generations to the necessity of adapting ways of life (even the idea of ways of life) to the degree that would be required if the population increased tenfold or a hundredfold (or whatever the figure would be). Yet even here there is a difficulty about the present generation deciding to interfere directly (i.e. to act for the sake of interference) with the situation to be inherited by the coming generation. Not knowing the resources or wants of the next generation, the present one can hardly but be flying blind whenever it might contemplate this.

Organizational strength, and the threats and dangers which it poses, has already been referred to. The point from this area which requires consideration is the squeeze likely to be put on particular (especially individual) ways of life and the making of them.

There is the nasty possibility that the individual (and even some loosely structured groups) might have to fight against impossible odds simply to maintain their ways of life, much less to enhance them: that the only way they might avoid being driven to the wall is to join battle with forces that seem arraigned against them. This is immediately to lose the ground which one would really want to defend. For the defensive posture — the need to assume it and the cost of assuming it — is quite antithetical to the living, much more to the making, of a human way of life. The necessity to enter into some kind of uneasy yet virtually indissoluble alliance with others (where the only basis of alliance is facing a common threat) is hardly better, for here also there is an enormous amount of one's own way of life that must immediately be given up.

The recourse of people in general, of both individuals and groups that are not geared to push, has been said to be the state, or concretely the government. Certainly the roles of government and the state become tremendously prominent and demanding in times of dominance by lesser organizations. Only with the very greatest support, constructive criticism, and continuous goading from its clients can governments have any hope of standing up in this kind of circumstance.

There is, however, a quite different side to this whole matter of the threat of people's lives being swallowed up by the human world at large. For we may wish to interpret it less as a threat than as an interdependence which need not be viewed as necessarily detrimental. Insofar as ways of life do become increasingly enmeshed and interdependent, insofar as everything that happens or that is done has ramifications for everything else, there seems plainly to be a possibility of enhancement and enrichment, of deepening and expanding humanity. For there is always more to relationships than meets the eye — always a new perspective that one notices, always an additional bit of information, always a different way of handling things, always the addition of further concreteness to the generality and abstractness with which so much of life is conducted.

Increasing interdependence can hardly be expected to have no costs. There is more room for busybodies, for pettiness, for mean-mindedness. There is certain to be pressure in a simplifying direction, pressure to abandon individual ways of doing things including distinctive and eccentric habits. As facilities are increasingly centralized and made uniform, it becomes correspondingly more difficult to be original. Nevertheless, insofar as the value for all of interdependence is plain, and insofar as diversity of interrelationships is beneficial, it is good that pressures towards uniformity and conformity should be resisted, and that increasingly irresistible centralisation should be made difficult rather than easy. For if interdependence and diversity of interrelationships are indeed valuable, the conclusion is inescapable that humanity as a whole, both in particular and in general, is the loser when ways of life are eliminated or when distinctive characteristics are flattened out.

2. Humans On Their Own, And Making Ways Of Life

Implicit in much that has been said in general throughout the foregoing chapters, and specifically in the earlier parts of this chapter, is the fact that human beings are increasingly on their own in a collective rather than (or perhaps more than) an individual way. But the word collective may be less than adequate to the reality.

Each individual person remains his or her own measure. All individuals must decide upon the measures they will adopt, must decide for themselves what life is about, and must make their own ways of life. There can be no departure or escape from that so long as humans are humans. The same goes for each group and for each society. But the circumstances in which this is carried on have a great impact and a great significance for its character. If all people's condition of being on their own had to be played out in circumstances which could be best described as analogous to their being in a void, then the character of that condition would be very different from what it would be if penalties were attached to every departure which anyone made from some kind of standardised social norm.

But all persons are on their own in an environment which is redolent with suggestions, help, and pressure — which can hardly help having some bearing on how they interpret themselves, on the measures which they adopt, and on the ways they use them. Where people are living in societies which are both interdependent and diverse, it may be said that individuals and groups can choose, can really go their own ways – and do so in circumstances where they have all the help and suggestions they could hope for — and all this without any real pressures to go one way rather than another. All of this is true, and profoundly important. Indeed, I would not want to say that a more satisfactory kind of arrangement for human beings than this is really possible. Yet it is true nevertheless that in such circumstances, the options and measures are substantially predetermined. In a sense persons can choose what they like and choose from a selection that is both wide and good. They are not in any limited or small or rigged or phoney market. But of course they are still in a market. And its very excellence makes it the more difficult for them to do anything but choose from among the range that is available. To go it wholly alone is made difficult by the very attractiveness and plausibility, the persuasiveness and coherence of that which is available. In the midst of a supermarket, one needs considerable self-confidence and assurance to decide that nothing suits. Indeed, in a highly developed civilization, a degree of complexity and sophistication is called for which is extremely difficult to attain of one's own devising, without referring to anything beyond or outside of oneself. In addition, insofar as people (or a group) perceive the inevitability of interdependence, they are in large measure impelled towards going along with measures that they find in the world, and taking available options rather than trying to construct different or fresh ones which would be their very own. Some rare people must always arise who, absolutely individually and relying wholly on their own interpretations of everything that has gone before, construct their own measures (which then in due course may enter a common pool). Other independent people either carve out their own options or transform and rewrite those which are straightforwardly available to them. But these are departures from the norm — and if they were too prevalent there would be a fragmenting tendency which would become difficult to reconcile with interdependence.

It is not easy to say how the collective functioning of the human condition of "people being on their own" actually proceeds. One thing worth saying is that there is an amalgamating process — something over and above a mere accretion or combination of things. It is perhaps something like fashion in its general character — difficult to follow or fathom at the level of how it functions, yet unmistakeable in its major manifestations.

Human beings seem, increasingly perhaps, to be interdependent through and through. This interdependence obtains not only in respect of ways of life, but also in respect of the condition of being on one's own. If individuals are (or provide) the framework of themselves, they also have their being within a magnificent variety of frameworks made up of other people and groups — and not excluding themselves either. Thus frameworks possess a tremendous range, in size, in function, in their own mutual relationships. The range of frameworks depends to a degree on the openness of the society, on its liveliness, on how far groups are formed within it, on how stimulating the whole congeries of frameworks itself turns out to be.

The real point to drive home here is the importance of emphasizing the complexity of the idea of humanity. To say 'human' is to bring into consideration each person and all people, each group and every interlocking between groups. Humans, in their condition on their own, necessarily receive tremendous support from other humans, and in a crucial sense they could want nothing better. This support is not in any sense separable from, or in any way over and above people being people, but simply part of it — part of saying that people are on their own but not isolated or dwelling in any thorough-going kind of solitude. Of course, the frameworks may not give the kind of support that particular groups or individuals want — they may, for example, reinforce perspectives which one might want to get away from, they may tie together and interlock in ways that make various courses almost impenetrable.

And yet, no matter how much may be built up in terms of self-sustaining, self-supporting, even apparently self-perpetuating frameworks — no matter how much a kind of settled condition of the possibilities and potentialities for humans may seem to be arrived at — no matter how complete the range of options or measures may seem to be: humans still remain on their own. It is an illusion to think that humans somehow attain (or are reduced to) a condition of being less on their own as things become settled, as knowledge and understanding increase, as ways of coping with problems or simply of achieving various things are mastered. For no matter how far any of this went, there would still be people, present, fresh from life, at the threshold, with all that behind them and in the past – human beings, wanting to size it all up, and having absolutely no option but to do so. If it does not measure up, then it is necessary to go back to the beginning. And when it does measure up, it can only do so on the terms of those doing the measuring and sizing it up. It may be added that there are likely to be some transformations in what this kind of thing really comes to as new generations embrace, interpret, adapt, modify and develop even the most apparently fixed frameworks.

Humans are amazing beings in combining in themselves both originality and dependence — and this not just at the individual level, but at every level. They are continually a union of many opposites, and all of this by way of moderating their condition as being on their own. They measure and make and do things, and in all of this they form — are continually forming — themselves. But at the same time that they are originating themselves for themselves (even if not, without qualification anyway, wholly at their own behest or along lines of their own devising), they are affected to the point of being formed by what is done and what happens to them.

What humans do, and what happens to them, are not, furthermore, separate spheres of influence upon themselves. They interact, and more than this they impinge upon each other. One can have some control over what happens to oneself, but certainly never complete control — probably no more, indeed, than over the impact upon oneself of what happens to one. If nothing happened to one, if there were no impacts upon one apart from what one had arranged, then one's own purely inner resources would have to be enormously powerful for one not to dry up and run down. But such insulation is inconceivable anyway, except in some fanciful empty isolation.

Humans are always put, and always putting themselves, into positions where things do happen to them, more or less. Part of what happens is as a result of contact with their fellows and the human world at large, and part as a result of contact with the world of facts and mysteries. The dependence of humans in the sense of needing stimulation, not to say encouragement, is an easily overlooked aspect of their condition as being on their own.

Being on their own, it is in a way the more important that they not be left to their own devices, that they not isolate themselves from stimulation. They must digest what comes their way (and of course it is highly desirable that what comes their way should be digestible); part of the point is that they cannot but digest what comes their way, and put it to such uses as they do and can and want to — and then discard the rest.

Not merely are humans dependent, they are also vulnerable, and on a huge number of fronts apart from the purely physical. They need not only to be stimulated, but cosseted and to a degree valued and respected. Some people need less of this than others; some can stand firm, in their own right and on their own feet, no matter what buffetings may come their way.

And there are perhaps not many human beings who do not need the stiffening that comes from opposition and dislike – provided that they are supported and encouraged from other directions. To lose self-confidence is a distinct possibility for beings on their own, as is failure ever to acquire it. And the lack or loss of self-confidence is bound to result in a real sense in which persons cannot be themselves, cannot become or realize themselves, cannot really <u>make</u> (as distinct from simply falling into) their own way of life.

This vulnerability of people is a species of dependence on others — and to a degree on themselves. The facts and mysteries are neutral from this point of view, and their impact, when destructive, can only be countered by people themselves. One may need aid from one's fellows, and human affairs need to be organized in such a way that there is nobody for whom somebody else does not have a duty of care.

The provision of all of this is, in a sense, catered for by a curious blend of qualities in humans themselves. For humans are beings who both bring tears to the eyes and hate into the souls of other humans. This sometimes happens at the very same time with the very same people. But more commonly — and probably more usefully — persons will stimulate generosity and sympathy in one person at the same time that they stimulate wrath and hatred in another. And so there is likely to be a balance of opposing forces created, of such a character that the persons concerned can find their way through them, and not be dispossessed because of one. Of course, they need their own strength, their own character, to be able to maintain their stand, to take advantage of the sympathy and not simply be put down by the anger of others.

There is also a more important condition — diversity — on which the general attainment of this balance between sympathy and antipathy depends. Insofar as people become bland and characterless, or (more dangerously) insofar as a norm is set up towards which everyone tends to conform, the diversity of response towards oneself from others may be expected to diminish. The blandness is less worrying in this particular respect, for it will dampen down strength of reaction from every direction. But the dangers of the tendency to conformism seem to be almost without limit. The ideal in this connection may be viewed as the circumference of a circle — no matter where one is on that circumference, there will be some on one side who are favourably disposed, and some on the other side unfavourably disposed. Or possibly it would be better to view the ideal as represented by a series of concentric and criss-crossing circles, symmetrical and asymmetrical towards each other. For it is most unreal to proceed or talk as if everyone was on a kind of par, and this last image is clearly suggestive of thoroughly diverse lines and levels of relationships and responses. But if instead of on circumferences, people lie close or closer towards some centre (or even centres), with increasingly dense clustering towards the centre, then those who are way out will neither be well regarded by those who are closer in, nor will there be anyone further out to give them support. And insofar as this tendency begins to assert itself and to develop, it becomes self-generating. Diversity is thus likely to be eliminated at an accelerating rate. Those who would be the salt of the earth with even the faintest encouragement get none, and accordingly few of them have the inner resources to stand out on their own against all the pressures that draw them away from their real position and towards the centre.

In the end, the really crucial issue in connection with this concerns individuality, in the widest sense. For if individuality (whether in groups or individuals, although one suspects that it is needed in both) is lost, if it departs from the scene, then it would seem impossible that circumferences could maintain their integrity, that the drift towards the centre could possibly be arrested.

The meaning of individuality here is not easy to pin down. It does not necessarily imply being different from everyone else, or creating some entirely new perspective, or constructing some quite novel arrangement of known components. That is, it need not be spectacularly or brilliantly original.

But neither can individuality, at least across the whole face of it, consist simply in conformity that satisfies. Within limits, conformity is not inconsistent with individuality — but when (or as) it becomes increasingly universal, it is increasingly impossible to take seriously the view that there is nothing apart from their own interpretation of things which drives people to the position in question.

Individuality means being the self that one has made and found. But this is no more than an abstract statement. It says little directly about how we should identify genuine individuality in particular cases, or how a person or group can make sure it has not been conned into something.

In a time of expanded horizons and potentialities, when it would seem that all the opportunities which a true individualism on the widest possible scale could require have been provided, and when there is virtually endless rhetoric about the liberation of humans and the possibility for each to realize themselves, individualism is in fact in an extraordinarily vulnerable position. Perhaps this is not necessarily true, but in fact the tendency is strong.

For all this provision seems hardly imaginable without that kind of organizational capacity which seems to make organizational strength more or less irresistible, and which in turn seems calculated to set up all the pressure towards conformity, towards bland acceptance rather than the construction of what one will be which has been considered above. This is obviously a major danger when the position is that humans are on their own in a collectivist sense. Anti-individualistic pressures are likely to be set up, and the very fact that they are set up in this context makes it the more difficult to resist them effectively.

While it is imperative that the kind of collectivism I have been considering should not be allowed to break down individualism as discussed — and while it is foolish if no attempts are made, from within a collectivist milieu, to give some positive encouragement to genius and originality — it is probably inevitable in a world in which elbow room is at a premium that some differences are too great to be accommodated. Here there is indeed a kind of constraint on people, and on individuality. But there is a sense in which it may be regarded as a constraint which, if taken up in the right spirit, concentrates the mind.

Of course, taken up negatively, it could result in decisions which impose rigid boundaries which simply become barriers to quality. And it is certainly plain that rigid lines, no matter with what enlightenment they are drawn at a particular stage, will prove unsatisfactory either in the long run or in the face of genius. But if a society really does take an enlightened, constructive, developing approach to the matter of determining boundaries, if it takes account of what its members are up to and on about, if it takes account of social needs and social potentialities, then by a process of judicious encouragement it may be able to provide well not only for its future but also for its own greater coherence.

The task is one which can hardly be evaded (indirectly even if not directly) in the determination of what facilities and opportunities and encouragements are to be provided. It is surely best, at least in an enlightened and progressive society, that the business should be undertaken with a full commitment to the ramifications of all its aspects. There are dangers where there is undue awareness of every aspect of what one is doing, for going wrong on one point is then likely to be associated with error in every aspect. But dangers can never be avoided.

From one point of view, the boundaries that are laid down may be thought of as diminutions of freedom. And they can be genuine diminutions. But freedom is not a simple idea or ideal, and it is on the face of it unlikely that nothing more would need to be said about it than that. Indeed, virtually the whole of the contents of this and the foregoing chapters may be interpreted as an elaboration and commentary on the idea of freedom. At the foundation — humans on their own and makers of their own ways of life — is surely the assertion that human beings are free; and not merely an assertion but one which gives some content to a form of words which seems, from most perspectives, to be either false or unintelligible.

At all events, the assertion is immediately carried further anyway, and the fundamental freedom of human beings (inalienable as it is sometimes said to be) is carried immediately towards a substantive account of the conditions of human freedom. Humans assert their own freedom with the measures that they make, and they begin to make their freedom actual (i.e. they begin to do something with it) as they make and use machinery. The facts and the mysteries define certain limits within which their freedom may function. People's capacity to relate to others, their intimate relationships with others, reveal the expanding dimension of freedom. People's need for stimulation indicates that the basic freedom needs to be sustained and supported, facilitated, enabled and encouraged if it is to come to anything, or near its potential. And at the same time that the need of people to be subjected to rules and decisions reveals the need for a certain containment of freedom if it is to be adequately distributed and supported, the fact that people can be subjected to decisions that are inappropriate reveals the basis of threats to freedom.

Freedom thus emerges as a concept of quite central importance. It is not quite a value — or perhaps the way to put it is that it is more than a value. For as it has been presented, both implicitly and explicitly, it seems to be more a condition, a construct, a consequence, and a necessity. To talk about humans as this work does is, among other things, to talk about freedom. This talk gives a perspective on a great many things that have been said about freedom, and offers both formulations and solutions to a number of the classical problems that have arisen in connection with freedom.

This, surely, is the treatment which such a concept requires and deserves. And lest there be any misunderstanding of the comment that freedom is not a value but more than a value, it is important to explain a more general point. If freedom were simply a value (if the term 'value' was of sufficient adequacy to encompass all that freedom means), then it would be in order for readers to ask, as they come to the end of a discussion of what human life is all about, whether or not freedom is a value that is espoused therein — and even more vulgarly whether the author values freedom. And the point I have wanted to make is that freedom is not in this way detachable from everything else. It is absolutely integral to the discussion. If the foregoing discussion means anything, it means that freedom is a condition, a construct, a consequence and a necessity — with all the qualifications and amplifications that have been supplied in the course of the discussion. Simply to say it is a value does not begin to do justice to the position as it really is, the position that it truly occupies. It is impossible to do justice to a notion such as freedom, and then simply take it or leave it on the basis that one has called it a value.

I have done no more than give a sketch, in the foregoing paragraphs, of what needs to be said about freedom in order to do it justice and really come to terms with it. And yet the sketch, necessary though it doubtless is, really suffices: for a concept such as freedom has both the advantage and the disadvantage of being, by itself, simply a summary word. The disadvantage is that attention to the concept is all too easily focussed on the word; and the result of this procedure is that a cluster of aspects of life are abstracted from something much larger — abstracted, even though they are really integral to that from which they are abstracted. And the further results of dealing with these aspects in abstraction is that they are inevitably distorted, and that a proper perspective on them (which involves a grasp of their relationships with some other aspects of life) is unavoidably lost.

But the advantage of freedom as a summary word is that it leads up to a sketch of the kind offered above, which points to how the concept of freedom can be employed not only to highlight key points in a general account of human affairs, but at the same time to reveal how it becomes a critical probe with which to come to grips with such an account.

There is, however, a concluding comment to be made about freedom, about what I would call its ultimate fate. For if there really is some major threat to the human world that needs to be taken into account in the contemporary era – or probably any era — it lies in the territory of freedom.

Freedom, pluralism, diversity are all bound up with each other, integral to human beings, and decisive to the continuing capacity of human beings to follow their own nature. The threat, of course, lies in humans themselves — in each person and group taken individually, in those with whom each person and group are interdependent, in those who call various tunes. If we ask what freedom and diversity come to in the end, the answer is that they are always the lifeblood of the human world. So nothing is more central, more basic, more integral. If humankind does not persist with diversity and freedom, if everything falls into some centre, then all is lost, though not for ever. For some real meaning is given to that faith in youth which is always the hope of the future if we take into account that an implication of humans being on their own is that each generation is on its own.

What then of rights? The account that has been offered is out of sympathy with thinking of human affairs in terms of rights. Humanity is too diverse a measure, certainly, for there to be any basis in it for laying down anything like universal, absolute, specific rights. And insofar as the main point of 'rights' talk is always to protest against depriving some section of some group of something which some other section has, the problem previously posed about there being no-one but the majority (which is clearly disqualified) to determine minority rights not only presents an insoluble dilemma, but also applies equally to the determination of the rights of any person or group by any other person or group. And it is certainly clear that in terms of the account offered here, rights are not part of the nature of things.

But while rights talk has no place in terms of the account given, the strengths of such talk are by no means ruled out by it – whereas the weaknesses are. The real defects of rights talk, as soon as it goes beyond a few very broad generalities, are its universality and its absoluteness — its inflexibility and its incapacity to take account of particularity. Nothing reveals the real depth of these shortcomings as does the realization that humans are on their own and that they make their own ways of life — each person, each group of people. Where rights talk drives towards uniformity, ways of life talk drives towards a conception of particularity in respect of needs, of prerequisites, of opportunities, of wants, of scope, of activities, of being, of attainments and of satisfactions. A stress on rights, insofar as it seems always to involve protest and demand, is calculated to place a strain on constructive relationships. If persons insist upon their rights, there arises the tendency for them to get (and want) them, neither more nor less – which means nothing different, nothing as well, nothing outside, apart from, or additional to that which the right has to do with: the corollary of the attitude of mind which says 'give me my rights' is 'and you and I may stand off from each other apart from that'.

The great strength of rights talk is that it draws attention to the point that those in authority must consider, not only their own conceptions of what they are responsible for and what they have a duty to do, but also the conceptions of what life is all about (and of what they are on about in their own lives) of those over whom they have authority. This thrust is anything but universal, absolutist or rigid. It is much more a matter of sympathy, of adjustment, of adaptation, of fitting in, of giving due consideration and taking due account.

Of course those over whom authority is exercised have a right to expect that they will be taken into account — their wants, requirements and so on. This kind of perspective, of cooperative attitude, may desirably be brought into play in all the interactive relationships which pertain to human beings. The concept of responsibility seems to sum up these considerations more satisfactorily than any concept of getting one's way: responsible decisions and exercises of power, responsibility generally (which surely means trying to give every consideration its due) in dealings between human beings. The language of natural law, indeed, seems more in harmony with the overall perspective and attitude that has been presented here than does the language of natural rights — for law talk can hardly proceed at all without taking particularity, responsibility and the like into consideration.

A comment is in order here on a specific issue which has

some significance for human affairs, concerning the need for congruity between the degree of political or governmental involvement which people may desire, and that which may be necessary for the human world at large to flourish. There has already been comment on various problems that can arise for humans if they do not take the right line in supporting government (or restraining it, or doing whatever else may be required); and also on the damaging situation of needing to place oneself in some kind of defensive posture. It does not seem likely that there would be a natural congruence of the kind referred to — for there is no reason to suppose that there is any direct linkage between the factors which generate an interest in such involvement and those which generate a need for it. The implication of this is that humans must accept the responsibility to undertake that degree of involvement which they judge to be required, rather than that which they might simply be inclined to. For otherwise, the human world is put at a risk that may be fatal. It is more likely that fatality will result from some dereliction on the part of government than from any other source. And unless the people are perpetually alert to this necessary involvement with government, not only is there a greater likelihood that such fatality may ensue, but there is also surely a greater likelihood that the involvement necessary when affairs have become palpably serious will be less attractive and more detrimental to the human world than it would have been if the situation had been continuously monitored.

What humans must perpetually be alive to is the need to keep available the conditions under which ways of life are most capable of being made by every person and group. Everything else must be made subordinate and subservient to that. Nothing else — no political or governmental system, no social structure, no set of laws, no educational arrangements, no provision of opportunities — is ever to be prized for its own sake. For to do so would not merely belittle human beings, but would also distract attention from the need to gear everything else to the service of human beings as makers of ways of life.

For the truth that humans are makers of ways of life does not mean that particular persons cannot fail to make their own ways of life. Those with the resolve and strength to make their own way in the face of great odds are probably few — and it is probably also true that those who will make their own ways to the fullest extent are few unless there is a favourable and supportive milieu. To fail to make one's own way of life is a matter of reacting rather than acting, going along with things rather than going one's own way, accepting things rather than adapting them, taking fundamentals for granted rather than taking them further.

To fail in making one's own way of life is not to fail to live at all, or to be without contentment or satisfaction or fulfilment or comprehension or anything at all of this kind. Indeed, the persons who do make their own ways of life may neither be conscious of, nor even perhaps attain, these desired qualities. But ways of life are not made for the sake of anything beyond themselves: for they are the totality for those who have made them. They are at once the most comprehensive and the most concrete human manifestations. In their ways of life, that is, human beings become truly human.

In the most fundamental of senses, then, ways of life are neither good, nor good or bad, nor better or worse. Of course, some are detrimental to others, and may need to be restrained or even stopped off. Equally, some are greatly stimulating to others, and productive of the most fruitful, energising consequences. Again, some people may value or deplore the ways of life made by others. But all such valuations are relative to some perspective that is external to any particular way of life in itself — and they relate to those involved in or making some way of life of their own, or to some enabling or protecting decision being contemplated or enacted by some decider.

But essentially, any way of life stands by itself, for itself, in itself - as that which its maker is and does, what he or she has been and will be. It both is, and represents the concreteness of that person, the measure that person is and the measures that person makes. It is the manifestation of persons making the most of themselves, of their integrity and coherence. It is in the ways of life they make that people become authentic. Others may evaluate a way of life relative to themselves. But no one can evaluate anything at all except relative to themselves. So no one can evaluate their own way of life, since they are it and it is they. In the end, the ways of life which human beings make stand as the absolutes in the human world.

End Notes

1. For an attempt at a definition of what a political philosophy is, see D. M. White, *The Philosophy of the Australian Liberal Party*, (Hutchinson, Australia), 1978, p. 11.

2. This is in a sense a challenge to the following famous 'very simple principle' asserted by John Stuart Mill in his *Essay on Liberty* - except that Mill's principle, as amplified in the twenty-five line paragraph in which he asserts it, is actually anything but simple. While the full paragraph is too long to quote here, the following sentences illustrate how far it is from being simple: 'The object of this Essay is to assert one very simple principle, as entitled to govern absolutely the dealings of society with the individual in the way of compulsion and control... That principle is, that the sole end for which mankind are warranted, individually or collectively, in interfering with the liberty of action of any of their number, is self-protection. That the only purpose for which power can rightfully be exercised over any member of a civilised community, against his will, is to prevent harm to others... The only part of the conduct of any one, for which he is amenable to society, is that which concerns others...' (*Utilitarianism, Liberty and Representative Government*, London, Dent, 1948, pp. 72-73).

3. I finished writing the book at the start of 1980, but did not publish it until 2013. I was partly inspired to publish the original edition, (titled *The World of Man*), even though it was thirty years since I had written it, when I heard Barack Obama say in his first Inaugural Address:

    'We will not apologize for our way of life, nor will we waver in its defence."

    I found it fascinating that in the first decade of the third millennium, a United States President would give centrality to "our way of life", rather than to ideas such as "our inalienable rights", or "freedom", or "democracy", or "justice", or "our more perfect Union", or any other ideal or value.

4. Atkinson's 1918 University of Melbourne *Litt.D* thesis is in the library of Queens College, an affiliated college of that university.

5. I actually started with '"Men' make ways of life". 'Man' at that time in such a context meant what 'human' means now.

6. As put by Socrates in Plato's *Republic*, 'Whithersoever the wind of the argument blows, there lies our course' (Book 3. S 394d).

7. The Eighteenth Century was the heyday of 'nature' as the philosophical key to knowledge and understanding. Its inability to open philosophical doors became apparent as definitions of 'nature' multiplied: I recall one commentator noting that more than 200 different definitions of nature were

identified as the Eighteenth Century progressed.

8   The pronouncement of Friedrich Nietzche (e.g. in *Thus Spoke Zarathusta*) that 'God is dead' is taken to mean that people stopped believing in God.

9   As put by Paul in his *Letter to the Philippians*, 'Therefore my brothers… work out your own salvation with fear and trembling' (Ch 2, v. 12, RSV of The Bible).

10 As put by Hegel in *The Philosophy of History*, 'Amid the pressure of great events, a general principle gives no help. It is useless to revert to similar circumstances in the Past. The pallid shades of memory struggle in vain with the life and freedom of the Present' (Dover, p. 6).

11 As put by Protagoras in *Truth (Aletheia)*, "Of all things the measure is man: of those that are, that they are; and of those that are not, that they are not". The Stanford University Encyclopaedia of Philosophy states that this is one of the few authentic Protagoras fragments to have been preserved and many ancient sources confirm that the statement was originally formulated precisely in these terms.

12 As put by John Keats in his 1819 *Ode On A Grecian Urn*, "Beauty is truth, truth beauty. That is all you know on earth, and all you need to know".

13 As put by Michael Oakeshott in his 1956 *On Being Conservative*, 'Some unfortunate people, like Pitt (laughably called 'The Younger'), are born old, and are eligible to engage in politics almost in their cradles; others, perhaps more fortunate, belie the saying that one is young only once, they never grow up. But these are exceptions. For most there is what Conrad called the 'shadow line', which, when we pass it, discloses a solid world of things, each with its fixed shape, each with its own point of balance, each with its price; a world of fact, not poetic image, in which what we have spent on one thing we cannot spend on another; a world inhabited by others besides ourselves who cannot be reduced to mere reflections of our own emotions.' (*Rationalism in Politics and other essays*. Methuen, London, 1962, p.196).

14 Robert Browning wrote of an excited bird which, in the springtime,

> '… sings each song twice over,

> Lest you should think he never could recapture

The first fine careless rapture!' (*Home Thoughts From Abroad*).

15 John Mulvaney wrote in his description of 40,000 years of Australian Aboriginal cultures, languages, and practices about the emergence of toolmaking, and spoke of toolmaking as defining humanity. (See *Prehistory of Australia*, Smithsonian Institution Press, 1999).

16 Henry Kissinger quotes a comment of Charles de Gaulle about the defects and ultimate futility of dictatorship: 'It is the fate of dictatorship to exaggerate what it undertakes… The nation becomes a machine on which the master

imposes a regime of unchecked acceleration. In the end something has to give way. The grandiose edifice collapses in blood and misfortune. The nation is left broken and worse off.' (pp 89-90 in *Leadership: Six Studies in World Strategy*, Penguin Random House, 2022).

17 Max Weber pioneered a century of analysis and research into authority in its various forms, including his ground-breaking tripartite division into traditional, charismatic and legal-rational authority. (*The Theory of Social and Economic Organization*, and *Politics as a Vocation*, are recommended seminal works.)

18 Mao Zedong launched the original Cultural Revolution in the People's Republic of China (PRC) in 1966. It followed The Great Leap Forward, and continued until Mao's death in 1976.(Wikipedia).

19 As Banjo Paterson wrote in *Clancy of The Overflow*,

'… For the drover's life has pleasures that the townsfolk never know.

And the bush hath friends to meet him, and their kindly voices greet him

In the murmur of the breezes and the river on its bars,

And he sees the vision splendid of the sunlit plains extended,

And at night the wondrous glory of the everlasting stars.'

(*Singer of the Bush, A B Paterson Complete Works 1885-1900*, ed. R Campbell and P Harvie, Lansdowne Press, Sydney, 1983.)

20 Alexander Pope's line that *'the proper study of mankind is man'* has been irresistible to commentators for centuries, although one might wish that its import was more clear. (*An Essay on Man*, a poem published in 1733–1734.)

21 Immanuel Kant began the conclusion to his *Critique of Practical Reason* with the following observations:

'Two things fill the mind with ever new and increasing admiration and awe, the oftener and more steadily we reflect on them: the starry heavens above me and the moral law within me. I do not merely conjecture them and seek them as though obscured in darkness or in the transcendent region beyond my horizon. I see them before me, and I associate them directly with the consciousness of my own existence. The former begins at the place I occupy in the external world of sense, and it broadens the connection in which I stand into an unbounded magnitude of worlds beyond worlds and systems of systems and into the limitless times of their periodic motion, their beginning and their continuance. The latter begins at my invisible self, my personality, and exhibits me in a world which has true infinity but which is comprehensible only to the understanding...' (p. 166, Tr. Lewis White Beck, Liberal Arts Press, 1956).

22 Karl Marx started a world-shaking ball rolling when he wrote that:

'In the social production of their life, men enter into definite relations that are indispensable and independent of their will; these relations of production correspond to a definite stage of development of their material productive forces. The sum total of these relations of production constitutes the economic structure of society - the real foundation, on which rises a legal and political superstructure and to which correspond definite forms of social consciousness. The mode of production of material life determines the social, political and intellectual life process in general. It is not the consciousness of men that determines their being, but, on the contrary, their social being that determines their consciousness...' (Contribution to a Critique of Political Economy, 1859).

23 Aristophanes lampooned Socrates' philosophy for being in the clouds:

'He (Socrates) must always, always, be able to confound the true...' (Aristophanes, *The Clouds*, http://classics.mit.edu, 419BCE).

24 Miguel de Cervantes's timeless *Don Quixote*, initially published in 1605, with its unforgettable portrayal of a person 'tilting at windmills', gives immortality to this aspect of human nature.

25 Wordsworth in *French Revolution As It Appeared To Enthusiasts At Its Commencement* penned in timeless lines written in 1805 that

'..... the meek and lofty

Did both find, helpers to their heart's desire,

And stuff at hand, plastic as they could wish:

Were called upon to exercise their skill,

Not in Utopia, subterranean fields,

Or some secreted island, Heaven knows where!

But in the very world which is the world

Off all of us, - the place where in the end

We find our happiness, or not at all.'

26 This takes to another level Edmund Burke's profound remark that the 'the objects of society are of the greatest possible complexity'.

27 Jean-Jacques Rousseau wrote of 'the general will' in the following famous words. 'Each individual, as a man, may have a particular will contrary or dissimilar to the general will which he has as a citizen.... In order then that the social compact may not be an empty formula, it tacitly includes the understanding, which alone can give force to the rest, that whoever refuses to obey the general will shall be compelled to do so by the whole body. This means nothing less that that he will be forced to be free; for this is the condition which, by giving each citizen to his country, secures him against all

personal dependence': in The Social Contract, London, Dent, 1938, pp. 17-18.

28 The tower of Babel is the biblical story about the confusion caused by different languages: Genesis, 11, 1-9.

29 As an American politician profiled by John F. Kennedy in his *Profiles in Courage* put it, 'The people speak with a fine, clear voice.... The people, yes..." (Harpers, N.Y., 1955).

30 C.f. an unidentified comment by Bertrand Russell in relation to the unavoidable need for punishment in some circumstances: 'You always have the ruffians'.

31 Cf a comment of Michael Oakeshott about a 'conversation of machine guns'.

32 Cf Exodus Chapter 20, vv. 1-22, where God delivered the Ten Commandments to Moses on Mt Sinai, and told Moses to tell the people that He had talked with Moses from heaven.

33 See Max Weber's timeless "Politics as a Vocation" in *From Max Weber: Essays in Sociology*, Ed H. H. Gerth and Mills, Galaxy, NY, 1958.

34 In the Oxford English Dictionary, 'determinator' appears as a rare but not obsolete word, and is defined as 'he who or that which determines in various senses of the verb; a determiner'.

35 See earlier footnote to Bertrand Russell's comment that 'You always have the ruffians'.

36 See Footnote 13 above.

37 This perhaps extends the import of the saying that 'democracy is the worst form of government except for all the rest'.

38 This is the author's synthesis of two Alexander Pope aphorisms:

"Of forms of government let fools contest, Whate'er is best administered is best', and

"The proper study of mankind is man'.

39 If the question be asked 'Where does this leave democracy?' the answer is that it leaves democracy meaning 'government by the people'; that this timeless form of words continues to call for explanation and its meaning for determination; and that more thought needs to be given to explicating the category into which 'democracy' should be assigned.

40 George Berkeley argued as follows in his *Principles of Human Knowledge*: 'That neither our thoughts, nor passions, nor ideas formed by the imagination, exist *without* the mind, is what *every body will allow*. And (to me) it seems no less evident that the various sensations or ideas imprinted on the sense, however

blended or combined together (that is whatever objects they compose), cannot exist otherwise than *in* a mind perceiving them.... (I think an intuitive knowledge may be obtained of this, by anyone that shall attend to *what is meant by the term exist*, when applied to sensible things. The table I write on, I say, exists, that is, I see and feel it; and if I were out of my study I should say it existed, meaning thereby that if I was in my study I might perceive it, or that some other spirit actually does perceive it.) There was an odour, that is, it was smelled; there was a sound, that is to say, it was heard; a colour or a figure, and it was perceived by sight or touch. This is all I can understand by these and the like expressions. For as to what is said of the absolute existence of unthinking things without any relation to their being perceived, that seems perfectly unintelligible. Their *esse* is *percipi,* nor is it possible they should have any existence, out of the minds or thinking things which perceive them." In *A New Theory of Vision and Other Writings,* Everymans Library, London, J. M. Dent & Sons Ltd, First published 1709, First published in this edition 1910.

Bibliography

Acton, Lord, *Lectures on Modern History*, London, Collins, 1960

Anderson, John, *Studies in Empirical Philosophy*, Sydney, Angus and Robinson, 1963

Anselm, St., *Proslogium, et al*, (tr. S. N. Deane), Chicago, Open Court Publishing, 1903

Aristotle, 'Nicomachean Ethics' and 'The Politics', in *The Basic Works of Aristotle*, (Ed Richard McKeon), New York, Random House, 1941

Augustine, St., *The City of God*, (Tr. Henry Bettenson), Harmondsworth, Penguin, 1984

Austin, John, *The Province of Jurisprudence Determined*, London, Weidenfeld and Nicholson, 1965

Australian Constitution Annotated, The, Canberra, AGPS, 1980

Australasian Federation Conference Melbourne 1890 (Debates and Proceedings of the), National Library of Australia website

Australasian National Convention, Sydney, 1891 (Debates of the), National Library of Australia website

Australasian Federal Convention of 1897-8 (Debates of, in Adelaide 22 March-5 May 1897, Sydney 2-24 September 1897, Melbourne 22 January-17 March 1898). National Library of Australia website

Bacon, Francis, *The Advancement of Learning*, London, Cassell, 1905

Bagehot, Walter, *The English Constitution*, London, Collins, 1965

Bell, Daniel, *The End of Ideology*, NY, Collier, 1962

Bellamy, Edward, *Looking Backward*, NY, Signet, 1962

Bentham, Jeremy, *The Principles of Morals and Legislation*, NY, Hafner, 1948

Berger, P L and Luckmann, T, *The Social Construction of Reality*, Harmondsworth, Penguin, 1966

Bergson, Henri, *Time and Free Will*, (Tr F L Pogson), London, Allen and Unwin, 1959

Berlin, Isaiah, *Four Essays on Liberty*, London, OUP, 1969

Blackham, H J, *Six Existentialist Thinkers*, London, Routledge, 1956

Bodin, Jean, *Six Books of the Commonwealth*, (Tr. M J Tooley), Oxford, Blackwell, 1957

Bosanquet, Bernard, *The Philosophical Theory of the State*, London, Macmillan, 1965

Boswell, James, *The Life of Johnson*, London, OUP, 1953

Bradley, F H, *Appearance and Reality*, Oxford, Clarendon Press, 1959

Brown, D. Mackenzie, *The White Umbrella: Indian Political Thought from Manu to Gandhi*, Berkeley, Univ California Press, 1958

Burnett, John, *Early Greek Philosophy*, NY, Meridian, 1959

Braithwaite, R B, *Scientific Explanation*, Cambridge, CUP, 1968

Brecht, Arnold, Political Theory: *The Foundations of Twentieth Century Political Thought*, NJ, Princeton University Press, 1969

Browne, Sir Thomas, *Religio Medici*, London, Cassells, 1905

Burke, Edmund, 'Reflections on the Revolution in France', 'Appeal from the New to the Old Whigs', 'Speech to the Electors of Bristol', and 'Speeches on American Taxation', in *The Works of the Right Honourable Edmund Burke*, (16 vols), London, Rivington, 1826

Burton, Robert, *The Anatomy of Melancholy*, NY, NYRB, 2001

Butler, Joseph, *Fifteen Sermons Preached at the Rolls Chapel*, London, Bell, 1953

Butlin, N G, et al., *Government and Capitalism*, Sydney, Allen and Unwin, 1982

Calhoun, John C, *A Disquisition on Government*, NY, The Liberal Arts Press, 1953

Cassirer, Ernst, et al, *The Renaissance Philosophy of Man*, Chicago, Phoenix, 1948

Chafee, Zechariah, *Documents on Fundamental Human Rights*, (2 vols), NY, Atheneum, 1953

Charter of the United Nations and Statute of the International Court of Justice, NY, UN, nd

Churchill, Rt Hon Sir Winston, *The Second World War (6 vols)*, London, Cassells, 1948

Collingwood, R G, *The Idea of History*, Oxford, OUP, 1961

Collingwood, R G, *The Idea of Nature*, Oxford, OUP, 1945

Davies, A F, *Australian Democracy*, Melbourne, Longmans, 1958

Davis, S R, *The Federal Principle*, Berkeley, Univ California Press, 1978

Della Casa, Giovanni, *Galateo or The Book of Manners* (Tr Pine-Coffin R S), Harmondsworth, Penguin, 1958

Descartes, Rene, *The Philosophical Works of Descartes* (Tr E S Haldane & G R T Ross), (2 Vols), Cambridge, CUP, 1912

Durkheim, Emile, *The Rules of Sociological Method*, (Tr Solovay & Mueller), NY, The Free Press, 1964

Duverger, Maurice, *Political Parties* (Tr B & R North) London, Methuen, 1964

Eliot, T S, *Notes towards the Definition of Culture*, London, Faber, 1948

Fraser, Malcolm, *Common Ground*, Victoria, Penguin, 2002

Green, T H, *Lectures on the Principles of Political Obligation*, London, Longmans, 1927

Hamilton, A, Madison, J, and Jay, J, *The Federalist Papers*, USA, Mentor, 1961

Hart, H L A, and Honore, A M, *Causation in the Law*, Oxford, Clarendon Press, 1959

Hayek, F A, *Law Legislation and Liberty*, London, Routledge, 1982

Hegel, G W F, *The Philosophy of History*, (Tr. J Sibree), NY, Dover, 1956

Hegel, G W F, *The Philosophy of Right*, (Tr. T M Knox), Oxford, Clarendon Press, 1958

Hobbes, Thomas, *Leviathan*, Oxford, Blackwell, 1960

Hobhouse, L T, *The Elements of Social Justice*, London, George Allen and Unwin, 1922

Hobhouse, L T, *The Metaphysical Theory of the State*, London, George Allen and Unwin, 1960

Hooker, Richard, 'The Laws of Ecclesiastical Polity' in *The Works* (3 Vols), Oxford, Clarendon Press, 1874

Hume, David, 'An Inquiry Concerning Human Understanding' in *Essays, Literary, Moral and Political*, London, Ward Lock, n.d.

Hume, David, *A Treatise of Human Nature*, Oxford, Clarendon Press, 1958

Jung, C G, *Psychology and Religion: East and West* (Tr Hull, R F C), London, Routledge, 1958

Kennedy, President John F, *Profiles in Courage*, NY, Harpers, 1619

Kirk, G S, and Raven, J E, *The Presocratic Philosophers*, Cambridge, CUP, 1960

Kissinger, Henry, *On China*, , USA, Penguin, 2011

Kissinger, Henry, *World Order*, UK, Penguin, 2015

Locke, John, *Two Treatises of Government*, (Ed. Peter Laslett), Cambridge, CUP, 1960

Machiavelli, Niccolo, *The Prince and The Discourses* (Tr Luigi Ricci, Revised E R P Vincent), NY, Random House, 1950

Marx, Karl & Engels Frederick, 'Contribution to a Critique of Political Economy' (1859), 'Theses on Feuerbach', 'The German Ideology', and 'The Manifesto of the Communist Party', in *Selected Works* (2 Vols), Moscow, Foreign Languages Publishing House, 1951

Maximoff, G P, (ed), *The Political Philosophy of Bakunin*, NY, Free Press, 1964

Menzies, R G, *The Forgotten People and other Studies in Democracy*, Australia, Angus and Robinson, 1943

Menzies, Sir Robert, *Afternoon Light*, Australia, Cassell, 1967

Menzies, Sir Robert, *The Measure of the Years*, Australia, Cassell, 1970

Michels, Robert, *Political Parties* (Tr E & C Paul), NY, Dover, 1959

Mill, John Stuart, *Utilitarianism Liberty Representative Government*, London, Dent, 1964

Mill, John Stuart, *A System of Logic*, London, Longmans, 1967

Montesquieu, Baron, *The Spirit of the Laws* (Tr Thomas Nugent), NY, Hafner, 1959

Morris, William, 'News from Nowhere' in *Selected Writings*, London, The Nonesuch Press, 1948

Morrison, Lord, *Government and Parliament*, London, OUP, 1966

Mosca, Gaetano, *The Ruling Class* (Tr Hannah D Kahn), NY, McGraw Hill, 1939

Nethercote, J R (ed), *Menzies – The Shaping of Modern Australia*, Redland Bay Australia, Connor Court, 2016

Nicolson, Sir Harold, *Diplomacy*, London, OUP, 1965

Oakeshott, Michael, *Rationalism in Politics and other essays*, London, Methuen, 1962

Ockham, *Philosophical Writings* (ed & tr Philotheus Boehner), Edinburgh, Nelson, 1959

Orwell, George, *Nineteen Eighty Four*, Harmondsworth, Penguin, 1956

Owen, Robert, *Report to the County of Lanark a New View of Society*, Harmondsworth, Penguin, 1970

Paine, Thomas, *The Rights of Man*, London, Everyman, 1963

Pieper, Josef, *Happiness and Contemplation* (Tr R & C Winston), London, Faber, 1958

BIBLIOGRAPHY

Plamenatz, J P, *Consent, Freedom and Political Obligation*, London, OUP, 1968

Plato, 'The Crito', 'The Republic', 'The Statesman', and 'The Laws', in *The Dialogues of Plato* (4 Vols), (Tr and Ed B Jowett), Oxford, Clarendon Press, 1953

Rawls, John, *A Theory of Justice*, Oxford, Clarendon Press, 1972

Redner, Harry, *Beyond Civilization*, New Brunswick, Transaction Publishers, 2013

Riesman, David (et al), *The Lonely Crowd*, NY, Doubleday Anchor, 1953

Ross, W D, *The Right and the Good*, Oxford, Clarendon Press, 1950

Rousseau, Jean-Jacques, *Emile* (Tr Barbara Foxley), London, Dent, 1961

Rousseau, Jean-Jacques, *The Social Contract*, (ed. G D H Cole), London, Dent, 1938

Russell, Bertrand, *The Problems of Philosophy*, London, OUP, 1962

Ryle, Gilbert, *The Concept of Mind*, Harmondsworth, Penguin, 1963

Sabine, George H, *A History of Political Theory* (3rd ed), London, Harrap, 1964

Salisbury, Harrison E, *A Time of Change – A Reporter's Tale of Our Time*, NY, Harper & Row, 1989

Salisbury, Marquess of, (Lord Robert Cecil), *Essays* (2 Vols), London, John Murray, 1905

Satre, Jean-Paul, *Being and Nothingness* (Tr Hazel E Barnes), London, Methuen, 1957

Shaw, Bernard, *The Intelligent Woman's Guide to Socialism and Capitalism*, London, Constable, 1928

Schumpeter, Joseph A, *Capitalism, Socialism and Democracy*, London, Unwin, 1965

Schopenhauer, Arthur, *The World as Will and Idea* (Tr R B Haldane & J Kemp), (3 Vols), London, Routledge, 1957

Stephen, James Fitzjames, *Liberty, Equality, Fraternity*, Cambridge, CUP, 1967

Tawney, R H, *Equality*, London, Unwin, 1964

Thomas Aquinas, St., *Summa Theologica*, (Tr. Dominican Fathers), NY, Benziger Brothers, 1947

Tocqueville, Alexis de, *Democracy in America* (Tr Henry Reeve & Frances Bowen, Abridged by R D Heffner), NY, Mentor, 1956

Weber, Max, "Politics as a Vocation" in *From Max Weber: Essays in Sociology*, Ed H. H. Gerth and Mills, NY, Galaxy, 1958

Wheare, K C, *Modern Constitutions*, London, OUP, 1951

Wittgenstein, Ludwig, *Philosophical Investigations,* (Tr G E M Anscombe), Oxford, Blackwell, 1958

Yohannan, John D (Ed), *A Treasury of Asian Literature,* London, Phoenix, 1958

INDEX

Absolutes, ways of life as, 374
Achievement 17, 27, 77, 152, 332, 349ff
Administration 93, 107, 110f, 379
Aristophanes 141
Artificial intelligence 278
Artists, artistic 161, 219f, 255, 294ff, 298
Atkinson, Charles Watson 12, 375
Authority 27, 75, 85, 110, 170, 191, 203ff, 218ff, 263, 371, 377
Babel, tower of, 205
Berkeley, George (Bishop) 379
Broking, politics as, 228-232, 235, 237-240, 243-250, 255, 260f, 263f, 267-270, 274
Browning, Robert 376
Budgets 231-234,
Burke, Edmund 378, 382
Causation, social, 278, 285, 293
Cervantes, Miguel de 378
Cogito, the, 12
Collective, collectively 20, 145, 170-175, 182, 188, 220, 263, 295, 299, 357, 359
Complexity 100, 173, 287, 290, 358, 360, 378
Computers 100ff
Conflict 11, 59f, 136, 206f, 222, 228, 246, 248, 250, 267, 305, 306, 350
Conformism, conformity 50ff, 90, 103f, 263f, 284f, 298, 339f, 357, 363ff
Conrad, Joseph, 59, 376
Conservatism 217, 290f, 376

Control 26ff, 33, 57, 71f, 92, 95, 113ff, 159f, 172, 190f, 209, 223, 228ff, 238ff, 260f, 266, 270, 275, 278, 280ff, 288, 295ff, 300ff, 315, 328f, 361, 375
Culture 24
De Gaulle, Charles 376
'Deciders' 41, 210, 237, 260, 283, 293, 295, 298, 331, 350
Deciding 89, 127, 228, 236, 270, 286f, 306, 314, 321, 323, 355
Democracy 232, 375, 379
Descartes, Rene 12
'Determinators' 8, 14, 277ff, 379
Dialectic 64, 117, 175, 190
Dictatorship 376
Dignity, human 49-52, 85
Disadvantage 348f
Diversity 13, 65ff, 195, 198, 204, 253, 274, 294, 357, 363f, 369
Economics 110, 113, 233f, 306
Equality 9, 345f, 348
External world, the 128f, 137, 167, 377
Facts 3, 23f, 26, 76, 124f,128, 130-145, 157, 165ff, 172, 174, 287, 333, 338, 341ff, 362, 367
Family 161, 184, 192ff, 292ff, 335
Freedom, free 10, 14, 17, 19, 28, 114, 118ff, 132, 184, 187, 197, 207, 221, 238, 261, 282f, 318, 349, 366-369, 375f, 378
Free market 207, 261, 282f
Govern, government 9ff, 14, 17, 55, 83, 110, 192f, 205, 214, 220-223, 228ff, 232-243, 259ff, 266f, 270f,

275, 278f, 281, 284f, 300, 304-329, 331, 350, 356, 372, 379

Governance 225, 230, 261, 304

Groups 14, 19, 21, 24f, 48, 71, 121, 170, 172-224, 228, 230f, 252ff, 256-260, 263, 272-275, 279f, 283, 290, 296, 305f, 309, 311, 316f, 319, 321ff, 334, 336, 339, 349f, 355-360, 364f, 369-372

Hegel, G W F 376

History 10, 22f, 27, 71, 121, 130, 140, 143, 145, 153, 193, 200, 202

Human Beings 9, 12, 19, 21f, 25-28, 35, 43ff, 48, 52, 62, 91, 93, 97, 115, 127, 129, 132f, 139, 143, 147, 162, 170, 180, 225, 239, 257, 259, 271, 275, 277, 287, 291, 318, 334, 337, 340f, 343, 347, 349, 357, 359, 367, 369, 371, 373f

Human Nature 10, 12f, 40, 42, 56, 81, 91, 122f, 190, 332, 336f, 341, 345, 351f, 369, 378

Human World, the 17, 19, 26f, 78, 81, 83f, 91f, 94, 108, 111, 113, 121f, 125, 128, 132, 135f, 157, 160ff, 167, 169, 171f, 178, 180, 183, 185, 190, 197ff, 203, 206ff, 216, 219f, 223, 227ff, 243, 248, 253f, 256, 258, 261ff, 267, 272f, 275, 277, 290, 292, 294, 296, 302, 314, 317, 327f, 331, 334, 341-345, 350, 353, 356, 362, 369, 372, 374

Individualism 50, 54, 144, 365f

Influence 11, 26, 33, 48f, 58, 71, 89, 128, 130, 140, 159, 196, 212, 261, 265, 267, 277ff, 282, 293f, 299, 302, 321, 361

Justice 110, 187, 204, 234, 375

Kant, Immanuel 377

Keats, John 376

Kennedy, John F 379

Kissinger, Henry 376

Knowledge 24, 26f, 33, 114, 128, 130, 137-155, 161, 163, 165ff, 178ff, 208, 218, 307, 334, 347, 360

Law 71f, 83, 86f, 93, 133, 261, 296, 313, 327, 371f, 377

Leadership 109, 198, 304-309

Liberty – see Freedom

Life, way(s) of 12f, 19ff, 23-28, 33f, 35, 53, 59, 61ff, 66f, 76, 78, 85, 89, 92, 94ff, 98, 112ff, 115f, 123f, 127ff, 133-136, 138, 140ff, 144-148, 150f, 153-156, 158, 161ff, 165ff, 169, 171-174, 182-189, 196ff, 206, 208ff, 218ff, 224, 227, 229, 243, 245, 253, 258ff, 262, 265, 268, 270f, 273f, 277, 283, 285, 288, 293, 296, 303f, 306-309, 312ff, 320f, 327-330, 332, 334, 337-344, 346, 349-359, 362, 367, 370, 372-375

Love 32, 132, 135

Machine(s), machinery 13, 26, 64, 78ff, 81-126, 127f, 133, 135, 154, 157, 161f, 218, 241, 260, 283, 290, 295, 312, 323, 328, 351f, 376

Mao Zedong 377

Market – see Free Market

Marx, Karl 377

Meaning 17, 71, 76, 99, 134, 137, 150, 156, 162, 181, 206, 211f, 364, 370, 379f

Measure, measurer, measuring, measurement 13, 25f, 31-79, 81, 89, 93, 100, 110, 116, 119f, 127, 131, 136, 140ff, 154, 157f, 178, 190, 217, 224, 227, 233, 265, 270, 275, 334, 337, 342, 348f, 354, 357-362, 367, 370, 374, 376

Mill, John Stuart 375

Money 71f, 160, 198, 231, 288, 354

Monopoly 188, 241, 254, 260, 296, 298-300, 303, 312, 322

Morality 24, 39, 46, 59, 75, 98ff, 132f,

180, 257, 354f, 377
Mulvaney, John 376
Mystery, mysteries 13, 23, 26, 41, 46, 65f, 76, 91, 125, 127-167, 172, 174, 201f, 287, 338, 341, 343, 362, 367
Nation, national 10, 20, 173, 181, 189, 191, 205, 225f, 231, 278, 376f
Natural law 371
Nature 22f, 36, 40, 47, 49, 91, 110, 124, 134, 136f, 157, 162f, 214, 217, 227, 263, 314, 341, 370, 375
Needs, human 10, 112f, 115, 142, 146ff, 150f, 153, 155, 161, 217, 282, 284f, 286, 302, 324, 319, 325
Nietzche, Friedrich 376
Oakeshott, Michael 59, 376, 379
Obama, President 375
Objectivity 44f
Obligation 10, 301
Opportunity 9, 19, 115, 185, 187, 259, 348
Optimism 28, 136, 176, 336
Organizations 26, 28, 110
Originality, human 49-54, 59, 178, 338, 361, 366
Parenting 115, 294, 306ff, 310, 348f
Paterson, A B (Banjo) 377
Paul, Saint 376
Philosophy, philosophical 9-15, 17, 19, 28, 52, 375
Plato 131, 375
Political Philosophy 9, 375
Politicians 14, 62, 109, 215, 225-275, 299, 323, 331
Politics 9, 11, 17, 27, 62, 195, 184, 225-275, 279, 299f, 322f, 331, 376
Politics as broking – see Broking
Pope, Alexander 377, 379

Population 10, 110, 355
Power 10f, 27, 90, 106, 112, 118, 149, 160f, 189, 199, 201, 207ff, 219-223, 235ff, 240f, 247, 262ff, 270-274, 278f, 287ff, 298, 301, 314ff, 319, 324, 329, 350, 371, 375
Private 20, 176f, 189, 295f, 315, 350
Protagoras 376
Public 20, 87, 176f, 232f, 295f, 299, 306
Reason 14, 17, 21f, 43f, 210
Regulation – see also control 172, 177, 191, 220, 223f, 229f, 259, 261, 266, 275, 281f, 328
Relationships, human 9, 12, 19f, 25, 27, 48, 68, 91, 93f, 108, 128f, 169-172, 182, 184, 194, 291, 299, 316, 327, 356f, 359, 364, 367, 369, 371
Religion 11, 13, 17, 22f, 65, 273, 307, 328
Responsibility 13, 122, 186, 222, 247, 270, 301, 343, 347f, 350, 371f
Right, The 187, 220
Rights 160, 217ff, 344, 370f, 375,
Rousseau, Jean-Jacques 378
Russell, Bertrand 379
Science, scientists 17, 52, 55, 63-66, 110, 130ff, 135, 143, 149f, 228, 308
Society 70, 91, 98f, 106, 187, 198, 212, 215, 217, 220f, 252, 256, 259f, 263, 274, 279-283, 293, 296, 298, 304, 309ff, 316ff, 323, 325f, 328, 351f, 360, 366, 375, 378
Socrates 22, 141, 375, 378
Standards 11, 21f, 24f, 35-40, 49f, 60, 67, 71, 73, 187, 252, 255, 354
State, the 202, 292f, 296, 323, 356
Status 49f, 54, 71, 98, 170, 198f, 204, 296, 345
Totalitarianism 221

Tune-callers, tune-calling 278, 286-327

Value(s) 12, 56, 74ff, 118, 125, 146, 160, 165, 187, 190, 198, 208f, 231, 268, 275, 284, 302f, 306, 341, 354, 357, 362, 367f, 373, 375

Way(s) of life – see Life, ways of

Weber, Max 377

Whip-cracking 278, 281

World, human – see Human world

Wordsworth, William 378

www.ingramcontent.com/pod-product-compliance
Lightning Source LLC
Chambersburg PA
CBHW052055300426
44117CB00013B/2137